THE GIFT OF
THOMAS JOSEPH WHITE
M.D., L.H.D., F.A.C.P.
TO THE LIBRARY OF
CABRINI COLLEGE
1981

WASHINGTON DATELINE

WASHINGTON DATELINE

BY

DELBERT CLARK

FREDERICK A. STOKES COMPANY
NEW YORK   TORONTO
1941

This book is for Lucia,
Who ought to have been
A newspaperman herself.

Contents

CHAPTER   PAGE

I. For Background Only 11

II. Senators-at-Large 20

III. There Were Giants in Those Days . . 35

IV. President and Press: The First Thirty Years 53

V. President and Press: Mister Big . . . 74

VI. Reporting the Nation's Business . . . 92

VII. A Day Among the Handouts . . . 118

VIII. Democracy's Show Window 142

IX. Congress — Uncensored 165

X. Syndicated Oracles 187

XI. The Submerged Tenth 205

XII. Champagne Punch 220

XIII. The Party Line 232

XIV. Tabloid News 243

XV. OGR — School for Censors 255

XVI. Press Control in the Making 271

XVII. If War Comes 297

For the Uninitiated 313

Index. 315

I

For Background Only

Washington is the largest village in the world, and it has but one topic of serious conversation. That topic, in turn, is the principal source of income and chief preoccupation of more than five hundred newspaper correspondents who report, and interpret, the news of the government to the United States and the world.

These five hundred are the élite corps of the American press; without them the nation would know little of the daily proceedings of its government; without them the government would have no valid means of gauging public opinion; without them, democratic government in the United States would cease to exist save as a meaningless form. Without them, save the mark, there could be no Gallup Poll.

The Washington correspondents have made reputations and ruined them; they have helped insure the success and foredoom the failure of legislative acts and administrative policies; they have commanded the wholesome respect and the bitter hatred of politicians. They wield a power such as is enjoyed by the press in no other capital in the world. They built up a promoter into a "Great Engineer"; they made over a half-pint New England politician into a homespun oracle; they took a cunning Texas Congressman with bushy eyebrows and remodeled him into a statesman.

Here in this vast, sprawling macrocosm of all the small towns in America the correspondents mingle daily with the great, the small, the nobles and the knaves who make up a government and its camp followers. No other great capital offers them the same opportunities, because no other capital is like Washington. Nowhere else would they find a city so devoted to the science of government that there would be nothing else to write about, nothing else to think about.

Washington is a one-industry town. Without that industry it would quickly lapse into oblivion as a dreary, unendurable suburb of Baltimore. It was created to shelter the government of a new Republic, created because the politicians could not agree on any city already in existence, and there is little in it worth mentioning but the government.

Washington is magnificent and tawdry, beautiful and unsightly, its broad, tree-shaded avenues lined with huge marble temples where democracy is guarded by 150,000 bureaucrats. Behind the broad avenues and the marble façades are narrow, squalid back streets strewn with slums inhabited by poor whites and Negroes. Washington is "a pouter pigeon, squatting on a row of tenements."

In summer the heat is unendurable, and the humidity makes breathing a burden. In winter it alternately rains and snows, freezes and thaws, and the people come down with influenza. Few cities have been deliberately laid out on so uninviting a site, a site selected after long deliberation by the Father of His Country, whom no one ever suspected of possessing a sense of irony. The city crouches miserably in a reclaimed marsh, and lifts up its eyes to the hills of Virginia and Maryland, which cut off the breeze.

It is populated by government employees, diplomats, lobbyists, lawyers, newspaper correspondents, and those nameless ones required to feed them, wash their clothes, and transport them about the streets. The names and faces periodically change, the pattern never.

In this artificial *milieu* live and work the Five Hundred. Fires, police news, traffic accidents concern them not at all, unless the fire is in the White House, a Cabinet officer is arrested, or a Senator gets into a traffic jam. They are concerned solely with the government in all its manifestations, and unrelated incidents are generally ignored. Once in a long while the exception occurs, when a major event requires old-fashioned leg work, and then the well-dressed correspondents flex unaccustomed muscles and go back to the techniques of their earlier days. Even then there is usually a political connection.

The Washington assignment is a century and a quarter old. When the Government met in Philadelphia a few seats were reserved for the press, but they were never occupied. In Washington, however, the picture soon changed. The first Washington correspondents were on the staff of a local paper, and they combined the functions of newspaper correspondent and official Congressional stenographer, occupying seats on the dais next to the presiding officer.

As the government became firmly established, out-of-town correspondents began to pay visits to the Capital and write letters of observation and comment back to their papers. Some of them represented several large papers at once, and the compensation they received would turn a reporter of today green with envy. They were the first columnists.

By 1820, in the administration of James Monroe, resident correspondents who sent out not only letters but also spot news began to appear in considerable numbers, and many of them greatly enhanced their income if not their integrity by using "inside dope" as a basis for stock-market speculation. This was particularly the case during the Civil War, when advance knowledge of imminent events could be of great financial value.

The end of the war put an end for the most part also to this source of collateral income, and Francis A. Richardson, a Washington correspondent for thirty-five years, commented ruefully in a memoir that he arrived on the scene too late.

After the Civil War and on up to the end of the century, it was a common practice for public men to sell news and interviews to the press, and General Ben Butler went further, writing his own interviews. A Speaker of the House, noted for his vituperative tongue, boasted that he averaged $100 a week selling news, but complained that his earnings were not as much as they might have been because for a long time, being inexperienced, he had allowed himself to be interviewed without fee!

The first formal co-operation of government with press came in 1823, when Congress set aside a special gallery for the correspondents, then twelve in number, but the Executive Branch did nothing to facilitate the gathering of news, and gave the press no official recognition.

Correspondents obtained their information, other than

on Congressional debates, from Cabinet members and Congressmen, and each had his pet, exclusive tipsters, who would call on him at his office to relate the day's budget of inside news and gossip. The correspondents made a point of cultivating politicians whose views coincided with those of the paper, and in consequence the reports tended to be extremely onesided and partisan. Anyone accustomed to the generally fair and full accounts in the press of today would have been appalled at the vicious distortion and discoloration habitually practiced, for example, during the administration of Andrew Johnson.

The impartial reporting which is now the rule, the honest effort to give a rounded, intelligent summary of the news, was unheard of. Even later, when the big papers did try to present a reasonably complete picture of what was going on, news accounts were as heavily interlarded with editorial expression, as full of personal interpretation and bias, as are the syndicated columns of today. It was not, really, until the turn of the century that the emphasis began to shift materially and news was offered as a commodity in its own right, rather than as a vehicle for influencing the policies and fortunes of government.

In those days — the latter half of the Nineteenth Century — the correspondents, despite their somewhat precarious relationship to the government, had nevertheless developed an extraordinarily high regard for themselves, and Richardson, toward the close of his career, expressed the general view in these florid words:

"Indeed it may be said that there are few departments of newspaper work which weigh more than the Washington

Correspondents, and the men who labor in this field constitute a not inconsiderable fraction of the flower of journalism. In the thirty-five years I was an active Washington correspondent, among my professional associates have been those who average well in intelligence, in culture, in sagacity with most of the men in public life with whom they came in contact."

(The correspondents' opinion of themselves has changed little in a generation.)

The growth of the Washington press corps from two local reporters taking down stenographic records of Congressional proceedings, to a highly diversified body of men and women whose activities and influence penetrate the remotest recesses of the national government has been strictly parallel to the growth of the government itself. As government grew, more correspondents came to report its activities. As the number and efficiency of the correspondents increased, and with the development of the telegraph and later the telephone, their influence began to be more and more apparent to the officers of government.

Their ultimate recognition as a force to be reckoned with, and placated, led to the setting aside of special facilities for their use, with workrooms and later typewriters, free telephones and stationery. Now every government department and independent agency, as well as the White House and the Congress, has provided full accommodations for the working press, with one or more press officers to assist them. The press release, or "handout," has become a major product of the governmental factory.

By 1902, when Theodore Roosevelt instituted the White

House press-room, the place of the Washington correspondent was firmly established in the government's scheme of things; but it was not until much later, when government became not only big but consistently controversial, that the elaborate press services of today grew up. Even as late as the administration of Herbert Hoover, whose sensitivity to the press was almost pathological, the publicity men of the various departments performed their functions in a desultory fashion. They were on hand if information was wanted, but they volunteered little, and the flood of handouts was a mere trickle compared to what it had become in the Roosevelt regime.

With the advent of Franklin D. Roosevelt and the launching of the longest and most intensive period of domestic reform the nation has ever experienced, the importance of cultivating the press became more than ever apparent. Presidential press conferences became a fixture; Cabinet officers and heads of emergency agencies followed suit; press officers became press departments, and in some cases were subdivided into "press" and "information," a subtle distinction lending itself to a variety of interpretations.

Not only was it important to the administration to have the news fully and accurately reported to the nation; it also became increasingly desirable that the press receive such expert assistance that the news would be reported in a favorable manner. Press releases in some cases began to sound like Fourth of July orations, with flamboyant introductions designed to give the impression that the news that followed was by all odds the most constructive and important to be had. Unadorned statements of fact tended to be the exception rather than the rule, and the embarrassing incidents were glossed over or omitted.

Thus news took on a propagandist tone, and in many agencies the honest search for facts not reported in the handout began to be discouraged. The propaganda appeared inevitable and excusable in a regime which had to sell itself to the nation in order to effectuate its avowed ends; so long as the ballyhoo was not offered as a substitute for facts, it was never more than a minor annoyance.

There is nothing really new in all this: it is the normal and logical trend of bureaucracy everywhere and in every age. The bureaucrat at best works hard and long and believes implicitly in what he is doing; at worst he is a charlatan and a leech on the public purse. Both exist coevally, the former, fortunately for the nation, in overwhelming majority. But in either case public criticism, or the publication of facts conducive to criticism, is invariably resented, and prevented if possible. It is only when government becomes so efficient in concealing its inefficiency that the nation is not permitted to be fully informed that the situation becomes dangerous.

The history of the Washington assignment is the history of the free press in America. In no other country does the press have so great advantages; nowhere else are the members of the press permitted and encouraged to hobnob daily with the great. Freedom of the press, literally construed, is the freedom to publish anything at all subject only to the laws of libel; in Washington it has come to have a much broader construction, a construction which presumes that government will not only permit publication of news, but will also make it freely available, with sundry aids and conveniences to lighten the task of the reporter.

This was not achieved overnight; it is not in the Constitution and it is not written into any law. It represents a body of unwritten precedent which has become the priceless possession of the Washington correspondents. It represents a long and persistent struggle for a position of dignity and respectability in direct ratio to the importance of the corps. Yet the very mechanisms which government over a century has provided have become so elaborate that it would require only a slight shift in emphasis, along lines already discernible here and there, to transform it into an extremely effective form of censorship-at-source.

So the Washington correspondent finds himself in a continual struggle. His function is to hear, see, and interpret; he must tell not only the conventional "who, what, how, when and where," but also "why." He is the eyes and ears of the nation at the seat of the nation's government, and he has a much greater responsibility than he often realizes. In the discharge of this responsibility he not only has to find news and write it; he has also, with increasing frequency, to circumvent official efforts to conceal the unpalatable truth, and to endure post-publication displeasure.

But he has a pretty good time of it, and not many Washington correspondents would trade their jobs for any others with equal salaries. In Washington the reporter is somebody, a somewhat bigger cog in the wheel than he would be likely to be elsewhere. He loves it, and if he occasionally forgets that he is not the wheel itself, such forgetfulness is not difficult to understand.

II

Senators-at-Large

Washington correspondents spend so much of their time in close proximity to greatness that many of them conclude such juxtaposition cannot be accidental.

Probably no other assignment in the world offers so many hazards to the balanced ego; no other is so conducive to the development of the stuffed shirt. In other capital cities the press is kept strictly in what is understood to be its place; its social status hovers somewhere between the green-grocer and the barrister, and any honor its individual members achieve is earned by diligent application of intelligence and hard work.

In Washington it's different. Nowhere else in the world does the press enjoy the professional and social prestige which has been conceded as an inherent right in the United States Capital. "Freedom of the press" has been so liberally construed that the newspapers have come to view as a violation of it any official affront or refusal to make news available in full and at all times. The official press conference, in latter years, has become an institution, not merely for the dissemination of fact and propaganda, but for a measure of debate as well. The Cabinet member most critical of the press in general has the most frank and open conferences with the reporters and is most willing to engage in give-and-take with them.

All this inevitably has its effect upon the mental outlook of the correspondent. When he first arrives in Washington and views this promised land, he is inclined to be dazzled and a trifle humble. High officials, from the President on down, invite him to teas and receptions and cocktail parties. Ambassadors and ministers request the pleasure of his company. Members of Congress greet him cordially and find ways of doing small favors. The number of these invitations and courtesies varies in direct ratio to the importance of the newspaper he represents, but he does not always understand that.

Presently the dazzled feeling wears off, the humility fades, and the correspondent is in danger of forgetting that this official attention has no relation whatever to himself as an individual — it is a species of propaganda, verging sometimes on outright bribery, aimed at him as correspondent of an important newspaper. If he stopped newspaper work the invitations would cease as soon as word got around.

Naturally, even when the correspondent realizes that this is true he dislikes to admit it, because such admission damages his ego. He prefers to think that the Ambassador of the U.S.S.R. and Mrs. Oumansky invite him to a musicale because they like him; that the Ambassador of Cuba invites him to meet Colonel Batista because the Ambassador thinks the Dictator might be edified by the meeting; that the Japanese Ambassador spreads such a lavish array of hors d'œuvres and pours such good Scotch because the Ambassador wants him to be happy. (The Ambassador does, but there's nothing personal in it.)

At this point the correspondent is well on the way to becoming a Senator-at-large. He is asked everywhere; he receives a rare invitation to dinner at the White House, or an even rarer one to the British Embassy. He receives handsome Christmas cards from important persons, and is flattered with requests for his opinion on weighty matters. The vows of intellectual celibacy are in peril.

Thus it is that among the Washington correspondents, as nowhere else outside the private offices of certain editors and publishers, there exists and is nurtured a strong sense of the "dignity" of the newspaper craft. In New York, Chicago and San Francisco the reporter is still a reporter who is never permitted to forget the fact; in Washington he is a journalist.

There was a distinguished and extremely high-minded Washington correspondent, one who had never forgotten how to be a reporter, who best epitomized that attitude.

Senator Simeon D. Fess of Ohio had just become Chairman of the Republican National Committee and was receiving the press for the first time in his new capacity. He beamed on the correspondents and launched upon a long monologue, the substance of which was that he had always had the very best of relations with the "newspaper boys," would always be ready to see the "newspaper boys" at any time despite his recent beatification, and hoped that his amicable relations with the "newspaper boys" would continue.

Richard V. Oulahan of the *New York Times* listened in frigid silence, then said:

"Senator Fess, you have said a great deal about what you are going to do for the 'newspaper boys'; would it be too much to ask what you expect to do for the newspaper men?"

While many Washington correspondents fall considerably short of the standards of Oulahan, they all have, to a greater or less degree, that same attitude. Yet few of them will follow his example to the extent of defending their collective integrity in the face of slights or strictures on the part of officialdom. They have a high and carefully observed ethical code governing their relations with news sources, but virtually none for their relations with one another, and almost no mechanism for making common cause if occasion arises.

When, a few years ago, a writer of a confidential news letter passed on to his subscribers a false and peculiarly vicious piece of gossip about President Roosevelt, a story whose falsity was readily ascertainable, he was expelled from the National Press Club, not for conduct unbecoming a newspaperman, but for disseminating untruths about a fellow-member! The matter was dealt with upon a strictly social plane.

In precise terms, there is no such thing as a "Washington newspaper corps." There are several hundred newspaper correspondents, all engaged in much the same quest, but prosecuting it in the most anarchic manner imaginable. Socially they are in the main friendly; professionally, save for temporary working alliances between two or three reporters, they are at war, with no weapons barred.

They have organizations — the National Press Club, the Gridiron Club, the Overseas Writers Club, the two women's press clubs — but these are social or vaguely cultural in character, and not one of them embraces in its program any sort of code for mutual defense or for professional standards of any sort. Nor, for that matter, does the American Newspaper Guild, to which many of the correspondents belong. Many of us once hoped that the Guild might assume this responsibility, but its total preoccupation with wages and hours has dashed that hope. It is little different in its outlook from a union of hod-carriers or charwomen.

Perhaps the best illustration of the dog-eat-dog competition which characterizes the Washington correspondents at work is found in their response to the publication of an important exclusive story by a rival paper. It is dangerous to generalize too much, but the commonest reaction takes the form of attempts to obtain official denials. This is the result of a desire on the part of the correspondent who has been scooped to construct an alibi for the home office; if he can quote a denial, absolution is his until the next time.

More often than not the story is one which officials would have preferred not to see in print, and since technical denials are not considered dishonorable, they are not hard to get. On the other hand, it is a frequent practice to distort the story sufficiently, in angling for a denial, to insure one. This practice, naturally, is predicated upon the assumption that the official in question has not read the item, which is likely to be the case if he is caught early enough in the day.

It has been the personal experience of every large bureau chief in Washington to send along for publication stories which were based upon information of the utmost reliability, stories which within a day or two were proved to be entirely correct, and then to read, before noon the next day, official denials which were obtained by misquoting the story. And of course there have been occasions when an official and categorical denial was issued an hour or two in advance of the event which the story forecast!

The peculiar perversity which prompts supposedly reliable public officials to make such denials is discussed elsewhere; the very officials who inveigh most against the press for its lack of reliability have a way of being the most culpable in this respect, and so inevitably contribute to its unreliability. But whatever their reasons, and there is not always a clear pattern discernible, it is difficult to find an excuse for the newspaper correspondent who thus sloughs off his responsibility to his employer and to his craft — he calls it profession — for the sake of avoiding criticism.

For that is why it is done, in nearly every case. The correspondent is usually under great pressure from his editors, and he is often judged from day to day, not by the quality of the news he produces nor by the number of clean beats he obtains, but by the production rate of his principal rival. In fairness to the boss, most editors will appraise a correspondent fairly over a longer period, but from day to day and from edition to edition it is the misses that are counted more than the bull's-eyes.

It is for such reasons that these reporters are willing to solicit denials rather than seek to establish the facts. It is a lot quicker, and in the daily press a story isn't much good twenty-four hours after a rival paper has had it. For such reasons, also, some correspondents will manufacture stories virtually out of the whole cloth for the sake of a beat. There are not many such, but they do exist and operate in Washington.

Such a fake story is concocted usually in one of two ways. One is the thumb-sucking method, whereby a correspondent puts two and two together to make five, after diligent sucking of the reportorial thumb. The other is the revival method. Here the correspondent assembles a mass of previously published and related facts, selects the most sensational of them for a lead, and then ties them to a current development to give the impression that the whole horrid mess is new and important, which it is not. Editors by the exercise of constant vigilance can reduce this practice to a minimum, but since they handle great masses of copy daily, it is easy to see how occasionally they are duped by their own men. Of course no reputable newspaper will tolerate such a practice once discovered.

Then there was the strange case of General Ma, wherein one of the most simon-pure fabrications ever put on paper did not get published. A correspondent of the United Press turned in a long and unqualified story telling just why General Ma Chan-shan was resisting the Japanese advance into Manchuria, despite the general orders of the Chinese central government not to resist. The "lobster trick" man received the story already written when he came to work at midnight, but the writer had long since gone about his personal nocturnal pursuits, and could not be consulted.

General Ma, said the story, was in the pay of the Japanese army. He and his little band had been bribed to put up a show of resistance and thus provide the desired incident which would justify a full-dress invasion. The story continued at some length in this vein, quoting no authority but likewise indulging in no if's or maybe's.

The lobster trick man, unable to check with the author and being generally suspicious, held out the story for the Bureau Manager. The latter was able to solve the mystery. It appeared that he and the reporter had been having a social drink a few nights earlier, and had been idly speculating upon the unorthodox conduct of the obscure Manchu general. They wondered, specifically, if he could be in the pay of the Japanese. The reporter, on a subsequent dull day, wrote it all as fact.

This reporter was simply trying to build a record for himself, and the story would have been, at the time, difficult to disprove. The fake story, the archaic story with its face lifted, the solicited denial, are all part of the same picture. A correspondent seeks to make a "good" record or avoid a bad one.

And it is this same sort of cutthroat competition, of irresponsible conduct on the part of a minority, of failure to observe any genuine code of ethics within the craft, which does more to diminish the stature of the Washington correspondents as a whole, and to incite general indictments of the integrity of the press, than any other thing.

If the freedom of the press, as written in the Constitution and interpreted these many years by common consent, should ever be impaired, it will be in part because the press by its faults has laid itself open to attack. And when the attack comes, it will come in Washington, at the seat of government, and the Washington correspondents will have to bear the brunt of the onslaught. They should understand this and be vigilant, and the best sort of vigilance is maintenance of a high standard and a clean record.

Toward the officials who are their principal news sources the correspondents maintain a scrupulously deferential attitude. They are respectful in their questions, they observe confidences, and they are extremely careful to avoid wounding the sensibilities of Cabinet officers or administrators by pursuing a subject too far. Naturally, in a group so large this is not invariable: confidences are broken or indirectly violated, and correspondents have been tactless and even rude. But the reverse is the rule, and for good reason. The government's general policy of helpfulness toward the press is entirely voluntary and pursuant to no legal obligation, and the correspondents value it too highly to do anything designed to alter it.

But deference is one thing and spinelessness another. Whether the growing inclination to accept statements at their face value, to permit invidious remarks to go unchallenged, is an indication of timidity or pure laziness is a matter for argument: probably each fault enters into it. Be that as it may, there are fewer and fewer correspondents who will, politely but firmly, debate an issue with a Cabinet officer when there is just cause for such debate, rather than take what he says with an inward grimace and an outward

smile. And since the reporter is required to write only what
he sees and hears, and not what he thinks, very often the
only means of getting at the truth is by the exercise of the
right to ask questions.

Actually, of course, the press has it in its power to retali-
ate against bad treatment or to expose official prevarication,
in an effective and entirely correct manner, but too often
the individual correspondent lacks the courage, the imagination, or the energy to act in such cases. And likewise the
correspondents en bloc betray the same weakness. They
have little of the cohesiveness which is beginning to char-
acterize the government press agents, and are far from being the compact, single-minded society sometimes imagined
by the outsider.

There was a time, in the administration of Theodore
Roosevelt, when the correspondents, then relatively few in
number, united in an absolute boycott of Charles Joseph
Bonaparte, the Attorney General, because in his relations
with the press he had begun to exhibit some of the attributes of his most famous relative. The issue was clear
enough: Bonaparte insisted that the reporters publish only
what he chose from time to time to give them, whereas
they believed that in return he should occasionally permit
them to seek information on their own initiative. The boycott turned the trick, and the Attorney General was quite
cordial toward the "newspaper boys" from then on.

During the latter part of his administration President
Hoover virtually boycotted the correspondents for weeks
at a time, canceling press conferences with the explanation
that there was no news, and ordering comic-strip detective

investigations when the reporters contrived to pick up harmless tidbits whose publication he had not authorized. There was plenty of news; and written questions, as required, had been submitted in large numbers. Mr. Hoover simply didn't care to meet the correspondents, but was reluctant to say so in so many words.

By the exercise of a little self-control the press corps, had it been a corps, could have made Mr. Hoover quite uncomfortable by neglecting to report even the things he wished to have published. But it did not do so. Twice a week without fail the correspondents appeared at the White House to read the notice of "no press conference today."

This is not an argument for the boycott, a dangerous and two-edged weapon. It is intended rather as an illustration of the relative impotence of the correspondents as a whole in the face of unjustified slights to the individual or group, slights which nibble at the first amendment to the Constitution.

The absence of any corps spirit, any ability, except on the rarest occasions, to act effectively and in unison, presents an interesting paradox in view of the energy and high professional standards of most of the top men among the correspondents. But they do most of their talking around the luncheon table or ranged along the Press Club bar, and very little of it face to face with the men whose acts they are reporting and interpreting each day.

It would be possible, interviewing leading correspondents, to gain an impression of unanimity of thought and purpose on such matters as responsibility toward news sources and toward one another which would completely belie the generalizations just written. But ask those same men to form a united front, or to reduce to a code their professional conduct toward one another, and you have a different story. Any one of them will profess a belief in virtue and an abhorrence of sin, but by and large he is too busy, too lazy, or too rugged an individualist to implement the belief when occasion demands.

In part this is because of the anomalous status of the working correspondent. He likes to think of himself as "professional," and to a great extent his working conditions smack of the professional, yet he labors for a wage and is not in any sense his own man, unless he is a free-lance columnist. He writes not what he might choose to write if he were really independent, but rather what his paper considers most important. He is more or less on an assignment basis.

All this inevitably generates a certain indifference to anything that does not directly and immediately interfere with the performance of his duties: he has no genuine code because he is not truly a professional worker, and he is tempted to leave to the boss back home the defense of his rights and prerogatives.

In brief, while he prefers in his more romantic moods to be classed as a professional, the emotional conflict between his dreams and the reality of a weekly pay-check results in a stalemate. He is really neither one thing nor the other, and so he is neither a good "professor" nor a good trade unionist. He is unwilling or temperamentally unable to assume the onerous responsibilities of the true professional, while readily conceding the desirability of the end in view.

When you add to this fundamental emotional blockade the fact that newspapermen are notoriously bad organizers, are in fact almost anti-organization, it is not at all difficult to comprehend why there exists no "Washington press corps." They are individualists almost to the point of anarchy. And yet, unless the correspondents do learn to coöperate for their own good, they are in danger sooner or later of finding themselves reduced to a state of ineffectiveness which will be approximately coincident with the destruction of the freedom of the press.

If the élite corps of the American press — the Washington correspondents — are incapable of taking joint action, or of devising and observing minimum ethical standards, then what indeed may be expected of the press as a whole? And what respect may they look for from bureaucrats, traditionally resentful of unfavorable publicity, if they offer no semblance of defense when occasion demands?

The only self-discipline to be found among the Washington correspondents is that imposed by the various associations of reporters covering related news. There is a White House Correspondents Association, a State Department Correspondents Association, a Treasury Correspondents Association, a Standing Committee of Correspondents at the Capitol, and the like. These organizations are carefully fostered by the press officers of the agencies they cover, because they are useful as disciplinary bodies to enforce upon their members the rules of news-gathering. They are useful also as a defense corps to insure fair and equitable treatment of their special segments of the press, but they rarely exercise this function and have a suggestion of the company union flavor.

There have been outstanding exceptions. The Treasury correspondents acted vigorously and in unison through their association to prevent undue blocking of news channels by the Secretary in 1934, and to thwart an outrageous case of favoritism toward the columnists Alsop and Kintner in 1939. But such examples as these are easy to recall because they are so few.

Far-seeing journalists are aware of the need for professional standards, but they do little about it other than talk. The lone-wolf attitude is dominant, and the colleague in trouble has to fight his battle unaided. So that when a President of the United States capriciously bars a reputable columnist from his press conferences nearly all the man's associates know about it but, knowing, merely shake their heads and wonder what the world is coming to. All but one or two, who published the facts and through this publicity accomplished the rescission of the order.

One reason for this supineness as a group is the vast mushrooming of the reporter's job in Washington in recent years, and hence the multiplication of correspondents. With the expansion of the "corps" in numbers comes an inevitable contraction in quality, plus a growing diversity of interests which makes it more and more difficult to accomplish any semblance of cohesion within the group. When a single press association has seventy or more on its Washington staff, and a single New York newspaper has twenty active correspondents, it is not hard to understand where the corps spirit has gone if there ever was one.

For all this jeremiad, the fact remains that probably nowhere else in the country would it be possible to find standards as high as those instinctively observed here. For all their rapid numerical growth, for all the incipient shift in emphasis from seasoned journalists to relative greenhorns, for all the urge for speed at the expense of accuracy, for beating the other fellow at the expense of simple honor, the Washington correspondents are still the élite of the nation.

None but a stupid sentimentalist would attempt to impose upon the craft the romantic chivalry of a Bayard, the foolish politeness of Alphonse and Gaston. The correspondents ought to be rough, tough and courageous. They ought to be energetic, imaginative and discriminating. They ought to show no mercy in the legitimate pursuit of their occupation. But they ought, too, to be scrupulously honorable, toward one another and toward their news sources; they ought to engage in a greater measure of self-discipline, and they ought to be toughest and most courageous when their integrity, or that of any of their associates, is threatened from without.

III

There Were Giants in Those Days

"I WRITE OF THE CORRESPONDENTS AT
Washington," said an oldtimer in a long newspaper article
back in 1888; "there is no brighter class of men in the
country. Their average intellect is above that of the Congressmen, and their energy is only equalled by the Corliss
engine."

Thus an anonymous correspondent, writing of his fellows. Today we may be a bit more reserved in our judgment — the great expansion of the press corps, with the
multiplication of relatively inexperienced reporters, has unquestionably lowered the general level of intellect and ca-
pability — yet on the whole the correspondents in 1941
have very nearly as high an opinion of themselves as their
predecessors did half a century ago. Perhaps we feel less
pontifical — unless we are syndicated columnists — because
we lack the flowing beards and handlebar mustachios of
those veterans of an earlier and less complex era. For they
were pontifical indeed, considered themselves the equal of
anyone and the superior of most, and missed few opportunities to advertise the fact.

Indeed, they thought so highly of themselves in 1872
that they adjourned in a body to the Republican National
Convention in Philadelphia and there, by persistent lobby-

ing, prevented the renomination of Schuyler Colfax as Vice
President, the only occasion of record when the Washington newspaper corps was able to present a united front on
anything. Colfax, a reporter and publisher himself over a
period of some seventeen years, had turned to politics, and
had served fourteen years in the House of Representatives,
the last six as Speaker. In 1869 he was elected Vice President as running mate to General Grant.

During those ten years in which he presided first over
the House and then over the Senate he contrived to incur
the intense hatred of the Washington correspondents by
his high-handed treatment of them, and they were determined that he should not have another term if they could
prevent it. Despite the fact that many of their editors and
publishers were also present in Colfax's behalf, they ham-
mered away at the top men in the Grant machine until
they were able to sidetrack the Vice President in favor of
Senator Henry Wilson of Massachusetts, a patriot whose
Senatorial career, begun during the Civil War, was the
direct result of galls acquired riding a horse as aide to General McClellan. It is difficult to conceive, fifty years later,
of the Washington correspondents and their employers
lobbying at a national convention on opposite sides of an
issue, for the modern journalist is much more of a hired
hand.

Perhaps the truculence of the correspondents in the old
days stemmed in some measure from the generally anarchic
conditions in the nation and its Capital, when graft and
bribery were the order of the day, and men never hesitated
to call one another thieves and traitors in public addresses.

The correspondents were not immune to these influences, and in many cases became wealthy gambling in the stock market on the basis of confidential information they obtained. In a time when Vice Presidents and Senators were taking graft in large sums, it was not surprising to find some of the correspondents finding ways to line their own pockets, and the knowledge that the elected delegates of the people were rascals may have served, by inverted logic, to elevate their opinion of themselves.

Particularly in times of national stress, as during the hectic administration of Andrew Johnson, the press of the period made not the slightest effort to be impartial or even judicious in the reporting of news. The vilest rumor, with not a shred of available proof, would be printed as established fact, with much detail and color, and it was this sort of journalism that for many years fixed upon Johnson the bad reputation concocted for him by his enemies. An example of the reporting of that time was a Washington correspondent's account of the Senate's passage of the Civil Rights bill in 1866 over Johnson's veto:

"The battle opened early in the Senate. Lane, of Kansas, presented a resolution based upon the President's letter to Governor Sharkey, and made it the occasion of a bitter personal attack upon Mr. Wade, in vindication of the President. It was the speech of a demagogue, couched in the language of a bully, and delivered in a manner which would disgrace the stump. It was but an occasion to make known that he had sold himself to Mr. Johnson. . . . To this attack Senator Wade replied in a speech which brought out all the lion in him. He met the Senator from Kansas

on a field of his own choosing, and completely foiled him.
Several other Senators, by questions, placed this political
trickster in the light he deserved to have cast upon him.
. . . To the infinite disgust of everybody, Mr. Davis rose.
It was a terrible infliction, but something which is certain
to come to pass whenever any measure distasteful to rebels
is likely to pass. . . . Senator Saulsbury followed in a
speech which, for plainness, treasonable sentiments, and
villainy, was never surpassed. . . ."

Thus American journalism, and Washington correspondence, in the 1860's. Thousands of newspapers all over the
country daily reported national news in this vein; "news
items" of this stripe were the only source of information
of hundreds of thousands of readers. Yet the press of today,
pure as Galahad by comparison, is accused of bias! Indeed,
it is doubtful even in those times whether most of the editors were actually unscrupulous, or whether instead they
were not the victims of extreme party bias at a time when
partisan feeling was at the boiling point, and when means
of collecting and distributing news were utterly unreliable.
To aggravate an already vicious condition, the newspapers
were heavily dependent for their revenues upon political
patronage in the form of government advertising, and each
administration systematically starved the opposition press
and surfeited the loyal publishers. It was charged that the
New York Times was forced by such economic pressure on
the part of the traitors within Johnson's own Cabinet to
abandon its support of him.

The development later on of the telegraph and its swift
adaptation to the needs of the newspapers altered the char-

acter of the Washington dispatches; and eventually, with the organization of impartial press associations, any publisher who desired to be fair had ample opportunity.

The earliest Washington correspondents, of course, were not reporters in any real sense of the word, but observers who wrote for their papers letters full of pungent commentary, heavily partisan in tone, on what they saw during their occasional visits. Usually they were the editors themselves, and such news as they happened to include served only as a springboard for their editorial observations. The first of these was James Cheetham, editor of the *New York Citizen* and a strong supporter of Thomas Jefferson and the Democratic Republican Party. Though born in England, he was a whole-hearted American citizen, and made many visits to the new capital to further the policies of Jefferson and call down ruin upon the Federalists. For this was why the editors came — their letters were neither for entertainment nor for instruction, but for partisan political purposes, and as the press expanded in the new republic, they made it the most powerful single political force.

James Duane, Irish-born editor of the *Philadelphia Aurora*, followed in Cheetham's footsteps, but by this time the desirability of making the Capital a year-round headquarters had impressed itself upon a number of journalists, and in 1822 Elias Kingman of Providence, R.I., moved to Washington to stay. A graduate of Brown University and a man of marked talent with a winning personality, he established his own news bureau and for forty years contributed on a regular basis to the leading journals of the country. His letters were printed simultaneously in the

New York Journal of Commerce and Commercial Advertiser, the *Baltimore Sun*, the *Charleston Courier* and the *New Orleans Picayune*. He amassed a small fortune, and upon his retirement achieved the status of an elder statesman, receiving at his home a stream of politicians who turned to him for advice.

His example was quickly followed by others, who came to represent one or more papers. Among them was the elder James Gordon Bennett, who corresponded for the *New York Enquirer* for five years in the style of Walpole, and then returned to New York in 1832 to found the *Herald*. Bennett was the first to concern himself with gossip and personalities, and thus paved the way for an eventual pestilence of columnists.

Matthew L. Davis, a Tammany organizer and bosom friend of Aaron Burr, has been credited with being the most influential of all the correspondents of that early period. Writing as "The Spy in Washington" for the *New York Courier and Enquirer*, he wielded a ferocious pen, at one time bringing about a duel between two Congressmen by a bribery exposé in one of his letters. It is told of him that, after the election of Jefferson as President and Burr as Vice President, he went to Washington and boasted to the President that his election was due entirely to the machinations of the newly organized Tammany Hall. Jefferson said nothing, but when a large fly buzzed past his nose, reached out and caught it. Exhibiting it to Davis, he invited the journalist to observe what a very large head it had in proportion to the rest of its body. Davis was not quite sure what was meant, but decided that in any event it was not too complimentary, and ceased his boasting.

Later in life Davis, who in addition to his letters to New York corresponded for the *London Times* under the nom de plume of "The Genevese Traveller," was presented to the British Minister, Lord Ashburton, as the author of the letters.

"I am delighted to see you," exclaimed Ashburton. "They are extraordinary letters, and I have read them with great pleasure. I hope, sir, that you are well paid by the *Times*. If not, sir, let me know it; I will take care that you are paid handsomely."

Davis hastily replied that he was well paid indeed — two guineas per letter.

Major M. M. Noah, an eccentric casual "tripper" from New York, developed a considerable reputation with his letters, and a great deal of personal popularity in Washington, but before he became a newspaper correspondent — and afterward — he was a professional politician. He took to literature after a number of years as consul at Tunis, writing a book about his travels, but his greatest exploit, following his return to America, was his attempt to reassemble the Jews in a new Jerusalem on Grand Island in the Niagara River. He issued a formal proclamation to the Children of Israel calling on them to repair forthwith to the island, but while it created a considerable sensation it failed to lure many colonists, and he quietly dropped the project and turned to corresponding for several New York evening papers. Eventually President Jackson gave him a government job, and as with many another since in that situation, journalism knew him no more.

Just prior to the Civil War the press gallery boasted a list of names many of which later made history, in and out of journalism. There was O. G. Halpine of the *New York Times*; J. L. Crosby of the *New York Tribune*; Joseph Medill of the *Chicago Press* and *Tribune*; J. Russell Young, later editor of the *New York Tribune*, Henry Villard, A. R. Spofford, and Whitelaw Reid, later publisher of the *Tribune* and ambassador to London. Contemporary of these and outliving most of them on the Washington scene was Ben: Perley Poore of the *Boston Journal*, who began work as an amateur writer in the time of John Quincy Adams and continued steadily for sixty years until the first Cleveland administration. He was a ponderous man with a huge beard, and his literary style, by our current standards, was as ponderous as his physique, but his two volumes of "Perley's Reminiscences" are a priceless eye-witness story of the formative period in our national life.

The device of the interview, so integral a part of present-day newspaper practice, oddly enough was not thought of until about 1867, two years after the close of the Civil War, and it took an Irish immigrant and a disfranchised rebel to create this journalistic form. Perhaps they played posterity a sorry trick; certainly the interview has been sadly perverted from all semblance of anything but doubtful entertainment, when illiterate manufacturers and millionaires and strip-tease dancers are regularly sought out for their opinions on momentous topics of which they know little or nothing, and concerning which their views are worth less than nothing. Be that as it may, John B. McCullagh, Washington correspondent of the *Cincinnati Commercial*, wrote the first full-dress interview of record, and had there been a Pulitzer Prize he most certainly would have won it, for the man he interviewed was Alexander H. Stephens, who had been Vice President of the Confederacy.

The interview was really "hot," too, and not the casual vaporings of a politician trying to get his name in the papers without saying anything. McCullagh spent three whole days at Stephens' home in Georgia, and in the course of several long conversations learned that Stephens disapproved of slavery, having retained his own slaves only because they had no other means of support, and that he considered Jefferson's and Lincoln's second inaugural addresses as the greatest American state papers. This latter was too much for the South, and McCullagh was attacked as a liar and a cad for having put praise of the "illiterate rail splitter" in the mouth of Mister Stephens, suh! So numerous were the expressions of incredulity that long afterward, when he next saw Stephens, the reporter asked him to verify the statement, which he did.

This first three-column interview proved so successful that McCullagh was encouraged to continue. His most eminent confidant was President Andrew Johnson, who the first time he was interviewed had no idea it was for publication. Neither had McCullagh, but he was so impressed with the strength and clarity of the President's views that he asked permission to print them. Johnson assented, and was so gratified with the accuracy of the article that he consented to receive McCullagh almost any time he was asked.

"I always prepared myself upon the subject which I wished the President to discuss before I went," said McCullagh thirty years later, "and to a certain extent I had an idea of the answers which I thought he ought to make. His talks were entirely informal; many of them were more in the shape of chats than stilted interviews. We each had a rocking chair and President Johnson would rock back and forth as he talked. He spoke very freely, saying whatever came uppermost in his mind, and at the close of each interview I would ask him if there was anything he had said which he did not wish reported. He would then tell me to run over the subjects we had discussed. I would do this, and if there was anything which he thought should not be published he would tell me. As a rule, however, he allowed me to use my own judgment."

At a time when the President, fighting for his honor with few journalistic defenders, most needed favorable publicity he found it in the columns of McCullagh's paper, and frequently called in his friend for a conversation. During his impeachment trial this became a standing procedure, and Johnson remarked that "everybody seems to read the interviews and nobody seems to read my messages."

With the expanding use of the telegraph and the organization of press associations, the individualism of the Washington correspondents began almost imperceptibly to diminish, until it was possible for L. A. Gobright, manager of the Associated Press, to say to a Congressional investigating committee:

"My business is to communicate facts; my instructions do not allow me to make any comments upon the facts which I communicate. My dispatches are sent to papers of all manner of politics, and the editors say they are able to make their own comments upon the facts which are sent to them. I therefore confine myself to what I consider legitimate news. I do not act as a politician belonging to any school, but try to be truthful and impartial. My dispatches are merely dry matters of fact and detail."

During the Civil War, with the Capital in imminent peril of siege, the correspondents suffered, but not in silence, under a military censorship. There was no "voluntary" pledge to refrain from the publication of military secrets, but a straight-out control over all dispatches coming out of Washington. Bitter charges of stupidity and favoritism (familiar words!) were made by the correspondents, but the government paid no attention. To a certain extent it appeared to have been driven to this first — and to date last — venture into thorough-going censorship by the influx into the Capital of a rabble of fly-by-night "reporters," representing no responsible journals and bound by not the slightest measure of professional ethics or personal honor.

At any rate the honest correspondents suffered, as they always do at the hands of the unscrupulous among them, and at length obtained a Congressional investigation which bore out all their complaints. But Lincoln and his Cabinet paid no heed and the blue-penciling of copy continued. Some of the more enterprising adopted the device of traveling to Baltimore or Philadelphia to send out their news, since the censorship applied only in Washington and in the field of operations. One correspondent early in the war went down to Manassas, Va., with a large party of Congressmen to witness the rout of the Rebels at Bull Run. He witnessed instead the rout of the Congressmen, who stampeded fairly early in the battle. Knowing he could never get his story past the censor, he took the next train to Philadelphia and filed it from there.

As the government after the war expanded and with it the press gallery membership, direct contact with high-ranking government officials slowly but surely became less the rule and more the exception, and it was no longer safe, in a culture growing steadily more polite and less exciting, to call a President a blackleg or a thief. Presidents and Cabinet officers began to single out solitary individuals in whom to confide if at all, until, in the current century, the press had achieved such a high degree of respectability that the press conference and press agent system developed. This is not to say that all romance has gone out of Washington newspaper work: it is simply that the job has taken on so much of the neutral tone of big business that the individual, save for a few, inevitably is submerged.

Some are not. Judson C. Welliver of the *Washington Times* won the favor of Theodore Roosevelt, and eventual fortune as a business executive, by disagreeing with the President in open meeting. Roosevelt never held regular press conferences, but did on important occasions summon from one to a score or more of correspondents to his study to give them a piece of news. It was on one of these occasions that Welliver, in an encounter faintly reminiscent of that between Cyrano de Bergerac and young Christian de Neuvillette, displayed the temerity that endeared him to T.R.

Roosevelt had invited a group of newspapermen in to explain to them a new method of regulating the railroads which he was planning to adopt as a policy, and after he had concluded, he perfunctorily inquired what his guests thought of it. Obviously he expected nothing but praise, and that was all he would have got had not the audacious young Iowan, a newcomer to Washington, been present. Welliver, who had studied the problem enough to make him at least as much of an expert as the President, ventured to be the "no-man" in the crowd, and while his colleagues stood abashed and trembling in his behalf, explained courteously but fearlessly why he considered that Roosevelt was approaching railroad regulation from the wrong angle.

But the thunderbolt was never hurled. T.R. listened attentively, and when Welliver had finished expressed his gratification at the lecture. He invited Welliver to return alone for more of the same, with the result that the reporter finally went abroad with a presidential commission to study transportation methods in Europe. From that first encounter he was a White House pet.

Some years later, when T.R. was a candidate for the nomination against Taft in 1912, Welliver was covering the Chicago convention, but in the days just prior to the actual opening of that historic meeting the correspondents found little of real news to write. As a result they resorted to "blacksheeting." One would write a story and his friends would beg carbon copies, which they would either rewrite slightly or send without change.

On this occasion, on a Saturday afternoon, George E. Miller of the *Detroit News* hatched an idea, whereupon three correspondents of Washington papers, one from the *Star* and two, including Welliver, from the *Times*, independently asked him for blacksheets. Each, unknown to the others, sent off his carbon copy with no change other than the substitution of his own name at the top for that of Miller. Next day Welliver's editor received two identical dispatches from his two men, but before he could recover from his ire discovered that the same thing had already been printed in the Sunday morning edition of the *Star!*

A related incident occurred sixteen years later, when the *Baltimore Sun*'s correspondent at the Democratic convention in Houston neglected to remove from the blacksheet the name of the local political writer whose work it was, so that the story as received in Baltimore bore embarrassing evidence of its origin.

But probably the best blacksheet story of all, as told of an old-timer among the correspondents, has as its hero L. C. Speers, for more than thirty years a reporter on the *New York Times*. Speers was accompanying President-elect Hoover on his battleship junket around South America, and at one of the more attractive ports of call he decided it was time to lay aside for an evening the cares of his assignment. Speers always was a lone wolf, but since on this trip all news was officially released and all copy censored, it made little difference, except for style, whether he or someone else wrote his story, so long as it was written and

cabled. So he asked a colleague to fill in for him, just on
the off chance that he should not get back in time. An
hour or so later, having forgotten his precaution, he ran
into another correspondent and made a similar arrangement. His memory grew weaker as the evening wore on,
until he had asked in all five or six of his friends to cable
blacksheets of their stories to New York in his name. All
faithfully complied, and the *Times* that night received half
a dozen stories from the South American port, all contain-
ing the same news, all signed by Speers, but all written in
different styles. When Speers returned to home base the
late Adolph S. Ochs, the publisher, meeting him in the
city room, merely remarked:

"Well, Speersie, you certainly gave us good coverage,
didn't you!"

Speers used to wear a handsome and extremely expensive
scarfpin with a remarkable history, the history of a first-
run story produced by a man who couldn't let a holiday
make him forget he was a reporter. Speers was on vacation
in a Southwestern State, and while there got wind of a
major scandal in the State government. Immediately he
wired his managing editor asking whether the *Times* would
be interested, and getting an affirmative response, went to
work. Virtually single-handed he exposed the whole mess
and brought the culprits to justice, and the grateful citizens
of the State took up a subscription to buy him the pin.

Speers was sent to Mexico to cover some of the civil wars
there, and eventually became a close friend of General Plutarco Elias Calles. But he was not on such good terms with
the Mexico City police, and was continually being arrested

for one minor infraction or another. One day Calles asked him if there was anything he could do for him, and the newspaperman, by this time grown weary of being thrown into Mexican jails, said yes there was — the General would be doing him a great favor if he would give him some sort of safe conduct. Calles promptly wrote out a pass which informed all and sundry that *Señor* Leland C. Speers was not to be arrested for any cause whatever.

Speers took the card and promptly, with fire in his eye and a song in his heart, returned to a café from which he had been escorted under guard on several occasions. Almost immediately there ensued an altercation with the proprietor, who with virtually no preliminaries called in the police. "You are under arrest, *Señor*," they told him. "Who says I am?" retorted Speers, flashing his card. "*Señor!*" exclaimed the officers, bowing low, "is there anything we can do for you, *Señor?*" — and backed respectfully out of the place. Speers had no more trouble in Mexico City.

The development of the correspondents' corps in Washington has had no parallel in the development of a first-class press native to the city, with the result that the Capital of the greatest country in the world is at the same time the only capital without a truly national newspaper. The oldest of the lot — and the only one with sufficient wealth and local prestige to have any possibilities in this direction — has been consistently preoccupied since it was established with local and regional news.

The first "Washington" newspaper was founded before there was a Washington — in Georgetown in the year 1789. It was a weekly, the *Times and Potowmack Packet,* and it lasted fewer than six years. Since then close to a round thousand newspapers and periodicals have been bravely launched in what is now Washington, of which four daily newspapers and one weekly remain — the *Evening Star*, oldest of the lot, founded in 1852; the *Post*, founded in 1877; the *Times-Herald*, composed of two former Hearst papers upon which Mrs. Eleanor Patterson, their publisher, forced a shotgun marriage a few years ago; the *News*, a Scripps-Howard organ only twelve years old, and the *United States News*, a factual weekly record of governmental activities published by the columnist, David Lawrence.

Most of the very early ventures were subsidized party organs, set up in the Capital by the administration in power because of the need for a medium for informing and instructing the civil servants in party politics. At that time it took anywhere from two days to two weeks for Washington news to be transmitted to established newspaper centers, and by the time it was printed and returned by stagecoach it would be too late to be of much value to the political leaders. The subsidy then appeared to be about the only possible means of support for a paper, as was proved by the *Impartial Observer and Washington Advertiser*, first to be published within the actual boundaries of the new city. It was founded in the spring of 1795 by Thomas Wilson, a Norfolk printer, and it lasted precisely one year, despite Wilson's attempts to raise revenue by the sale of "Carey's war map, writing paper, writing ink, ink powder, etc."

Within six weeks after the removal of the government to Washington in 1800, six papers sprang up, two Republican and two Federalist, but only one, the *National Intelligencer*, endured for long. Its owners made every effort to publish an intelligent and literate journal, and as the official organ of Jefferson, Madison and Monroe it attained considerable distinction. By 1843 its editors, Joseph Gales, Jr. and William W. Seaton, had obtained permission to report Congressional debates, which they continued to do until 1860, when Gales died and the *Intelligencer*, after sixty years' existence, expired. During the War of 1812 the *Intelligencer* underwent a brief suspension of publication, not for lack of readers but because its editor was at the front defending Washington while the British troops were upsetting his type fonts.

Why Washington in its 141 years should have developed no nationally influential newspaper is a mystery no one has attempted to solve: only two since the pre-Civil War period — the *Star* and the *Post* — have come within hailing distance of such a consummation, and the *Star*, which since 1867 has been the property of a single family, has never appeared to have any ambitions in that direction. The correspondents of the press associations and the out-of-town journals began early and still continue to be almost the sole interpreters to the nation of the policies and projects of its representatives.

IV

President and Press: The First Thirty Years

ONE DAY IN 1895 WILLIAM W. Price, a reporter for the *Washington Star*, walked up Pennsylvania Avenue to the White House and took up a position just outside the front gate. When politicians who had been calling on President Cleveland emerged, "Fatty" Price buttonholed them and milked them of what news they were willing to give down. He was the first White House correspondent.

Price suffered many rebuffs. The *Star* had great local prestige, but in those days no reporter ranked high enough socially to stop strangers on the street and ask them impertinent questions. It took a lot of nerve but it paid dividends in news for the *Star*, and before long reporters for other papers, and out-of-town correspondents, joined Price in front of the Executive Mansion and with him ambushed the great, fresh from their communion with the Burning Bush.

Seven years passed, and the little knot of men outside the old iron fence grew larger. Had it been a generation later they might have been mistaken for pickets, instead of honest reporters earning their daily schnapps. The politicians and Cabinet officers and diplomats grew accustomed to seeing them there, accepted them first as an unavoidable nuisance, then as a partial blessing, a band of heralds who could be relied upon to publish to the world the well-considered philosophy of the statesman.

Seven years they walked their beat, in the rigors of winter and the ghastly summer heat, in rain, snow, and sleet. Then one day it rained, a cold, dismal rain characteristic of Washington winters. From a window in the White House, warm and protected from the elements, Theodore Roosevelt looked out and took pity. Or perhaps he had an inspiration.

At any rate, the first President to know the full value of publicity, the first President of a new century and a new era, called in his secretary and then and there directed that a special room be set aside in the newly built Executive Offices for the sole use of the press. The Washington correspondents had come of age.

Many years earlier the Congress, peculiarly sensitive to the sweet uses of publicity, had made full provision for their convenience in reporting legislative proceedings, but the Presidents had remained aloof, some seeing an occasional favored reporter, some seeing none, but all looking with a measure of distrust upon the correspondents as a whole. Theodore Roosevelt took them in, literally and figuratively.

In the nearly two-score years since Roosevelt I saw a golden opportunity from his study window, the White House run has grown and expanded and become ritualized to a degree that would have amazed Fatty Price and his fellow-pioneers. There have been as many motifs in presidential press relations as there have been Presidents, but there has never been any real retrograde movement as a whole. Theodore Roosevelt showed his successors how to make use of the press, and they all followed his example, some reluctantly and with disastrous results like Hoover; some gladly but ineptly, like Harding, but only one with a finesse that surpassed that of T.R. The White House correspondents have never known but one Franklin D. Roosevelt, and they probably will never know another.

Let no one assume that when Theodore Roosevelt gave the reporters a press room he also gave them his confidence. The press conference had not yet been evolved, and the chief advantage of the workroom was that it gave a point of vantage, indoors out of the weather, from which to pounce upon the President's callers. Roosevelt himself never worked with the correspondents *en masse*, but played favorites, giving private interviews to those he favored at the moment.

He originated the "trial balloon," a device for disclosing prematurely a tentative policy, and then charting his course by the public reaction. If the reaction was good, the policy went into effect; if bad, the reporter was roundly repudiated, denounced as a malicious liar and a friend of the trusts, and the policy was laid away in mothballs.

The trial balloon has been used extensively since, but T.R. was the first to realize that he need not burst unannounced on an unprepared nation with a novel proposal.

Allowing for the difference in generations, T.R. in his relations with the press was very like Roosevelt II, who revised and perfected the instrument of power invented by his relative. T.R. captivated the correspondents by his personal charm, he fascinated them with his barber-chair interviews, shrill voice emitting expletives, arms waving, while the dexterous valet fenced at the presidential whiskers.

He let no scruples stand in the way of a favorable press. He courted reporters and then consigned them to the Ananias Club for perfectly accurate recitals if the public response was bad. He used the press to the limit. He was arbitrary and arrogant. The press loved him.

Yet he was the first, and to the time of this writing the only, President to use to the full his power to deny a correspondent normal access to the news. The entire episode was a comedy of errors, and T.R. came out of it slightly the worse for wear.

A correspondent named Jesse Carmichael was told by what he considered to be a thoroughly reliable source a bizarre tale involving the Roosevelt children and a Thanksgiving turkey, and he wrote it, with all the trimmings, in the *Boston Herald*. According to this story, a huge turkey which someone had given the President escaped in the White House grounds, and the boys pursued it with bows and arrows, finally bringing it down, while Daddy cheered them on.

The story turned out to be false, and it was not only the turkey's feathers that flew. T.R. was enraged, not only because the yarn was untrue, not only because of the sharp criticism of the turkey lovers, but even more, perhaps, because he considered that his family was not a legitimate news topic. He ordered his secretary to bar Carmichael from the White House and from all other Executive agencies.

He went further in his anger, and forbade the Weather

Bureau to furnish its forecasts to the *Herald*, but here he stubbed his toe, for the law requires the Bureau to furnish such service to all papers. The *Herald* promptly threatened civil suit, and the order was canceled.

But the interdict against Carmichael himself stood — for a while. All the other correspondents meanwhile provided him with carbon copies of everything they wrote, with the result that never before, without going near a government office, had he done such a complete job of covering Washington. When the President realized that he was checkmated, he withdrew the interdict as gracefully as he could.

There was another correspondent who incurred T.R.'s displeasure in a rather unique fashion. He had just arrived from Chicago and didn't know the ropes, but seeing a large and imposing delegation of Chicagoans entering the White House to make some appeal or other to the President, he mingled with them and went in as one of the delegation. The ensuing conference made an outstanding exclusive story, but this man was too conscientious just to walk out with it. He lingered behind, introduced himself to the President, explained how he happened to be there, and then asked how much of the story he might print.

T.R. leaped to his feet, shook his fist across the desk, and in his shrillest tones shouted:

"If you print one solitary word of that conference I'll publicly repudiate it!"

The correspondent backed out in haste, and was told by the President's secretary that the incident probably would result in his being barred from the White House. Taking this as an indirect order, he stayed away for a good while, until informed that he had not been excommunicated and all was forgiven.

Five Presidents and twenty-five years intervened between Roosevelt I and Roosevelt II. Under these Presidents — Taft, Wilson, Harding, Coolidge and Hoover — White House press relations expanded and became regularized, but there was no marked advance, from the point of view of the correspondents, until F.D.R.'s famous first conference in March, 1933, from which the reporters emerged dazed and babbling like so many children at a party.

Taft, fat and amiable, made a genuine attempt to go on from the point where his predecessor and political godfather had left off, but he lacked the rare talent a President requires to deal successfully with the press. He instituted weekly conferences with all the correspondents, and from the beginning they liked the big, good-humored man who had taken the place of the strident, dynamic Roosevelt.

But the correspondents were never permitted to pin anything directly on the President: the most they were permitted to say was that "the President is concerned about" something or other, or "the President is considering" some course of action. Meanwhile Taft communed frequently and intimately with Gus J. Karger of the *Cincinnati Times-Star*, owned by the President's half-brother, and thus tried to keep the news in the family. Karger nevertheless occasionally "leaked" to his associates when he was able.

But the memorable feud that terminated the Taft-Roosevelt friendship also terminated the amicable relations of Taft with the press. The return of "Teddy" into the news, pitted directly against the President, caused many of the correspondents to desert the incumbent and return to their first love, and Taft felt the defection keenly. He considered that the correspondents were being unfair, and an atmosphere of hostility developed which was never dispelled.

Woodrow Wilson, the Princeton professor with a program of reform, invited the correspondents at the beginning to co-operate with him, to bring him reports on the trend of public opinion while receiving from him full and frank discussion of his acts and policies. For two years he held mass press conferences twice a week, but they were never a success. Wilson brought to the White House the atmosphere of the college classroom, and assumed the didactic pose of a professor lecturing a group of backward freshmen.

Despite his glowing half-promises, he seldom took the press into his conference, and the reports he had asked them to bring were not delivered. He was excessively cautious and aloof. It was he who, imitating the European technique, invented the "White House spokesman" as a mask for himself. (The President himself addressed the reporters, but they quoted him as "a spokesman.") On the other hand, he did permit himself for a time to be directly quoted — until he had been seriously misquoted on several occasions.

Perhaps the chief trouble with Wilson was that he was more humanitarian than human, more mind than man. He could never bring himself to be jovial with the reporters, and his attempts at humor were ponderous and pitifully professorial. Like Theodore Roosevelt, he sternly objected to the publication of personal news about himself or his family, and criticism of members of his Cabinet drove him

into something like a cold fury. He never really understood
what it was all about, and was essentially anti-press. Later
he described his experience in these words:

"I came to Washington with the idea that close and
cordial relations with the press would prove of the greatest
aid. I prepared for the conferences as carefully as for any
lecture, and talked freely and fully on all large questions of
the moment. Some men of brilliant ability were in the
group, but I soon discovered that the interest of the majority was in the personal and trivial rather than in principles
and policies."

If the testimony of correspondents who attended his conferences can be relied upon, Wilson must have adopted this
latter attitude almost at the outset, for there is no body of
proof that he ever carried out the lofty project in press relations which he himself outlined. He appeared always to
have maintained a standard of absolute perfection — for
others.

With the *Lusitania* incident as an excuse, Wilson broke
off direct relations with the correspondents, and never saw
them again in a body, so that for some six years there were
no White House press conferences. Had Wilson had the
political cunning of a Roosevelt and been less of a social
introvert, it is not beyond the realm of possibility that
many of his post-war defeats might have been avoided, or
at least mitigated. It is at such times that a President most
needs the friendly support of the Washington correspondents, and it was, perversely, during just this period that
Wilson didn't see the press at all. It would be difficult to

conceive of Franklin D. Roosevelt denying himself such an asset.

With the advent of Warren G. Harding and his ungrammatical "normalcy" the Washington correspondents rapidly regained all the ground temporarily lost in the Wilson administration. Harding was a small newspaper publisher himself, and with his limited intellect probably looked upon the more important correspondents as his superiors rather than as his inferiors. At any rate, he revived the open press conferences and was frank to the point of loquacity.

Unfortunately for the new regime, however, he had neither the high intellectuality of Wilson nor the mental alertness of Roosevelt, and almost from the start he began putting his foot in his mouth. Naturally, he was popular with the correspondents because he did treat them well, but as his mouth grew larger his foot grew correspondingly smaller, and a series of extremely embarrassing incidents followed. Harding persisted in a progressive revelation of his own incompetence, and his wooden Indian façade could not long conceal the utter void behind it.

Ultimately, after several minor lapses, he precipitated a first-class international incident which resulted in curtailment of the press conference privileges.

During the naval disarmament conference of 1921, the President, in response to a direct question, gave an interpretation of the treaty which was diametrically opposite to the one previously divulged by Secretary of State Hughes and understood by all the delegates to the conference. Publication of his interpretation caused a great sensation, and Hughes insisted upon an official correction. He also insisted that thereafter the President should answer only questions submitted in advance, in writing, and at his next conference Harding, greatly embarrassed, announced the new policy. Later it was modified to permit "follow-up" questions leading out of those submitted in writing.

Despite all his intellectual limitations and his general ineptitude, the correspondents developed a genuine fondness for this political accident, and frequently protected him from the consequences of his own stupidity. Without this affection his administration might well have been punctured long before it was.

Harding ignored all the social restrictions of his high office whenever he could get away with it, and sought out the society of ill-assorted cronies with whom he could forget that he was President. The poker parties in the "little green house on K Street" are a matter of history; the games of Hearts at the old Press Club are less well known, but there are correspondents now in Washington who had occasion to curse the President under their breath when he passed them the Queen of Spades.

The Coolidge administration provided the correspondents with more amusement and less news than any other. Coolidge continued the weekly conferences on a more restricted basis than Harding's, but he never directly courted the favor of the press. Talkative to the point of garrulity, he seldom discoursed extensively or intelligently on important matters, and it was this silence on anything that counted, plus his fiction of the "White House Spokesman," that gave him the wholly synthetic reputation of a "strong, silent man."

Prevented by the blank wall of the conferences from writing much real news out of the White House, the correspondents diverted themselves by relating homely incidents involving the President as man. Reversing the trend of his predecessors, he reveled in this sort of publicity and saw to it that there was plenty available. At the same time he resented any criticism of his policies, and never made any worthwhile use of the press conference.

He could not be quoted even indirectly, and would not permit his refusal to answer a question (often an important piece of news in itself) to be mentioned. Because so many correspondents quoted the "Spokesman" as saying such a variety of things, the White House press conferences reached their lowest ebb as a reliable news source, yet Coolidge's only remedy was to deny stories, as had Roosevelt I, when the public reaction was bad.

An amusing incident early in his administration admirably illustrated his extreme sensitivity to public sentiment, even in very small matters. At one of his conferences he donned the mask of the "Spokesman" and made some mildly disparaging remarks about fishing as a sport. The story was widely published, and the fishermen of the nation took it very badly. Within the year President Coolidge was fishing at every opportunity, incongruously garbed in business suit, choker collar, fedora and wading boots, and the news photographers were invited to take his picture as often as they pleased.

Undoubtedly he was bored to distraction, but was not the man to overlook little opportunities for cultivating public favor. He relieved his feelings during these piscatorial sorties by snagging with the hook the fingers of the Secret Service man whom he took along to keep it baited.

The trivia that was published about Coolidge greatly exceeded in volume the important news, and much of it he himself directly inspired, telling homely stories about himself to the Secret Service men, who dutifully passed them on to the reporters. The whole absurd Coolidge legend, in fact, was almost entirely a creation of the press.

J. Russell Young of the *Washington Star* once wrote a little story about Coolidge feeding peanuts to the squirrels on the White House lawn. Next time he saw Young the President exhibited a big bag of peanuts, saying, "I've got some!" It was said of him at the time that thereafter he walked as often as possible about the grounds, tossing one peanut to a squirrel and eating two.

Perhaps one reason the correspondents delighted in writing these homely bits about Coolidge was that his type of wry, sterile humor, and the mounting evidence he gave of being a very small, very solemn man in a very big job, intrigued them by reason of the contradictions involved. At any rate, the output increased steadily right up to the time he retired to a journalistic career, and when he died the correspondents sent over the wire many columns of nothing but anecdotes that had been told about or by him.

When he was alive he delighted in every one of these stories, and was equally gratified when he could make an original wisecrack about a reporter. One such was Charles R. Michael of the *New York Times*, who possessed the faculty of asking questions which could not be answered without embarrassment, and who had incurred the temporary displeasure of the President. Adolph S. Ochs, publisher of the *Times*, called on Coolidge at his summer camp, and Michael hung around the cottage to talk to him when he came out. As the publisher and the reporter walked away together, Coolidge turned to an aide and remarked:

"There go the Ochs and the ass."

Another reporter, Al Reck of the *Washington Daily News*, had the adolescent habit of telephoning press relations officers and announcing himself as President Coolidge or Chief Justice Hughes or what have you. When the submarine S-4 sank to the bottom Reck was on night duty covering the Navy. Around midnight the phone rang in the Navy press room and a nasal voice said:

"This is President Coolidge; I'd like the latest word on the S-4."

The officer in charge replied:

"Aw, cut out the horseplay, Al, and come on down here out of the cold."

There was a moment's silence, then the voice again, twangier than ever and much more emphatic:

"This is Calvin Coolidge, President of the United States! I want to find out about the S-4."

The officer nearly had heart failure, and waited anxiously for days for the axe to fall, but it never did.

Once someone gave the President a raccoon named Rebecca. This furnished copy for quite a while, and then one day Rebecca went into a decline, and the reporters were advised indirectly of her condition. The daily bulletins finally revealed that Rebecca was diagnosed to be pining for love, and the publication of this distressing fact brought an immediate gift of an anonymous male 'coon.

Editors wanted to know the name of Rebecca's husband, but the correspondents couldn't find out, so they agreed that it should be Horace, and Horace got a deal of publicity. Then one day the "White House Spokesman" stood up in press conference and said, through his nose:

"You boys have been calling this raccoon Horace. His name is not Horace."

This was the Great Stone Face's idea of a priceless joke on the press; it never occurred to him that it was a very sorry joke indeed for news of the national government to be so manhandled, through the absence of a reasonable official co-operation, that the nation never really knew accurately what was going on and was compelled to batten on humorous anecdotes.

All this time, up the street in the Commerce Department building, a big, fat-faced man was handing out intelligible news of the government in general and discussing administration policy with illuminating frankness. The press intelligence system he developed, and the extremely cordial relations with the correspondents that resulted, had much to do with making him President. Before his nomination, Herbert Hoover came to be accepted as God's gift to the correspondents; before his election there arose occasion for some slight misgivings; his first major contact with the press after the election — his battleship tour of South America — was distinguished by an absolute and literal censorship.

After his inauguration it soon became apparent, even to

those most reluctant to concede the obvious, that all the frank, informal talks with reporters, all the amiability of the man they had ballyhooed as "the Great Engineer," were a cold and brutal build-up for the presidential nomination. When this finally trickled down into the consciousness of the corps as a whole, President Hoover began to be treated as a news source rather than as a portly demigod, and to be judged accordingly.

The outcome of this unillusioned judgment was one of the most complete and disastrous collapses of a myth that could be imagined. Hoover of course was the cause of his own collapse, and his misguided presidential ambitions constituted a great personal tragedy because of his fundamental unfitness for the office; but the correspondents, no longer laboring under the spell of his pre-presidential affability, experienced no emotional compulsion to make him look better than he was.

The requirement that all copy from his South American "goodwill" tour be submitted for censorship was the tip-off; his attitude as President bore out the forecast. Hoover was morbidly sensitive to publicity; it is said that he read religiously everything written about him, and all but memorized the unfavorable stories. In Coolidge's place he might have done very well and gone down in history as one of our better Presidents; it was his fate to inherit the office at a time when a superman, which he was not, was indicated. He couldn't stand the gaff.

Hoover continued the semi-weekly press conference and partially abolished the "spokesman" device by permitting some indirect quotation, although he did adhere to the requirement that original questions be in writing. He enjoyed making important formal announcements, which he read from a prepared text, his eyes assiduously avoiding those of the reporters, but the informal aspects of the conference, once things began going awry in the nation, were agony for him.

As matters became worse and he fumbled distractedly with the machinery of government, his press conferences became more and more perfunctory, his manner colder and more ill-at-ease. He began slighting the press corps as a whole, favoring instead a chosen few, notably Mark Sullivan, William Hard and Richard V. Oulahan, while attempting the professional ruin of those who were not "in his corner."

Early in his administration President Hoover started spending week-ends at his fishing camp on the Rapidan River in the Blue Ridge, about a hundred miles from Washington, and it was on one of these excursions that an incident occurred which brought to a head all the growing hostility between press and President. Generally the White House correspondents were notified of the trips in advance, but sometimes the President tried to slip away without the usual escort of five or six reporters, and then there would be a mad scramble to hire cars and follow him.

Actually the correspondents never molested him at his camp and were not in a position to do so had they wished. They were there just for "protection," in case anything happened to the President. They put up at a hotel at Orange or Luray, Va., a good distance from camp, and arranged for perfunctory telephonic reports from his secretary on the news, if any. The camp itself was heavily guarded by Marines, and no one was permitted near the entrance.

On Sunday, July 5, 1931, during the German debt moratorium negotiations, Hoover was at camp as usual, and the correspondents were idling about their hotel in anticipation of the customary drive back on Monday morning. But suddenly they were informed that the President had left for Washington.

They followed as quickly as possible, and next morning the papers carried graphic but entirely sympathetic stories of the hasty departure and the dash back to the White House on urgent government business. The President had left without lunch over the protests of his official party, and a station wagon, following him with sandwiches, overtook his car only after a hazardous ride over the winding Virginia road. The trip had taken a remarkably short time, and the average speed was given.

The President was furious. The dramatic accounts of his ride, entirely truthful and without a suggestion of criticism, were taken as a personal attack, and he instituted what became known as the "leak" investigation, to find out who was providing the correspondents with these intimate details. He was particularly enraged at the revelation of the speed with which he had traveled, a very simple thing to compute, and blamed it all on the wagging tongues of Secret Service men.

Very likely his wrath was heightened by the coincidence that not many weeks earlier Frank Connor of the *New York World*, trying to keep up with the reckless speed of the presidential caravan, was forced into the ditch and with

his wife was gravely injured. (The President steadfastly refused to be preceded by a motorcycle escort, with the result
that ordinary motorists on the highway could not know,
unless they saw and recognized the White House license
numbers, that this was an official party.)

At any rate the investigation was pursued in a mood of
deadly seriousness, though it rapidly took on most of the
more ridiculous aspects of a comic opera. Secret Service
men known to be friendly with the reporters were under
suspicion, and just to make it funnier, one of the best of
these news sources was unwittingly assigned to the investigation. After a while the correspondents got into the spirit
of it, and began writing any number of harmless little stories of the sort that would have delighted Coolidge, but
which they knew from experience would annoy Hoover.

One of these was the tale of the patched window curtain, and it was told in the most charitable manner imaginable. A curtain on a White House window had been
mended, and the fact was disclosed as an evidence of depression economy. But again the President took it as a criticism, and looked harder than ever for his "leak."

Eventually the correspondents began writing daily accounts of the progress of the investigation, thus publishing
it to the world in all its childishness.

Actually there were many stories that the reporters could
have printed and didn't: stories of the President's petulance
over minor matters, of his pitiable indecision when confronted with the necessity for an important stroke of policy,
of his distrust of his closest advisers. But they didn't print

them, and what they did print was, by and large, legitimate news.

Hoover lost favor with the voters because of his ineptitude in office; he lost favor with the correspondents because of his brutal, though clumsy, attempts at censorship, the result of his utter inability to appreciate the value of friendly publicity.

At the time of the "leak" investigation a group of correspondents and their wives whiled away a long evening at a lodge atop Stony Man Mountain, some miles from the Rapidan camp, composing a theme song to the tune of "The Infantry, the Infantry, With Dust Behind Their Ears," with this final stanza:

> Although Marines are stationed down at President
>   Hoover's camp,
> Don't ask them if the road is rough or if the weather's
>   damp;
> For answers to these questions you must search your
>   several beans:
> State secrets are well guarded by United States Ma-
>   rines.

All this time, however, there was a growing undercurrent of resentment at the treatment of the press by the President and his secretariat — the faithful ex-detective Richey; the affable but powerless Newton, a lame-duck Congressman; and the bumbling ex-journalist Joslin. This resentment ultimately came to the surface with the presentation of a series of "demands" on behalf of all the correspondents, demands reasonable enough and not at all out of line with previous press relations technique at the White House.

Most of them were agreed to, but with little genuine improvement in a situation which had gone too far to be mended except by a complete change of personnel, a situation which was the direct responsibility of a man unequal to his job, who trusted no one, and who feared personal publicity. One of the results of the "leak" investigation had been a virtual order to the correspondents to print nothing that did not come through official channels, the nearest approach to a direct attempt at censorship-at-source since the first World War. The press paid no attention to the order, but they had little or no co-operation from then on so far as the White House was concerned.

On a number of occasions, it has been repeatedly charged, the President resorted to direct and spontaneous falsehood when in difficulties or in response to unfavorable political developments, and his efforts to prevent the press from publishing anything he had not authorized continued. His secretaries fell in with his mood and instead of giving him good advice (knowing perhaps that it would be useless), abetted his attempted censorship. Once Theodore G. Joslin, the press secretary, lectured the correspondents on the necessity for consulting him before sending out stories. When this was published he called them in again, denied that he was trying to censor them, and then asked that they refrain from publishing either his original request or his denial!

Of course the attitude of the White House permeated the entire Executive establishment. Departmental press contacts were curtailed and became perfunctory. And finally the President himself arrived at the goal toward which he had been steadily moving — he simply stopped seeing the press. From June 1 to November 25, 1932, a period starting before the national conventions and running nearly three weeks past the election, Hoover met the correspondents only eight times, although normally those twenty-five weeks would have included fifty conferences. From September 13 on there were no conferences at all, and the only news from the White House, other than the weekly chronicling of the failure to hold conferences, was contained in the perfunctory press releases handed out by Joslin.

So the Hoover administration petered out, the debacle in press relations providing a striking symbol of the whole. As T. S. Eliot wrote in his poem "The Hollow Men" —

> This is the way the world ends
> This is the way the world ends
> This is the way the world ends
> Not with a bang but a whimper.

V

President and Press: Mister Big

On November 8, 1940, for the first time in the history of the White House assignment, a newspaperman was barred from presidential press conferences because of the political tone of his correspondence. Theodore Roosevelt had excommunicated a correspondent for a specific offense involving members of the President's family, but never before had a reporter been barred because of undefined "general inaccuracies."

Paul Mallon's refusal to take the order without questioning, and the prompt reportorial activity of Charles Hurd of the *New York Times*, resulted in swift rescission of the ban, but the unprecedented incident marked a crisis in the relations of press and government.

The atmosphere surrounding the President had been growing more and more tense, with regard to the newspapers, as his campaign for a third term progressed to a conclusion. As in 1936, the majority of the big newspapers were editorially arrayed against him, and he publicly resented their opposition, sneering openly in at least one speech at one of them.

His subordinates and satellites were quick to follow his lead: the press was "big business"; its writers were compelled to follow the dictates of the owners regardless of their own convictions; its editorial expression should, but did not, follow popular trends, hence it was not a "free press"; Wendell L. Willkie received more space, and a better position in the papers, than did Franklin D. Roosevelt.

When, on November 5, the nation returned Mr. Roosevelt with an impressive vote of confidence, there was a chorus of "I told you so's"; the newspaper readers had repudiated the newspapers again. Three days later, on a Friday morning, Paul R. Mallon, a veteran Washington correspondent and an independent columnist, was barred from the press conference by a Secret Service man. No specific criticism was offered, and there was but one conclusion to be drawn: the anti-New Deal tone of his column, widely syndicated in several hundred papers with a great variety of political views, had offended the administration.

The correspondents had been anticipating some sort of forthright criticism at the least — some, indeed, were entirely prepared for punitive measures — and when word of Mallon's punishment got around there was no doubt that the campaign had started. The removal of the ban (there had been a "misunderstanding") within a few hours was unable to obliterate the fact that it had been ordered.

Every one of the correspondents vividly recalled the press conference of Secretary of the Interior Ickes twenty-four hours earlier, a conference devoted almost entirely to a polemic against the newspapers along the now familiar lines. Ickes had long been the advance guard, the parachute trooper, of the more extreme New Dealers; the initial exponent of revolutionary policies. He was the *banderillero*, and when he started sticking darts into a bull, it had become a common assumption that a matador was not far away.

Ickes paid his respects to the press on Thursday. Mallon was barred from the President's conference on Friday. The following Tuesday, November 12, for the first time in his administration, Roosevelt canceled a conference with the old Hoover excuse of "no news," an excuse which the correspondents had long since come to recognize as meaning that the President was in no mood to see them.

But then something happened. On Friday there was the usual conference with more or less the usual atmosphere. Ickes sloped rapidly away from the fray, settling down instead to assemble a symposium of all shades of opinion on "the freedom of the press." And about two months later the President's secretary, Stephen Early, addressed these words to a gathering of journalists in St. Paul:

"Thank God our editors are subject to no limitations except those imposed by the law of libel. . . . A free press is absolutely essential to the democratic way of life. Since democratic government is in the last analysis government by public opinion, our whole democratic structure falls if freedom in the expression of opinion is curtailed or suppressed in any way."

Presumably, unless Mr. Roosevelt or Mr. Early some time writes an entirely frank memoir, no one ever will know just what occasioned the abrupt cessation of attacks on the newspapers; what brought about the restoration of normal press relations at the White House. It is safe to guess, however, that it came about somewhat in this manner:

One of two important government officials made representations to the President against the iniquitous Mr. Mallon, whose comments had frequently given them pain. Mr. Roosevelt, at the height of his own pique at the press in general, and flushed with his two-day-old electoral victory, acted impulsively, as he has been known to do, and ordered Mallon barred from the conferences.

Mallon's undaunted Irish response to the affront, the immediate inquiry into the facts by the correspondent of the nation's most influential newspaper and their publication next morning in that paper, caused Mr. Roosevelt and his advisers to take second thought. Perhaps their thoughts ran along this general line:

We are engaged in a great and historic campaign to put the United States in a position of armed non-belligerency as an ally of Great Britain; our campaign, generally popular in the nation, is founded on the premise that democratic procedure is worth fighting for; a free and untrammeled press (as Early said two months later) is one of the prime requisites for the effective functioning of democracy; anyhow, how would we feel if we should lose, on a collateral issue, the now almost unanimous support the press is giving our foreign policy?

In times of national stress, when the Executive must be trusted beyond all normal limits, there is an extremely short step from free government to dictatorship, particularly when the Executive is a man of great energy and self-confidence. There are many who feel that in the first two weeks of November, 1940, President Roosevelt was very close to that step, insofar as it affected freedom of the press.

There is, perhaps, considerable significance to be read into the fact that Early, the one of Roosevelt's three secretaries who is a bona fide newspaperman, had just started a long leave of absence when the Mallon incident occurred, a leave which was expected to terminate in his resignation; and that almost immediately he returned to work. Early is a fiery Virginian, related to Jubal Early the raider. He is irritable and quarrels with the White House correspondents, and they sometimes say unkind things about him. But by and large, he is probably their best friend, and the strongest exponent of a free press, at the White House.

It will, of course, be a long time, if ever, before the remarkably cordial relationship between the President and the correspondents which Roosevelt established in March, 1933 is fully restored. And that is a pity, so far as Roosevelt at least is concerned. No President since Theodore Roosevelt has enjoyed so full a measure of affection from the working press; none has gone so far in helping them with their work.

Even the minority among the regular White House correspondents who consistently and actively disagree with the President are unwillingly drawn to him by his lethal charm, and that, no doubt, accounts in large measure for the depth of their resentment against him. The majority disagree with him to a greater or less extent, but they like him, and are in a position to be of great assistance to him in interpreting his policies so long as they can know they are being treated fairly.

Yet no generation of correspondents has long maintained such a spirit of uncritical enthusiasm as permeated the corps early in 1933, and it would be bad for the press and the nation if this were otherwise. The newspaper readers would get very little beyond the official interpretation of government news; they would learn nothing of the details of policy and administration which have so vital a bearing on the whole.

At the same time, no President has ever been able to preserve full equanimity in the face of dawning disillusionment on the part of the correspondents, and this would be especially true of one who, like Roosevelt, had taken them to his bosom with so passionate an embrace. He would be a little more than human if the subsequent stings did not occasionally remind him of the proverbial viper.

The advent of Roosevelt, to the accompaniment of the din of crashing banks, had all the aspects of a popular revolution, and one of the immediate results of this revolution was the removal of the dust and cobwebs that had enveloped press relations at the White House during the Hoover administration. Hoover had gone out unwept by the correspondents, utterly withdrawn into contemplation of his own pitiful failure, providing no news, and striving more and more clumsily to hide his shortcomings under a bushel. The press corps fervently hoped that this new man with the genial grin would be different, and they were not disappointed.

On the night after Roosevelt's inauguration, the correspondents were waiting at the White House for the announcement of the bank holiday and the suspension of gold payments. After a series of postponements George Benson, hardshell Republican correspondent of the *Minneapolis Journal*, yawned and delivered himself of an all-time masterpiece of inaccuracy:

"It's going to be just like this all through this administration — just waiting around and nothing happening."

That very week Roosevelt held his first press conference, a conference such as had never before been seen at the White House or anywhere else, one which ended in a spontaneous and unparalleled burst of applause. The promised New Deal had reached the long-starved Washington correspondents.

The old order in press relations was swept completely away. Full-time press relations officers, mostly ex-newspapermen of broad experience, were put to work in all the departments and principal administrative agencies, and regular press conferences, once or twice a week, were made the rule. The new regime understood what the old had forgotten — that no democratic government can survive without full publicity.

Roosevelt himself struck the keynote at once. There would be no "White House Spokesman," no written questions. The President could be quoted directly only when he specifically authorized, but the substance of what he said could be freely attributed to him. "Background" information could be used but not attributed to the President or the White House, and was intended to improve the perspective of the reporter in writing his story. Finally, "off-the-record" remarks were not to be published in any way.

This was by far the most liberal form of press conference yet devised, and the correspondents hailed it with cheers, which were not diminished in volume after the first meeting with the President had demonstrated that he meant what he said. There had been nothing in the man's past relations with the press to prepare them for this display of skill and genial frankness, but there it was, like all the other Roosevelt surprises. Gone was the dour, almost furtive atmosphere of Hoover's infrequent conferences, gone the dreadful sterility of Coolidge's. The new President talked freely and at length, and his words were full of news.

Roosevelt brought with him to Washington three secretaries, of whom one, Early, was an experienced newspaperman. Steve took general charge of White House press relations, and kept an eye on the departmental press agents as well. And for the first time in history the White House relations with the correspondents were put on a really systematic basis.

Twice a week the President met the reporters at a fixed time. Every weekday Early met them in the morning to answer questions, explain the President's visiting list, and hand out such secondary information as was available. The President's conferences have continued without serious interruption, and even at Hyde Park or Warm Springs he has made it a matter of routine to receive the correspondents at the regular time.

The press conference, however, while the most spectacular manifestation of Roosevelt's keen sense of publicity values, was only a part of the revolution he accomplished. The whole creaking mechanism was overhauled and speeded up. When the President had a formal statement to make, mimeographed copies were ready for the correspondents within a fairly short time. The daily calling list, a matter of secrecy under Hoover, became public property. The press room was enlarged, redecorated and refurnished.

Yet, almost from the beginning, there were those who perceived an essential pragmatism behind all this genial front, who understood that while they were the beneficiaries of the most efficient publicity machine devised by any government, there was no trace of benevolence in it. Roosevelt, and all his subordinates, simply appraised with a remarkable detachment the uses to which the press could be put, and realized that it was to the utmost advantage of an administration with a controversial program to have the press on its side.

When the "honeymoon" began to wane and the press began to be slightly less lyrical about Superman, a parallel change in attitude appeared at the White House. Barely perceptible at first, it has become more pronounced as the years have passed, and something not far removed from armed neutrality has to some extent taken the place of the Rotary Club atmosphere of the first year.

The dawning consciousness, the first morning-after stirring on the bridal couch, is well illustrated in the published observations of leading correspondents between 1933 and 1935. In June 1933 Arthur Sears Henning, chief of the anti-New Deal *Chicago Tribune* Bureau, wrote that relations between the press and the White House had never been so happy. At the end of 1934 George R. Holmes, bureau manager of Hearst's International News Service, wrote that Roosevelt was "his own best press relations man," and added that he had "never known a time when the administration seemed more honest in giving out news." But early in 1935 it was possible for Arthur Krock of the New York Times, who had previously praised the President for his handling of press relations, to say that the administration was guilty of "more ruthlessness, intelligence, and subtlety in trying to suppress legitimate unfavorable comment than any other I have known."

A series of strategic blunders at the White House and a series of repudiations of true stories involving important policy decisions started the press on the road to disillusionment. Washington correspondents, being no more than human, do not love a President merely because he treats them well, but also because he seems to them to be an outstanding statesman, and it was the tactical errors and the failures of policy as much as the subtle shift in attitude toward the press that cooled their first fine ardor.

The first definite break came early — in 1933 — but it was an isolated instance and was not immediately duplicated. Arthur Krock had written an embarrassingly premature revelation of the President's program for the London Economic Conference, and the White House in a formal statement (a rare phenomenon in such matters) not only denied it, but in doing so cast reflections on Krock's motives. This resulted, at the moment, in little more than strained personal relations between Roosevelt and one of his most outstanding journalistic supporters, but it was the first faint portent of what was to follow.

Early in 1935 the President in response to a question said he would not support State NRA legislation, but when publication of the news brought a protest from Governor McNutt of Indiana, a pioneer in such activities, the President repudiated what all clearly understood to be his own position in a public telegram to McNutt, which said:

"I have no hesitation in making perfectly plain to you the extraordinary misinterpretation put upon my reply at press conference."

The next time he met the correspondents Roosevelt scolded them, advising against "unwarranted inferences."

In June of the same year, after a conference of legislative leaders at the White House, Senator Robinson, Majority Leader, and Senator Harrison, Chairman of the Finance Committee, told the reporters that the President had asked them to press for immediate passage of "soak-the-rich" tax legislation. But when the editorial writers shrieked in dismay, Roosevelt flatly denied that he had made any such recommendation.

On the policy side, the correspondents began to have honest doubts of the validity of some of the President's moves. They felt that his "horse-and-buggy" harangue after the Supreme Court had invalidated NRA was an extremely impolitic display of bad temper; they were dismayed at his letter to a Congressman urging the passage of a bill to assist the bituminous coal industry regardless of doubts as to its constitutionality, "however reasonable."

And when, early in 1937, Roosevelt offered his plan to

pack the Supreme Court, even those who agreed with him in principle were aghast at the brutal disingenuousness of the arguments he advanced and the tactics he employed to obtain passage.

All these things, and others like them, inevitably turned the eyes of the press corps toward the newly discovered clay feet of its idol; when the discovery was published to the world, the atmosphere at the White House began to cool off. As the years passed and opposition to the New Deal coalesced, the correspondents eventually realized that while Roosevelt II was the ablest publicist ever to occupy the White House, he was at the same time as ruthless and arbitrary when occasion arose as was Roosevelt I.

Specifically, "freedom of the press" was found to mean, in the last analysis, freedom to publish news which was authorized or "constructive," but decidedly not news which might cast an unfavorable reflection on an administration policy, or embarrass the administration in any way.

In short, Roosevelt ardently desired and sought to facilitate unlimited publicity, so long as it was flavored to his taste, and to this end he exerted all the extensive powers of his high office. Letters eventually began to be received by publishers complaining of their editorial policy; individual correspondents began to feel the weight of official displeasure when they ignored official desires. The temperamental resemblance between the two Roosevelts became more and more manifest.

Press relations at the White House are still the best they have been in any administration, but the portents that have appeared have compelled the correspondents to realize how slight is their foothold, how easy it would be, in time of genuine crisis, to remove all the aids that have developed as a matter of precedent, and reduce their freedom to the slender confines of the Constitutional verbiage.

With all his cold-blooded manipulation of press relations to his own ends, President Roosevelt has simultaneously turned on full force a personal charm which even the most hard-boiled veterans have found it virtually impossible to resist. To the cynical this is one more trick in the bag of a very tricky politician; to the more charitably inclined it is a part of the essential geniality of the entire Roosevelt family. Probably it partakes of both.

Every Spring, beginning with 1934, Mr. and Mrs. Roosevelt have entertained informally at a dance for the correspondents, and these parties for the most part have been entirely felicitous occasions. The guests are not restricted as to costume, although either dinner coats or whites are customary for the men. The usual receiving line is there, but after the bulk of the guests have arrived, the President, informally dressed in linen or seersucker, sits at one end of the East Room, chatting amiably with whomever comes up, and Mrs. Roosevelt receives the late comers at the door with a smile and a hearty handshake.

The entire first floor of the mansion, as well as the gardens, is thrown open, beer barrels are set up in the main lobby, and fruit punch is available at strategic locations. A good jazz band is engaged, and Mrs. Roosevelt, with as many of her children as are at home, mingles with the dancers and acts as master of ceremonies for the "floor show." Supper is served at midnight, and the dancing usually continues for an hour thereafter.

Perhaps these parties have been made too informal; certainly they have been confined less and less to the newspapermen and their wives from year to year. Press telegraphers and office boys have found places on the invitation list, and at times the attitude of the guests has had a suggestion of the proletarian atmosphere of Andrew Jackson's day. Partially intoxicated correspondents have been observed on the dance floor, and the lineup at the buffet table in the dining-room has become such a mob scene as to outrage some of the dignified Negro butlers.

On the individual side, neither the President nor Mrs. Roosevelt has failed to keep in close touch with the correspondents who regularly cover the White House. A death in the family brings flowers and perhaps a personal call, and correspondents in special circumstances have been invited informally to Sunday supper at the White House.

Sometimes there is a distinct impression that Roosevelt would like to be much friendlier, much franker, than his high office and his political situation will permit, that he would occasionally like to be met as a social equal.

There are many examples of this, perhaps the most revealing one being at his Warm Springs retreat, when one evening he drove by the cottage where the correspondents were staying to ask if there were any objection to shifting the time of his press conference next day. The correspondents asked him if he wouldn't care to stop a moment, and to their great surprise he accepted. He went in and stayed an hour or more, had a bite of supper, and conversed freely and frankly on a variety of topics important and trivial.

Then there was the annual clambake at the New York State farm of Secretary of the Treasury Morgenthau. All the correspondents accompanying the President to Hyde Park are invited, and the other guests include such intimates as Archibald MacLeish, poet and Librarian of Congress, Tommy Corcoran, and the like. On this occasion, in the midst of the supper, most of the guests suddenly burst out chanting "We want Butch, we want Butch!" It developed that "Butch" was a new nickname Roosevelt had thought up for Felix Belair of the *Times*, now of the Luce publications, and it was his idea that it would be a great joke on Belair to pin the label on him in this fashion. No one laughed louder or longer over Belair's embarrassment at the extremely appropriate nickname than the President himself.

In the summer of 1933, after his first hectic "hundred days," Roosevelt was cruising up the coast of Maine in his sailing yacht, and a handful of correspondents were following in a chartered boat. One day they were invited aboard the yacht for an informal conference, and the President received them seated in the stern. Suddenly he noticed that some of them were forced to stand because he was sitting directly in the middle of the thwart. He called to Gus Gennerich, his bodyguard and court jester, and asked to be moved over. He was vastly amused when Gus, who had been a member of the family for many years, exclaimed:

"Gosh, Frank, you're getting to be a big fat so-and-so! You've gotta reduce!"

It is Roosevelt's unfailing practice to address everyone
he knows, or wishes to impress favorably, by his first name,
and this applies equally to British prime ministers and
Washington correspondents. In press conferences it frequently helps make a questioner appear slightly silly to
have the President look at him with a quizzical expression
and drawl, "Now, Charlie!"

Correspondents to whom the President has never been
introduced and whom he seldom sees go away from State
receptions swearing that he knew them on sight because
of his habit of rearing back, beaming, and saying:

"Hel-lo, Smith, glad to see you!"

And his faculty for listening attentively and with an air
of flattering interest sends many a newspaperman, as well
as many an axe-grinder, away from the White House beaming ecstatically, convinced that the Great Man has endorsed everything he said. Heywood Broun once headed a
delegation to the White House during the formative days
of the American Newspaper Guild, and when he emerged,
somewhat dazed, he said to a companion:

"Did you notice he agreed with everything I said?"

The friend replied:

"No he didn't; he just smiled."

Of course the White House correspondent who for
months or years has been subjected to this softening-up
process and then is put severely in his place in response to
an embarrassing question, feels not unlike a prize-fighter
who has been tickled into helpless hysteria for three rounds
and then knocked cold with a right to the chin.

In the technical routine of press relations, Roosevelt is

a past master. He knows how to time an announcement to get the best position in the papers, and has been known to hold a story up for a day because some other extremely important event was then commanding the front pages. And on the other hand, he has been known to put out a big story in time to blanket a Congressional development unfavorable to him, perhaps to the extent of pushing it entirely off the front page.

In the press conference itself he is extremely adroit and is seldom caught off base. There have been occasions when he betrayed a lack of information in response to a question, and his blithe habit of appearing to know all about everything tends to lead him into such pitfalls. At the same time, his fund of detailed information is so truly remarkable that the slips are few indeed compared with those of his predecessors, particularly when one considers the freedom with which he permits himself to be questioned.

Of course one of the reasons he is not tripped up oftener is that the correspondents as a whole don't think very fast on their feet and neglect to ask the one follow-up question which would expose the information they are seeking. One instance in which the President was caught completely off guard by an adroitly worded question resulted in the formation of his famous Dunce-cap Club.

After the Congressional elections of 1938 Robert P. Post of the *New York Times*, as a result of numerous suggestions that Roosevelt should run for a third term, decided that the moment was opportune to ask him about it once more. With the assistance of an associate he so framed his question that it could not be evaded, a precaution others asking the same question had failed to take.

Fred Perkins of the Scripps-Howard Newspaper Alliance had just put the query in the customary form:

"Mr. President, are you a candidate for a third term?",
and the President merely grinned and said, "Now, Fred!"

But then Post took his youthful courage in both hands and asked:

"Mr. President, would you accept a nomination for a third term?"

There was no way out. The President flushed angrily and snapped:

"Bob, go over in the corner and put on a dunce cap!"

Although trapped, he was alert enough to realize the fact and to know that his answer must be either yes or no or maybe — there was no way to slide around it. A Hoover might have attempted an answer and fallen into the pit; Roosevelt took the only course readily available to him — he employed his presidential prestige to silence the questioner with ridicule.

While much of the credit for President Roosevelt's unique success with the Washington correspondents must be given to Early, his irascible but astute secretary, in more recent years Steve has had an able assistant in William D. Hassett, a self-possessed, good-humored and thoroughly competent ex-newspaperman. Early undoubtedly has one of the most nerve-racking, thankless jobs in the entire government, a job on which many an apparently first-class man has fallen down. There have been times when he has slipped, but he has not fallen down, and he has been in the White House hotspot for more than eight years.

VI

Reporting the Nation's Business

EVERY NEWSPAPERMAN REVERTS AUTOmatically to the status of cub reporter when he starts covering Washington. The best police reporter, the best foreign correspondent, finds himself in a new and bewildering environment, and until he familiarizes himself with it his years of experience in other fields avail him little.

Not only is there a vast and complex new set of agencies to cover, but in addition there is a whole new set of techniques to master before he regains his normal efficiency. The active foreign correspondent or the man trained in a State capital has least to learn, and unlearn; the big city police reporter is on the toughest spot.

To mitigate this initial greenness, the government has made extraordinary provision for the press: the galleries at the Capitol, with their luxurious workrooms; the departmental press agencies with their handouts; the press conferences and the generally cordial atmosphere, help the newcomer over the rough spots. Yet if he relies too fully on these he is worse off than without them, for he is in danger of becoming little more than a transmission belt for official propaganda.

There are more than five hundred correspondents accredited to the Capitol press galleries, which means that they work for daily papers or press associations using daily telegraphic service. Some of them are correspondents of highly specialized trade organs; some represent the local papers; a few others are correspondents of foreign newspapers or agencies.

These five hundred-odd are maintained in Washington by more than three hundred publications and news-distributing agencies, some representing several papers, others being members of large bureaus serving a single paper or agency. Their employers range from the Associated Press, with seventy-five or more on its huge staff, to serve a worldwide chain of newspaper clients, to the *Hinton News*, which shares one correspondent with half a dozen other West Virginia papers. Their total number is about as great as the entire membership of Congress, and with their wives and children they could populate a good-sized village.

As the years have passed since the first stenographic reporters started covering Congressional debates, down through those early "columnists" of the 1800's, so like the ones we know today, to the present highly organized and routinized task of covering Washington, there has developed a code of sorts and a specialized technique to meet the peculiar demands of the assignment. It is this code, and this technique, which sets the Washington correspondent off from his colleagues elsewhere.

The Washington correspondent for a big newspaper or press association is no more like his predecessor a hundred or even fifty years ago than is the motorcar like a bicycle; the principal and virtually only resemblance is that both earned their living digging up news. Then the reporter roamed the field, and got his news where and how he could find it. There were no press agents, no handouts, no telephones placed at his disposal by a publicity-hungry bureaucracy. Except for formal announcements and Congressional debates, his sources of information were almost entirely personal. He was "a chiel amang ye takin' notes."

Nowadays there are, roughly, six classes of Washington correspondents qualifying for admission to the Capitol press galleries. They are the press association reporters; the members of large and well-organized bureaus of individual newspapers; the lone representatives of individual papers; the individuals who correspond for several small papers in the same geographical region; the correspondents of highly specialized trade journals, and the free-lance, syndicated columnists. Each of these six major groups has its special characteristics and special methods, and each is divided into subgroups.

The press association men, while including in their number some of the most brilliant and able of all the correspondents, have as a class little color. The reason is simple enough: a press association is an agency engaged in the business of gathering and selling news to a large number of newspapers all over the world, and it could not very well, with all these diversified masters, have a very distinct personality. Obviously its job is to get the news out as rapidly and as accurately as it can and with the fewest possible trimmings. It is not supposed to have any "policy," because if it did it would collide with the policies of its clients. The same reporters are serving the *Kansas City Star* and the Hearst papers, the *Chicago Tribune* and the *Boston Globe*, and an infinite variety of journals less well known, and departure from the established pattern is not encouraged.

The press association reporter's work is highly routine; each man has a particular "run" to cover, and there is no free-lancing around town in quest of a good story. The only thing that prevents the press associations in Washington from developing many genuine specialists is their policy of moving staff members around before they have an opportunity to dig deep into their jobs. A reporter may be covering the Treasury today, the Senate a month from today, and the State Department a month after that. The press association men in Washington who have made names for themselves have usually been the exceptions to this rule.

Outside the press associations, nearly every reporter is more or less a specialist, from necessity and from choice. The governmental machine is so vast and so ramified that no one man could possibly report it all intelligently, and so in the larger bureaus at least specialists are assiduously developed. One bureau will have, if it is lucky, a reporter who knows quite a lot about taxation; another who understands the anagrams which issue daily from the Securities and Exchange Commission; another who is acquainted with the deviousness of the diplomats and can tell when they are insulting one another and when complimenting.

As the number of correspondents in a bureau diminishes, so does the degree of specialization, so that a bureau with half a dozen reporters is compelled to spread out thinner than one with fourteen or fifteen. Nevertheless, even here a degree of specialization is developed. As in the medical profession, these correspondents become, not eye doctors, ear doctors and nose-and-throat doctors, but specialists in eye-ear-nose-and-throat.

The lone correspondent of a single paper or group of small geographically related papers becomes a specialist in the type of news desired by those papers. Within the limits of their interests he is a general practitioner, but he learns to know what they want and don't want, and restricts himself accordingly.

Thus a correspondent for a Pittsburgh paper is probably more interested in mining, smelting, and labor unions than anything else except Pennsylvania politics, whereas one from Knoxville or anywhere in Washington or Oregon is ahunt for news about hydroelectric power.

The correspondents of the trade journals, of course, are highly specialized, and except for perfunctory acknowledgment of their existence, are not in the generally accepted sense "Washington correspondents." One cares about nothing but oil, another iron and steel, another aviation, another drugs. They live their little lives in these narrow limits, and are the most circumscribed of all the correspondents, writing about a few things for a few readers.

The syndicated columnists, like the correspondents of the early Nineteenth Century who wrote "letters" of observation on government affairs, cover the world. Some have foreign affairs as their particular love, and some labor unions as their pet peeve, while others concentrate on economics. But all of them roam the range of public affairs, like a Swede making the circuit of a smorgasbord. They write with great authority about everything, though frequently with little evidence of genuine knowledge of anything.

They are, for the most part, simply free-lance editorial writers.

The "straight news" reporters make up the bulk of the Washington correspondents, and it is upon them that the reading public must rely in the main for its knowledge of what is going on. It is for them, also, that the government has set up a vast mechanism of news distribution through the medium of the press conference, the press agent, and the handout.

No two categories of Washington reporting have precisely the same set of rules, even though all conform generally to one code. But the State Department and diplomatic correspondents have a special technique far different from that of the man who covers Congress, and the financial reporter is something else again. Their varying methods conform, not only to the type of news they are gathering, but also to the type of men with whom they deal.

There was once a tough, New York Irish reporter who, while he never worked in Washington, understood the fine distinction between types of news and types of news sources. He was on his way to report a "bucketshop" raid and was conversing with his companion from another paper about the new Columbia University School of Journalism. He was a bit skeptical of the value of methods learned in a classroom, and opined that "de whole t'ing is de approach — git de approach an' you got de story."

When they reached the raided bucketshop they found a large room, elaborately furnished but in great confusion. Detectives were all over the place, and in a far corner one of the operators of the "shop" was cowering at his desk. The reporter who knew the value of "de approach" strode up to him and said:

"Hey you! Where's de odder bastard?"

Presumably he knew, instinctively, with whom he was dealing and how to handle him. In Washington, on the other hand, the code tends sometimes to become so rigid that the correspondents cease to be genuine reporters. They treat their sources with such elaborate and unwarranted courtesy, and pussyfoot so fearsomely around a story, that they often miss it.

A new correspondent for the Associated Press, recently imported from a Southwestern bureau, was told to check up on a tip concerning the Treasury. After a little while he turned in a very good story, liberally sprinkled with direct quotations from Secretary Morgenthau. The man who had given him the assignment said, sternly:

"Where did you get this story?"

"From Morgenthau," he replied.

"Do you mean to say you called up Morgenthau on this?"

"Certainly I did; why not?"

The other couldn't think of any reason why not just then, but next day the reporter was called in by the Bureau Manager for a bit of friendly advice. He was informed that it wasn't the thing to telephone Cabinet officers that way, that the way to get news was to go through the press agents, except in the most extraordinary circumstances.

Of course the inhibition against telephoning a Cabinet officer is grounded in good sense: he is a very busy man with a great deal of importance on his mind, and if he were bedeviled continually by reporters with secondary questions he would soon stop answering the phone and would never be available at all. Some Cabinet officers, in fact, can't be reached on the telephone. The Secretary of State, Cordell Hull, lived for eight years at the Carlton Hotel, as everyone in Washington knows, but it is to be doubted if any correspondent has ever reached him there on the phone.

One high-ranking bureau chief, a personal friend of Mr. Hull's, once in 1933 went to the extraordinary length of sending a staff member to the hotel to shove a note under the Secretary's door, asking him if he would call up his friend, and discuss a particular matter. It was of utmost importance to the nation and was shrouded in the densest possible fog, and the Secretary, evidently realizing the validity of the request, complied.

To avoid being annoyed at all hours, Cabinet officers and other high administrators instruct their press agents to be available for answering questions, and Washington correspondents in general respect this arrangement so long as it really operates. Only when the press agent can't be found or is unco-operative and the matter is really important will they call a high official at his home, particularly late at night. They know perfectly well that one of the easiest ways to alienate a news source is to get him out of bed or up from the dinner table with a trivial inquiry the answer to which could be had elsewhere with no trouble at all, or which is of no particular importance anyhow.

The principal direct contact of the Cabinet officer with the press is through the medium of the press conference. Otherwise the correspondent reaches the Secretary only indirectly, through the departmental press officer. This aloofness, necessary as it may be, frequently leads the correspondent into sloppy habits and causes him to lapse into a weak routine which is not, to say the least, worthy of the highest standards of reporting. He may even fail to canvass the sources which are readily available, and make up in speculation what he lacks in facts, a tendency which doesn't help the newspaper reader in his effort to understand the "why" of the news.

In the winter of 1941 the President let it be known that he was sending Lauchlin Currie, one of his administrative assistants and an economist, to China to advise the government there. The White House announcement came out in such a way that it was not possible to question the President about it, so the correspondents were left to find out for themselves just what was Currie's mission. Very few of them took the obvious course that one did. He called the Treasury press agent and asked, and was one who had a full and correct version in his paper next morning. There was no mystery, no sensation, but most of the others who wrote the story ran the gamut of romantic speculation.

This tendency on the part of a very large number of the Washington correspondents to take what is given them and not look further, or worse, to speculate instead of asking questions, is one of the more disturbing latter-day phenomena of Washington reporting. To a considerable extent it is the result of intellectual laziness which in turn is the result of the elaborate array of "crutches" provided by the government, so that the reporter writes the handout and nothing more, even when omissions of fact stare him in the face.

It is manifest, also, in the press conferences, when officials make the most obvious misstatements or omissions of fact, deliberately or otherwise, and no reporter corrects them. Or when a Cabinet officer makes an invidious categorical statement designed to mislead the reporters and distort their understanding of the news, and the correspondents simply stand and take it; retire murmuring "Thank you, Mr. Secretary," and go back to their offices and write what the great man said without any attempt to put things in their true light.

When the Attorney General, Robert Jackson, said in a press conference that all aliens were to be registered, a revolutionary announcement in itself, since it shattered all American precedent, perhaps fifty reporters were present, among them some of the highest ranking in Washington, but not one of them thought to ask by what authority this was to be done. Actually that was one of the important aspects of the story, since the Departmental attorneys were even then puzzling over whether it could be done under existing law or whether new authority would have to be asked of Congress.

When the Secretary of the Interior, Harold L. Ickes, read the press a not too logical lecture on its lack of freedom, only one correspondent, the only woman reporter present, had the courage to stand up and politely debate the issue. Every other reporter in that press conference, while knowing or sensing the fallacy in the Secretary's thesis, was perfectly willing to say nothing and write stories which would simply repeat what Ickes said.

With, no doubt, the best and most benevolent of intentions, the Executive Branch of the government has provided the newspaper correspondents with a large and increasing supply of lotus, and too many of them eat too much. They substitute handouts for enterprise, volunteered statements for the stimulus of question and answer. Too often a correspondent who has missed a press conference says: "Don't worry, I can pick it up."

To be sure, enterprise in a Washington correspondent can go beyond the bounds of tact and good sense, as many a correspondent has learned to his sorrow after some of the best news sources cut him off because of his tactics. There are times when a reporter has to grin and bear it: he must know when an issue between himself and a news source is sufficiently fundamental to risk sacrificing a "contact."

When the "national defense" constriction of the channels of news had become noticeable in early 1941, a New York reporter obtained, exclusively, a story forecasting a development in War Department policy. He checked it with the press agent and was told it was correct. But next morning the Chief of Staff (and perhaps behind him the President) raised such a fuss that the press officer was ordered to issue a denial, although explaining over the telephone that if the story had been put a little less flatly the brass hats wouldn't have objected.

He was a friendly and useful press officer, but the reporter was all set to write a story giving him the lie direct and by name, until his superiors convinced him that he would merely alienate thereby a good news source and gain nothing for himself.

There come times, of course, when the question is so fundamental, the issue so sharply drawn, that there is nothing for the correspondent and his paper to do but stand and fight, and if a news source is thereby estranged, it's too bad. It becomes then a matter of upholding the integrity of the reporter and through him of his paper and the press in general. And this is no mere philosophical point, for if unwarranted assaults on the veracity of the correspondent go unanswered, his value to his employer and his readers is diminished by that much.

The reverse of the picture is the atmosphere of mutual trust that is built up between a correspondent and his news sources, an atmosphere which enables the correspondent to score many valuable news beats. This applies not primarily to the conventional sources — the press officers and other obvious functionaries — but to important men in the background who are willing occasionally to talk to an individual in whose discretion and intelligence they have faith.

Every veteran correspondent worth his salt has one or more such private sources; the fortunate ones have several, covering a wide range of governmental activity. And since the activities of the government impinge so extensively upon the lives of the citizens, it is also easy to find unofficial sources who can reveal details of official news. The representative of the Investment Bankers Association may be able and willing to reveal anonymously an important decision of the SEC before it is officially announced; the head of a big labor union frequently knows what's going on in certain fields and has no objection to talking to a friend. And a reliable Congressman is the best-known antidote for close-mouthed bureaucrats.

There are, indeed, some individuals in the government itself, and in positions of great responsibility, who talk far more than they have any business to, and the reason for their garrulity is sometimes a considerable mystery. Such officials will actually jeopardize their positions by the news they give out; even though they know the correspondent will conceal the source of his information, there is always the possibility that the story will be traced.

Naturally sources of this type, if they are not mere gossips or office politicians with axes to grind, are extremely valuable to the reporter. It is not up to him to judge whether the assistant secretary is making a fool of himself by revealing a certain set of facts, but he sometimes wonders why it is.

In some cases, like that of James A. Farley, pure, unaffected geniality is the answer. Big Jim always had great difficulty keeping back bits of information desired by his friends of the press, and while what he told them was likely as not to be "off the record," it had a way of being printed, often to the great embarrassment of the Postmaster General.

There are others in official life who seem to have a passion for being the deus ex machina, the behind-the-scenes creator of a sensation. They do not require personal publicity or any credit at all — they simply like to see a big story

in the papers for which they are responsible. Some are
highly placed officials, others are little more than clerks,
but they count it a day well spent when they have given a
correspondent an exclusive story.

An astonishing beat was scored a few years ago in this
fortuitous manner. On a Saturday evening, just when a
correspondent was about to go home, an unimportant civil
servant whom he barely knew telephoned him and offered
him, for no apparent reason at all, documentary information which permitted him to forecast, several weeks in
advance, an extremely important decision of the Interstate
Commerce Commission. Now the ICC is somewhat like
the Supreme Court in the secrecy it maintains prior to
actual announcement of a decision, and an advance story
on such a decision is virtually unheard of. Clearly, the man
who, without compensation or recognition, gave this information would have been discharged immediately had his
responsibility become known. Evidently he was one of
those who ask no reward beyond the secret knowledge that
they have made the front page incognito.

These, to be sure, are rarities, and the best and most
reliable of private news sources are those responsible officials who, from long friendship and complete confidence,
will on occasion give a favored reporter a story, or the
explanation of a mystery. But the same officials will with-
hold, even from their best journalistic friends, information
which they deem it not to be in the public interest to
disclose.

The Washington correspondent, in proportion to his
imagination and ingenuity, resorts to many devices, fair

and unfair, to obtain news. Sometimes it is a question of getting to see the right man at the opportune moment, often a difficult proceeding. At other times it is a matter of having a story pretty well in hand, but without sufficient verification for publication as fact. Then the tricks play their part.

One correspondent, new to Washington but learned in the technique of newsgathering in Moscow, picked up a full and important forecast of a huge appropriation for airplanes to be asked by the War Department. The source was unofficial and the correspondent, while believing the story, considered it necessary to get something in the nature of a confirmation. This is how he got it:

First he called on the War Department press officer on another matter, and in the course of casual conversation brought up the matter of the appropriation, purposely giving incorrect details. The press officer, off his guard, corrected him on the details. This was confirmation, but the correspondent, as a double check, dropped in on the military aide to the Secretary of War, and began in an offhand manner to talk about the projected request for two billion dollars worth of airplanes. The aide's jaw dropped, and he stared at the correspondent in consternation, without saying a word.

One device that sometimes works is to call on the appropriate official, bluntly inform him that such-and-such a story is in hand and will be printed, and ask him if he wouldn't like to make sure that it is correct in every detail; or, if it is on a controversial matter, if he wouldn't like to get his side printed too.

Back in 1935 one correspondent and his bureau manager, by dint of something resembling an algebraic formula, were able to print with a high degree of accuracy the names and duties of the men who had been selected to administer President Roosevelt's first big "blank check" relief appropriation.

The bureau manager met at lunch an acquaintance who told him what Rexford G. Tugwell would be given to do; the tip was entirely logical, so he called in the reporter who covered relief activities and together they figured out the whole setup. If Tugwell was to have Resettlement (they didn't know the name then), what would Ickes, Hopkins, and some others have? By elimination they worked it out and published it.

An outstanding example of reportorial ingenuity was that of Felix Belair, then of the *New York Times*, and J. Russell Wiggin of the *St. Paul Pioneer-Press*, immediately after the outlawing by the Supreme Court of the original Agricultural Adjustment Act. Everybody, including the Secretary of Agriculture, wanted to know how the farm relief program could be saved; everybody was scratching his bureaucratic head in an effort to dig up a means of meeting the crisis.

Belair and Wiggin discovered a little one-page law, one of the many passed in the early days of the New Deal, called the Soil Conservation Act. Written for a limited and highly laudable purpose, this act, like many others of that period, contained in its brief compass almost unlimited authority, authority broad enough, in fact, to carry on, under another and entirely constitutional guise, the crop limitation program invalidated by the Supreme Court. The two correspondents showed it to the AAA Administrator, who had forgotten it existed, but who quickly touched it up where necessary and got it re-enacted as the "Soil Conservation and Domestic Allotment Act." It is to this day the organic act of the New Deal farm program.

By their familiarity with their special field, these two correspondents were thus enabled to score a decisive news beat and one which came true soon enough to be remembered, an important point to a reporter. In the dear dead days when everything that happened in Washington was completely routinized, if a correspondent obtained an exclusive story he could be sure that in a reasonable length of time it would be publicly confirmed. But in these cataclysmic times, when details of policy change as often as the weather, the beat that is quickly confirmed is a joy to the press. And sometimes, even though the story was 100 percent correct at the time, it is never confirmed because somewhere along the line the situation changed.

As the reader may gather, it is not the correspondent who wanders about asking people if they have any news who gets news. The Washington correspondent must study developments in relation to those of the past; he must keep abreast of important legislation, and he must be able to comprehend quickly the relationship between an incident in the Executive Branch and a possible new law. Thus equipped, he is in a position to see the right people and ask the right questions in order to get his story.

Seeing the right people, however, is not always as simple as it sounds, and sometimes it takes considerable ingenuity to get to them. Some high officials are generally easy of access, but others carefully shield themselves against informal press contacts, partly because they don't want to be bothered and partly because they don't trust themselves in the presence of a reporter.

Back in 1933 when the Senate Banking and Currency Committee was conducting an extended investigation of stock market and banking practices, J. P. Morgan was one of the more sensational witnesses. Morgan probably contributed little if anything to the sum total of the committee's information, but he was, after all, a Morgan, son of that other J. P. Morgan who once got the United States Government out of a financial jam and who fought publicly with Roosevelt I.

Much was made of his appearance, and the reporters and photographers rallied round to take his picture, including that famous one with a circus midget on his knee, prime achievement of Dexter Fellows, the Ringling press agent. Then one day a number of the correspondents caught Morgan alone in his hotel suite and started interviewing him. To their great surprise and greater delight he talked frankly, almost garrulously, on all manner of vital topics involved in the investigation. But before he had gone far in rushed one of his junior partners and exclaimed:

"Of course, gentlemen, you understand this is all off the record."

And so was killed one of the most extraordinary interviews the Washington correspondents ever obtained.

There was a young Washington correspondent who happened to be related to the publisher of a large and highly respected newspaper, and as chance would have it he had the same surname. This reporter found it no end of fun, and quite profitable, to capitalize his name in getting to talk to news sources difficult of access.

During the General Motors sitdown strikes Alfred P. Sloan, then President of General Motors, had been conferring in Washington with government officials who were as anxious as he to get the strike over with. After the conference he left in a hurry for New York and shut himself up in his house there, refusing to talk to anyone.

Our young reporter whose name, let us say, was McSweeney, looked up the Sloan telephone number and put through a long distance call. The Sloan butler answered, and the youth, in his deepest and most adult tone, said: "This is Mr. McSweeney; I should like to speak to Mr. Sloan."

There appears to be no doubt at all that the butler, and Mr. Sloan, thought it was the eminent publisher, because the embattled industrialist came promptly to the telephone and gave the young man a very good interview.

On other occasions young McSweeney made his way into the private offices of busy Cabinet members merely by sending in word that "Mr. McSweeney" wished to see them. Neither in the case of the Sloan interview nor in any of these did he ever say: "This is Patrick McSweeney of the *Kankakee Beacon*"; so that the officials, in admitting him, first thought that the publisher was waiting outside, and later, when they saw it was not the publisher, somehow got the impression that the young fellow was working for his relative's paper and must be pretty important.

Such tactics as these are good only until exposed, and cannot be used on the same person very often. And no Washington correspondent who cares for the ethics of his craft will obtain news under false pretenses, but will always announce himself correctly and campaign under his own colors. It is this sort of thing that militates against the press corps as a whole, and it is quite true that the Washington correspondents, as a group, are only as strong as their weakest members, particularly if these weak ones happen to represent papers or press bureaus of some consequence and respectability. The reporter in the movies, who resorts to all sorts of skulduggery to get his story, is as foolish and ineffective in real life as the Superman of the comic strips, who marches up to a man and says in effect:

"I'm a reporter; I have a tip that you are a crook. Tell me all about it."

Such tactics, at one extreme or the other, have no place in actual modern newspaper practice, and particularly not in the highly specialized job of reporting a government in action. The romantic, movie-hero reporter may be faintly reflected in a free-lance war correspondent, but never in Washington. Richard Harding Davis would have been a colossal flop in the national capital in 1941.

Neither is the modern reporter, and again, especially the Washington correspondent, the drunken bum so often depicted. Unfortunately our writers for stage and screen are either men who have never been inside a city room or are deliberately distorting the picture for the sake of plot interest.

Two or three years ago Frank Capra made a picture

called "Mr. Smith Goes to Washington," a picture full of high political idealism and, in its broad outlines, extraordinarily faithful to the actual scene. But in it he represented his Washington correspondents as generally inebriated and always venal, a characterization justly resented by the press after the preview.

Specifically, he had Capitol reporters bribing a Congressman's secretary in order to obtain an interview with her boss, and later depicted the same Congressman in a rough-and-tumble fight with a crowd of correspondents in the bar of the National Press Club. Now, in the first place, no bribery is ever necessary to get an interview with a Congressman, particularly a "freshman." In the second place, correspondents do not have the wherewithal to offer bribes if they so desired. And finally, they do not engage in brawls with members of Congress in the Press Club or anywhere else.

There are drunken correspondents just as there are drunken Senators and drunken bankers and movie directors; there are, unfortunately, venal reporters, who quietly accept a little unsolicited graft. But these are decidedly in the minority, and are held in low regard by their fellows.

Members of Congress to a limited extent, and lobbyists to a greater extent, go in for petty bribery of the press, and sometimes it is not so petty. Often the correspondent is hard put to know whether or not to accept a gift, even though it may come as a Christmas remembrance. But the test is not difficult as a rule. From experience with the donor he knows whether it is a genuine token of regard, an inconsequential "thank-you" for perfectly legitimate publicity, or an advance payment for services to be rendered at some future date.

It is not uncommon for some legitimate news source to send a bottle of Scotch at Christmas to correspondents whom he knows personally, but one reporter who received a whole case of whiskey promptly sent it back. Secretary of Commerce Jesse Jones regularly ships a few of his friends cases of Texas grapefruit at Christmas, and they are never returned because the recipients know perfectly well that "Jesse" is not trying to buy them.

As for getting into fights with Congressmen, the most outstanding example of that in recent years, an example which never materialized into an actual encounter, involved Carlisle Bargeron, then a reporter for the *Washington Post*, and never noted for the wearing of velvet gloves. "Barge" was reporting a debate in the House, and wrote of Mr. Blanton of Texas that he was wearing a white suit reminiscent of the organization of which he was reputed to be a member.

Blanton, a distinctly unpopular Congressman because of his general pettiness and his fondness for throwing monkey wrenches into the government of the District of Columbia, telephoned the *Post* and said that if Bargeron would come to his office he would beat him to a pulp, or words to that effect. Bargeron, a small man, dashed out of the office, leaped into a taxicab, and told the driver to take him to the House Office Building. Before he got there his feet began to chill perceptibly, and if it had not been for the wasted taxi fare he probably would have turned back.

Arrived at his destination, he loitered uneasily along the

corridors, horrid pictures of the burly Blanton passing through his mind, pictures of Blanton victorious astride a maimed and prostrate Bargeron. Twice he turned around, but finally contrived to reach the office door. There he stood, reassembling his courage, and finally, to put on the best possible show, jerked open the door, charged in, and announced:

"I'm Bargeron!"

Blanton's jaw dropped. Like many bullies, he was not prepared to have his challenge accepted. He jumped to his feet, thrust out his hand, and said:

"I'm glad to meet a man!"

Alongside these comic interludes, of which there have been many in the history of Washington newspaper correspondence, is a great body of straight, factual, and frequently distinguished news gathering, interspersed, rarely, with a job of action reporting to which the correspondents rise with considerable efficiency, considering the length of time most of them have been away from that field.

Such an incident was the "Battle of the Bonus" in the summer of 1932, when President Hoover, in his most egregious blunder, ordered out the Army to chase out of town at the point of the bayonet several hundred World War veterans whom he had tolerated for two months past. Suddenly virtually every reporter in Washington became without warning a strange combination of police reporter and war correspondent. It was hard going for many of them, but in the main they demonstrated that a good reporter can cover any story if he has to.

The Bonus Army, led by two or three fanatics with a

genius for organizing and inspiring their fellows, had started trickling into town around the first of May. By the end of June they occupied a number of condemned buildings along lower Pennsylvania Avenue not far from the Capitol, and a large, well-organized camp across the river in the Anacostia flats.

They had been virtually welcomed to Washington by the police. The nation was reaching the bottom of the depression, and these apparently penniless crusaders touched a sentimental spot in the heart of Brig. Gen. Pelham D. Glassford, the retired Army officer who commanded the police force. He saw to it that the veterans received shelter, bedding and food.

But when they didn't go away after a while President Hoover, already suffering from an acute attack of the jitters, apparently concluded that the government was in peril: perhaps he had been reading Flaubert's "Salammbo" and had in mind the mutiny of the Carthaginian mercenaries. At any rate, with no advance warning, he ordered the District of Columbia Commissioners to have the police evict the bonus army from the old buildings on the avenue.

The very police who had befriended the marchers now moved in on them, and a pitched battle ensued, with the police getting the worst of it, attacking, as they were, entrenched adversaries. Two or three lost their lives.

Then the President called out the Army — infantry, cavalry, machine guns, field artillery, tanks and General MacArthur, the Chief of Staff. The Army evicted the bonus seekers as directed, but then chased them on down the avenue and across the bridge to their miserable camp. Gas bombs were hurled, late at night, into the camp and the poor wretches, men, women and children, scattered into the Maryland countryside to watch their tents and pitiful effects burned by the troops.

This was the sort of story Washington correspondents were not accustomed to handling. Some were gassed, some got prodded by bayonets and cavalry sabres, but the graphic and detailed accounts they put on the wires left nothing to be said. Fat-flanked gallery-sitters, political dope writers, foreign affairs experts, all turned to and covered a small war because they had to.

And almost the only casualty, other than outraged sensibilities and blistered feet, was the trousers of stout Franklyn Waltman of the *Baltimore Sun*, now a seer for the Republican National Committee. Waltman, through error, was pursued by cavalry, and in trying to scale a wall to escape got stuck. The cavalry caught up and prodded him mercilessly where he customarily sat.

But barring the rare action stories of the sort Mr. Hoover dropped in our laps, there is still plenty of romance in covering Washington, and the correspondent who keeps his enthusiasm intact and does not become overly cynical is the best correspondent. That is why a new man in Washington, with a foundation of solid experience elsewhere, has a habit of turning up the most interesting copy. He sees points of interest in items which are "old stuff" to the veteran, who fails to realize that the lay reader doesn't know as much about them as he does. Everything is new to this newcomer, and he writes it with a fresh viewpoint which is invaluable to his readers.

Fortunate indeed is the correspondent who, after five or ten years in Washington, can still use his imagination in the search for news, can continue to realize that the national government is a constant source of romance and mystery to the "milkman in Omaha." Too often the freshness wears off, the horizon becomes limited, the imagination dulled, and the press handout grows in importance in his daily work, as indeed the press agent intends that it shall.

VII

A Day Among the Handouts

THERE IS ONE GOVERNMENT PRESS agent for every two bona fide newspaper correspondents in Washington, and the volume of handouts issued each year by all the government bureaus is staggering if not actually incalculable.

Prior to World War I, if a newspaper reporter wished to obtain a piece of news direct or interview an administrative official, he went straight to the source, dealing with the man or his secretary, depending on the individual. There were scattering factual statements from government agencies, but they were not the major industry of today. Reporting Washington was to a great extent on a par, technically, with big city police reporting: the correspondent looked for news until he found it, and the amount he produced was in direct ratio to the degree of imagination and industry he exercised.

Soon after the United States entered that war, however, the government concluded that some sort of censorship was a prime necessity; failing to get Congress to authorize a genuine muzzling of the press, President Wilson took second best, and created the Committee on Public Information with a newspaperman, George Creel, as director, and key Cabinet officers as members. It was the duty of this "committee" to provide authorized news to the public, and every effort was made to prevent news of the war from being made available in any other way.

Thus were born the institutions of the government press agent and the handout. War news was distributed in the form of carefully prepared stories, and by agreement with the publishers, correspondents did not attempt to go beyond these press releases. When the war ended and with it this voluntary censorship, the value of the press agent and the handout had become so apparent to the Executive Branch of the government that they were never discarded.

Press agentry on a large and well-organized scale came permanently into the governmental system, not in 1933 as many mistakenly believe, but in 1929, when Herbert Hoover, himself a successful promoter, became President; but it has reached its peak, short of the creation of a Ministry of Propaganda, under Franklin D. Roosevelt, the most resourceful publicity man not in the business. And the Ministry of Propaganda, slightly disguised, may not be so far in the future.

The press agents of Hoover and his predecessors were little more than information officers in the strictest sense. For the most part they were not highly paid, highly trained ex-newspapermen or professional publicists, but civil servants assigned to the task, or in some cases broken-down old correspondents grateful for an obscure berth in which to spend their declining years. Today there are 200 or more government employees in Washington and many more "in the field" engaged full-time in the dissemination of news and propaganda to the press and other agencies of information; and at the head of each important bureau of this sort is a genuine specialist drawing a very good salary. The government has learned that well-ordered publicity pays rich dividends.

When President Roosevelt assigned his secretary, Stephen T. Early, to organize press services in the various departments and important non-Cabinet agencies, the avowed purpose was to provide full and accurate publicity for all the government's activities, without propaganda in the invidious sense, and without suppression. "Do your job just as if you were working for a newspaper," Early told the press agents.

Obviously no such high-minded ideal could last for long. Pontius Pilate's trenchant question, "What is truth?", found a variety of answers as the administration's reform program became the focus of national controversy. To each administrative official truth is what he believes; and what he does not believe, does not approve of, or would prefer to forget, is not generally considered fit material for the press.

Consequently that early dictum of the President's Secretary was in many cases quickly forgotten. Routine facts, statistics, and developments which on their face could not be unfavorably interpreted were publicized fully and freely, but the other side of the picture was preferably concealed. President Roosevelt himself abandoned his promise to admit his mistakes frankly, and his subordinates, following his example, simply neglected to mention anything that did not redound to the credit of the New Deal, discouraging meanwhile independent research along these lines.

This second phase of the New Deal's publicity program reached its logical consummation when, in 1938, the administration consistently and violently denied what every responsible person in Washington knew — that the WPA was being put to outrageous political uses — and the honest, pro-New Deal correspondent who exposed the whole sorry mess was ostracized by his former friends in the administration.

Despite such extreme examples, the government press agents and the government handout serve a useful if not actually indispensable purpose; without them the correspondents would find it virtually impossible to give an accurate report of the manifold activities of government, and the public would receive from day to day an account which at best would be fragmentary and misleading. Reporting news of government without the aid of press agents and handouts would be about as effective, in these days, as for a general to attempt to instruct his army in person. Both were done, once upon a time, but governments and armies have far outgrown such intimacy.

The danger to the press, and through it to the public, is in the possibility that the correspondents will accept handouts and the dicta of press agents at their face value, and prepare their budget of news entirely from these official and naturally biased statements. When this occurs, and sometimes it does, the public is misled and democratic government is done a serious disservice.

It is not unnatural for press agents, and behind them their official masters, to desire that the correspondents should rely on the handout and the press conference for their news, since then only the authorized version would be printed. But until recently there were very few important officers of government or press agents who actively discouraged independent reportorial activity, except in extreme cases, and in fact their respect for the correspondents was and still is in direct ratio to his intelligent search for the news behind the press release.

Yet in the recent past there has appeared an increasing tendency to make it difficult to do such a job of reporting, and personal access to the man who makes the news has become rarer. The Navy has established a strict censorship at the source; the Army has set up an elaborate establishment manned by active and reserve officers; and other key agencies have followed the same course in greater or less degree. "National Defense" has become the excuse and apology for making the press agent the principal officer of his agency, so far as the public is concerned.

To accomplish this end, the government has elaborated, enlarged and refined in the past eight years the publicity system worked out by Early as the President's legate. Each important agency has, not one press agent, but several, with secretaries, stenographers, messengers, mimeograph departments, and in some cases field representatives. They deal with the newspapers, the weekly and monthly magazines, the radio and the newsreels. They write handouts for the reporters and speeches for the bosses. It has become their task to see to it, not that the correspondents' questions shall be quickly and accurately answered, but that the correspondents shall have at their immediate disposal such a volume of statistics and propaganda that questions will be reduced to a minimum, unless they are for purposes of elaboration in the spirit of the handout. Then the "information specialists" are overflowing with information.

It goes without saying, perhaps, that the quality and integrity of a governmental press agency depends entirely upon the quality and integrity of the individuals manning it. Some always have and always will conceive it to be their duty, regardless of the desires of their superiors, to answer as few questions as possible and conceal as much news as possible. They will go to great lengths to get favorable attention for a speech by the Secretary, or a spot on the society page for the marriage of the Secretary's daughter; they will be very kind and helpful in matters having little or nothing to do with the news. But they can be somewhat worse than useless when stories are breaking and information is required. Volunteered misinformation is of little value in enlightening the public.

In all charity, it must be said that such press officers as these have been and still are in the minority, but there is an increasing proportion who, regardless of their personal instincts to the contrary, find that they are unable to publicize their agency's acts and policies with any degree of freedom because the man at the top forbids it. Why such men, former newspaper correspondents of considerable distinction for the most part, prefer to continue to work under such conditions of intellectual prostitution rather than seek other employment where their souls are their own a greater part of the time, is a question to which the answer is complex, but in the main economic in nature.

When the New Deal came in, there was a large and im-

mediate demand for skilled journalists who could publicize
and interpret its acts to the correspondents. They were not
hard to find. This new administration had an aura of glamor
which attracted to it many newspapermen who for one reason or another were dissatisfied with their current employment, men who believed in the New Deal and who were
happy to do their part in putting it over. At that time, also,
there was an increasing number of competent newspapermen out of work because of the depression, and from the
ranks of these, as well as from the employed, the New Deal
recruited its press agents.

For the most part they received better salaries than they
had been accustomed to, and with these salaries a variety of
perquisites such as private offices, private secretaries, longer
vacations, and the like. A man who used to get $5,000 a
year and now gets $9,000, as a few do, and has accommo-
dated his scale of living to the higher salary, may well find
the prospect of a return to $5,000 or less extremely discon-
certing if not actually out of the question.

A number of highly paid correspondents went into government service for less, or no more, than they had been
receiving, because they believed in what the New Deal was
doing and their bosses didn't. I have no record of one leaving the service for a lower salary because he fell out of sym-
pathy with the New Deal. I know personally of two or three
who, while still ardent New Dealers, would like to go back
to newspaper work, but who have been out of it so long as
to have forgotten that they are getting at least twice as
much salary as they could command as reporters after so

protracted an absence. So they continue as government spokesmen.

Foremost among the government's press agents is one who might resent the term as applied to himself — Stephen Early. Early, first secretary to President Roosevelt, is nonetheless press officer of the most important of the executive agencies, and without question has the toughest job of the lot. In addition it was he who for a long period, prior to the advent of the Office of Government Reports, continued to exercise general supervision over the publicity machine he helped to create, in many instances actually selecting the man for the particular vacancy.

It was Herbert Hoover who first hired a newspaperman for his secretary, but Early is the only one to hold the post continuously for any great length of time. His predecessors were failures, sometimes spontaneously, sometimes because it was impossible to do a decent job of press relations for Herbert Hoover as President. Early, for more than eight years, has snapped and snarled at the correspondents and given them the best service they have ever had from the White House. His job is grueling, exasperating, and it takes its toll of his nervous system, never very placid anyhow, but he remains the true friend of the working press, and Mr. Roosevelt would find it very hard indeed to get along without him.

Early, in fact, has attained an importance as presidential press secretary accorded to none other — he holds his own daily conference and is quoted in his own right. The presidential secretaries have always released a considerable amount of news, orally as well as written, but they have invariably appeared in print as "a source close to the White House," "a White House attache," or even, by metonymy, "the White House." But when Early's morning press conferences began to be vehicles for expressions of presidential policy, and became as important, sometimes, as the President's own meetings with the correspondents, these devices of anonymity ceased to be adequate, and soon "Stephen Early, the President's Secretary," was an important and acknowledged source of White House news.

There was, of course, an additional reason — some say the sole reason — for this emergence of Early from anonymity. Several statements he made over a period of time turned out to be a trifle prejudicial or a trifle out of line with the facts as they later developed, and the correspondents, to protect themselves, began quoting him directly. But that is not all. His pronouncements have more and more the quality of genuine authority, and are recognized as such. Because they have this quality, it is important that it be known who makes them, true or false.

When "the White House" announced the agreement with the Danish minister, Henrik de Kauffmann, to take Greenland under our protection, a brief announcement was made, and a little later the State Department released the full text of the compact and the exchange of notes. But with the original announcement Early gave considerable oral elaboration at his morning press conference which was of great value to the correspondents. It was obvious for whom he was speaking, and what he said had a certain added value because it could be quoted directly with none of the circumlocution that protects the President. More and more Early has assumed the status of what in a private business would probably be known as "assistant to the President."

When a steel strike was called during a deadlock in negotiations between the Congress of Industrial Organizations and U. S. Steel over the terms of a new contract, home offices of all the Washington correspondents were pressing them for official reaction, but it was most difficult to get because it was late Saturday afternoon, with government offices closed, and most of the brass hats were warming up for the spring dinner of the Gridiron Club. Secretary of Labor Perkins assigned her chief conciliator to the job, but aside from that there was little to report from Washington.

Then without solicitation Early, who was at a pre-Gridiron Dinner party, phoned at least one Washington newspaper bureau and passed on the word that the C.I.O. strike call was actually a bluff, and that agreement had already been reached to continue at work while negotiating. The result was that reassuring stories were written by Washington correspondents, and the panicky headlines were toned down. Thus the President's Secretary, at a moment when he might possibly have been excused for laying aside the cares of his job, on his own initiative performed one of the primary functions of a government press officer — to assist the press in getting all the facts.

Early has been far from perfect, but the White House Executive Offices are haunted by the ghosts of those who have failed in that job, and on the whole he has done well. He has been known to deny a report which came officially true within the hour, or worse, to utter a misleading half-truth, but such occurrences have been spectacular because of their rarity, and it is generally agreed that they are the fault of the President himself for failing to keep his Secretary informed, as much as of Early's own desire not to appear uninformed or to spare "the Skipper."

Long tenure in such a position presupposes absolute and unquestioning loyalty to the man's superior, and unflagging devotion to President Roosevelt has been one of Early's outstanding characteristics. This devotion, which the President commands so extensively, is unquestionably the only thing that has kept his secretary this long in the hardest job of press agentry in the government.

Below the presidential offices there operate a wide variety of press agents, from the point of view of personality, efficiency, and importance in the composite governmental picture. Some rejoice in a quiet anonymity — true bureaucrats, however competent, who are content to draw their salaries and give satisfaction without courting fame. Some others consider themselves to be important cogs in the governmental wheel, and strive mightily to make themselves known. Having adopted public service as a career, they hope that some day they may be struck by the lightning of a presidential appointment. Or perhaps they are merely dazzled by the outward and visible pomp which surrounds them.

These are the men who, more and more, are the symbols of power in our growing bureaucracy. They are not the possessors of power in themselves, because at best they are only hired men, obscure Bruce Bartons of government, but inasmuch as they have become the principal funnels through which the press obtains its information it would be a serious mistake to minimize their importance.

They are not mere handout dispensers. They determine whether a correspondent may or may not see a Cabinet officer or other high official; they decide, even, whether to ask that officer a question transmitted through them by the correspondent. Many times a reporter honestly in search of legitimate news has asked a press agent to put a query to the top man, only to get no reply at all, or merely the word that the Secretary "has no comment." Most of the time this no doubt represents the facts in the case, but there have been occasions when there was every reason to believe the press officer never took up the matter at all, taking it upon himself instead to determine what the reporter should know.

This is not "information," or "intelligence," or whatever they choose to label it: it is volunteer censorship by an underling with delusions of grandeur and it contributes nothing at all to the cause of efficient democracy. It is worse than having press agents who are ignorant of what is going on in their own agencies, another phenomenon not at all uncommon. If the press agent doesn't know or won't find out, then the "free press" has an uphill task getting the news of government to the governed.

Much of this sort of thing is a result of a fundamental misconception on the part of the press officer as to his function. Some of them appear to think of themselves as so many hundred-eyed Arguses, to keep suspicious strangers away from their sacred cows. In some agencies correspondents have been driven to elaborate devices to get to speak, even briefly over the telephone, to a responsible official when the press agent himself was ignorant of news developments. Once in the early days of the Defense Commission a reputable correspondent, quite openly, called a commission aide from the press room, to ask for an appointment. But before the connection was made the press agent had taken the phone away, saying "Let me talk to him," and the correspondent never got his appointment.

The life of a government press agent is a miserable one at best, but Washington correspondents who take such jobs are perfectly aware of what they are letting themselves in for and ought to be prepared to do the job properly or not at all. They have no privacy; they must be available at their homes after hours; they must be at the beck and call of their bosses, and regular hours of labor are unknown. They must make it a point to keep constantly informed of what is going on in the agency they are publicizing, and be prepared to pass this information on promptly in response to inquiries.

All this they know, but there are those who just can't be bothered. They spend long lunch hours in the Press Club bar; they are uninformed when asked a simple question and manifest no desire to inform themselves and the inquirer; they go home early and are seldom available by telephone in an emergency. They are captious and irritable when called up out of office hours. They are not earning their salaries.

On the other side of the picture are those — and they are still in the majority — who remember Steve Early's original rule. They are on the job at all reasonable hours and they know what is going on, or if they don't will make an honest effort to find out. They try to maintain a normal contact between the press and the government, and arrange appointments with officials as if it were part of their job and not a reluctant acquiescence in brazen effrontery. They are among the most valuable of all government employees, because through them the public is kept advised of its representatives' actions.

Unique among the press agents, and the oldest of the top men in point of service is Michael J. McDermott, Chief of the Division of Current Information in the State Department. A brisk, genial, moon-faced Irishman, McDermott has been in this ticklish spot in the Department for fifteen years, and is the friend and counsellor of more newspaper correspondents than he can count, though he never was a reporter himself.

In an agency where much of the news is legitimately, if temporarily, secret, he has achieved an admirable balance between his duty to the Secretary and his duty to the press. There are occasions when he seems to resent the publication of important news from the State Department of which he has had no prior knowledge, but he has never implemented this passing resentment by trying to discredit the story or punish the reporter. He or an aide is always on the job, day or night, and he has never been known to mislead a reporter deliberately. He is an institution.

Over in the Department of the Interior Secretary Ickes has at his right hand a burly, red-faced philosopher, Michael W. Straus, who manages one of the largest and most efficient information divisions in the government for the government's most outspoken critic of the press. Whatever Ickes says about our shortcomings, he is always meticulous in his insistence that the correspondents have access to the news of his huge and diversified department, and in Straus he has a willing adjutant.

Straus is an old Hearst man, and the tone of his huge output of handouts betrays the fact. He dearly loves a sensational approach to the news, and when he puts it on paper, if there is the slightest touch of romance to it, the whole thing emerges a deep purple. For example:

"Giant generators whirling around the clock for Department of Interior power producing agencies are pouring a torrent of electricity onto transmission lines for a dozen States, but skyrocketing demands have made mandatory a wholesale expansion of the production program, Secretary Ickes announced today, speeding it up not by weeks or months but by years. . . . Today's necessities make federal power production plans of eight years ago, which then were attacked as 'fantastic' although merely considered adequate by public officials, now appear conservative. The critics' cries of 'useless projects' a few years ago have faded to a mocking echo as current examination reveals them ridiculous in retrospect."

But it must be said that after some four-hundred words of flamboyant introduction, Straus went on in that same release to give more than a thousand words additional of straight information about the power program, including a very useful table. I can see him, strolling into Ickes' huge private office, itself big enough to house a respectable power plant, and I can hear him say:

"Boss, don't you think we ought to dash off a little jazz to make a lead for this power stuff?"

And Ickes replying:

"Go to it, Mike. I'll make a statement raising hell with those so-and-so's who said we were building too many power dams."

Straus maintains a large and efficient staff of assistants, each with a specialty, and there is always news to be had from the Interior Department. One assistant publicizes the national parks, another the Reclamation Bureau, and so on. The Office of Indian Affairs has as an assistant to the Commissioner an experienced newspaperman, also with a flair for the romantic, who feeds out press material about the original Americans. He does not work directly under Straus, but is on speaking terms with him.

Straus's ménage for a number of years was a haven of refuge for competent journalists who found themselves out of a job, because he had a very generous allotment of funds in the Ickes budget. He handled news not only of the Interior Department, but also of the Public Works Administration, an emergency agency and a controversial one which produced a great deal of copy. The number of stranded correspondents taken under Straus's capacious wing is not inconsiderable. Later on, however, when PWA faded to a shadow and was absorbed by the new Federal Works Agency, it became impossible to expand the staff of the Director of Information any further.

Straus probably would consider the high point of his career of press agentry to be his publicizing of Ickes' new building for his department. Ickes got some millions of

PWA money allotted to this project, and not a brick was laid, not an elevator installed, that Mike Straus failed to put out a romantic handout about it. He laid the number of workmen on the job end to end, he estimated the relative capacities of the spacious cafeteria and the Grand Canyon of the Colorado, and each time Ickes changed his plans and the job was delayed another month or two, Straus found more material for press releases. Never was a subject so thoroughly canvassed, so utterly exhausted.

When Harry Hopkins was made Federal Emergency Relief Administrator in 1933 he brought in Morton Milford, a thoroughly experienced editor, to be his director of publicity. Milford assembled a fine staff of assistants, and it was one of these, Truman Felt, who succeeded him when he died. There is no suppression of news in the Works Projects Administration (successor to FERA) if Felt can help it. He and his aides are indefatigable in the service of the press, and have been known to spend hours on busy days digging up statistics which they knew perfectly well were to be used in hostile editorials.

There are others who could be mentioned as examples of honest and competent handling of government press relations — Guy McKinney of the Civilian Conservation Corps, a former *Chicago Tribune* correspondent; Marion L. Ramsay, ex-Hearst man and a real expert on public power, who has publicized Rural Electrification and one or two other agencies; Gordon Dean, now in private law practice, who removed the veil of unconscionable secrecy from the Department of Justice, and who held to the view that not more than five percent of all his department's activities had any reason to be secret; Samuel Bledsoe (late of the Associated Press) and his staff at Agriculture, where a tremendous volume of strictly factual press releases is handled daily, but where no question from a correspondent fails of an honest answer; the Treasury staff, headed by Charles Schwartz but assembled and trained by Herbert Gaston, a *New York World* man, who is now an Assistant Secretary; Carlton Skinner of the Maritime Commission, a former *Wall Street Journal* correspondent, who worked with diligence and intelligence and never considered himself to be a bigger man than his one-time associates.

All these, and many others, among them turn out a perfectly incredible number of handouts in the course of the year, some trivial or entirely propagandist in nature, but the majority conveying legitimate information which would be much harder to get in any other form.

The National Recovery Administration before the Supreme Court killed it was turning out releases at the rate of more than a hundred a week, and the Agricultural Adjustment Administration in its heyday about equaled that record. Straus's combined output from Interior and PWA ran about 6,300 in two years. These totals, of course, include texts of speeches by officials as well as ordinary factual information, and New Dealers have not been backward about making speeches. The advance text of a speech is extremely useful to the press: if it is being delivered just at a deadline, the handout enables the paper to carry a story at that time instead of later.

A striking example of this occurred in the Spring of 1941 when William S. Knudsen, Defense Commissioner, was to deliver an important address in New York on a Saturday evening. New York morning newspapers go to press normally about two hours earlier on Saturday to accommodate the great volume of mail subscribers to the Sunday edition, so that it was imperative to have a copy of the Knudsen speech in advance if possible.

It appeared that Knudsen had had a rough draft prepared and had taken it with him to revise on the train, with the understanding that when he reached New York he would telegraph the changes back to Washington, where the final version would be released. He took his time about revising the speech, and finally the press staff, which had foregone its customary half-holiday, took extensive corrections by long-distance telephone, getting mimeographed copies of the text to the Washington bureaus just in time to rush back to New York and other centers by telegraph.

The NRA, to raise old ghosts, maintained a magnificent press service, and to the best of my knowledge no Washington correspondent ever had just cause to complain about the volume or quality of its product. William Lawson, a seasoned newspaperman, was its chief, and he organized a full staff on the pattern of a newspaper city room, with himself as managing editor. His aides included a city editor, copy readers and reporters.

The NRA as it was nearly drove the correspondents mad because of the infinite variety of important things that were happening there all the time, and if it had not been for Lawson's service the public never would have had an accurate picture of its activities. He sent his reporters out to cover important code hearings and rushed mimeographed stories around to the newspaper offices, page by page if it was late. They were meticulously accurate and extremely well written, and could have been used as they were if necessary. News bureaus would have not one but half a dozen or more men covering NRA alone, but they could not possibly have personally covered more than a fraction of all that went on. This fantastic period undoubtedly proved the value of the handout, if it needed proof.

In those days the government agencies generally didn't worry too much about what kind of news the correspondents got — the men at the top for the most part were too new to bureaucracy, too busy with earth-shaking activities, too conscious of the overwhelmingly favorable attitude of press and public, to fret at the occasionally adverse story. The handout was strictly a supplement, and an indispensable one, to what the reporters were able to find out on their own.

It is not unfair to say that by now the converse is true — what the correspondent is able to learn by independent research is supplemental to the handout. As the New Deal consolidated its position, its members learned the methods of the bureaucrat, and the honeymoon of press approval faded; so faded, too, that first fine flush of free publicity. The crop of handouts has not declined, in proportion to the urgency of government activities and their multiplicity, but they contain more and more propaganda, and are offered more and more as a substitute for fresh information in response to questions.

They have to a considerable extent forced their way into the Cabinet press conference, so that the department chief, like some college professors, merely takes them as a text and elaborates upon them. When the correspondents arrive for the conference they are likely to find a fine crop of press releases waiting for them, starting off with "The Honorable Frank Knox, Secretary of the Navy, announced," or "Secretary of the Interior Harold L. Ickes said today that," or something of the sort. Then the press conference develops into a seminar based on these canned statements. Or perhaps the releases are handed out after the conference, and the reporters find to their chagrin that all they have heard is already written down and mimeographed in more readable form.

An excellent example of this is provided in the monthly press conferences of Secretary of Labor Perkins, mentioned elsewhere. Virtually no news of any consequence ever comes out of Miss Perkins' conferences. Once a month the Bureau of Labor Statistics prepares a long, factual release on the trend of industrial employment and payrolls, with analyses by categories. It is a good routine story — sometimes an important one — but it is all in the handout. Miss Perkins' "conference" consists of reading the introductory summary of this statistical handout, which always is phrased as an announcement by her personally. Such questions as are asked are answered perfunctorily and make little if any news.

Even Jesse Jones, Secretary of Commerce, whose conferences usually are full of meat, sometimes falls into this practice. In the spring of 1941 he called a press conference and a fairly important story resulted. But the story was ready in advance in the form of a handout, and there was no real reason for calling in the reporters if that was all he had to say.

The Navy Department, with the war-born stringency, releases no news except in handout form, save for the conferences of Secretary Knox, a newspaper publisher who thus finds himself in a very odd spot indeed; and the War Department, while freer with publicity, seeks to provide a handout in answer to every question, if possible.

It is difficult for anyone who has not sat through a busy day at the news desk of a large Washington bureau to conceive of the number of press releases received. First thing in the morning a considerable fraction of those given out the day before appear again, by mail. Then the fresh crop appears, and continues throughout the day. Bureaus support a special messenger service which goes from department to department collecting releases, and these messengers make the rounds at least twice a day. Most of the agencies also send copies of their handouts to the Press Club, where they are laid out on a big table for the correspondents. And some, having their own messenger services, send copies direct.

Thus one is likely to receive, in the course of the day, anywhere from one to six or more copies of each press release, including all the proceedings of the Interstate Commerce Commission and the Securities and Exchange Commission. If it is a large news bureau it arranges to get all press releases, even though most of them go straight to the waste basket, because the manager can't possibly know in advance which he will want and which not. The Agriculture Department, for example, issues many statements of a regional or highly specialized character, but it would be placing too much confidence in bureaucratic clerks to expect them to know which the individual newspaper desired.

In addition to the official handouts there is a sizable harvest of private releases. These come from all manner of agencies and individuals, from the Chamber of Commerce of the United States to the Congress of Industrial Organizations; from B'nai B'rith to the National Catholic Welfare Conference; from lame-duck statesmen seeking to reclaim a small spot in the sun to the mad economist with a new and unintelligible theory for saving the world.

Sometimes these privately sponsored releases are more pestiferous than those from the government, because often the pressure groups consist of little more than an executive secretary and a press agent seeking to earn their stipend, and they have a way of following up the handout with a personal visit or a telephone call. Sometimes too they will tell you, impressively, about their intimate friendship with your boss in the home office, the impression they attempt to convey being that if you don't send a handsome story about their little racket your boss will be terribly displeased. More often than not such fakers mispronounce the boss's name, or endow him with a nickname by which he was never known. The bigger and more influential your paper the more insistent they are, and heaven help you if it has ever manifested the slightest editorial interest in anything remotely resembling what they are trying to sell.

The result of it all is a steady stream of mimeographed matter flowing across the bureau manager's desk, most of it of no use to his paper at all. But a secondary result is that, in inspecting all this stuff, he must use a great deal of snap judgment as to its value, and not infrequently he makes a mistake, for a kernel of important news may be hidden in the verbiage of a carelessly written handout, or purposely tucked away at the end of an otherwise worthless release. Or the import of the release may not be immediately apparent.

E. P. Herring, in his book, "Public Administration and the Public Interest," remarked that "sifting out the news from the mass of prepared official statements is a task that discourages further curiosity regarding detail on the part of the busy journalist." The statement is far too comprehensive, but there is in it an element of truth. A reporter with a large volume and variety of news to write is often tempted just to rewrite a handout without further research, and it is also true that many correspondents find themselves so burdened with routine duties having little if any relation to the news, but imposed upon them by their employers, that their time for independent reporting is seriously curtailed. Certainly their superiors have no such idea in mind, but often they fail to appreciate the amount of time and effort required to get the answer to an apparently simple and direct question, time and effort subtracted from the subordinate's newsgathering.

It cannot be too strongly emphasized that when and if the handout becomes a substitute for independent reporting, all that will remain to differentiate between newspapers will be the selection they make from among the handouts, and the manner in which they rewrite them. It is difficult to believe that this is what the government desires.

VIII

Democracy's Show Window

THE CURRENT CROP OF DICTATORS must frequently wonder why American Presidents and Cabinet officers periodically subject themselves to questioning and heckling at the hands of newspaper reporters. If they really understood the possibilities of the open press conference, and were clever enough to make use of it, they would know that it can be one of the most effective devices for controlling, coloring and suppressing news.

The press conference is an American development and probably could not have become a fixture in any country with a lesser degree of freedom of the press. It grew out of demands of the American newspapers for a reasonable degree of direct contact with the men who make the news, rather than with their underlings. To a limited extent it has spread to other lands, but in none of them is it so accepted, so institutionalized, and it is at once laughable and pathetic to see a foreign dignitary being subjected to the process for the first time in his life.

As a fixture in the national government the press conference is relatively recent. William Howard Taft was the first President to essay regular meetings with the press, but departmental press conferences were a much later development, and did not reach their fruition until the time of

Franklin D. Roosevelt, when the full value of friendly and intimate relations with the press was for the first time realized.

It takes a good man, quick-witted and not too thin-skinned, to conduct a successful press conference over any considerable period, and the institution has been a failure in some cases simply because perfectly willing officials were not quite up to the job. Without doubt Franklin D. Roosevelt is the ablest man in press conference ever to come to Washington, and he is one man who has appreciated to the fullest that the regular conference works both ways: not only that it affords the correspondents an opportunity to meet face-to-face the Chief Executive of the Nation or the head of a Department, but also that it permits him at will to get his own version of the news to the press without the weakening device of an intermediary. It lets him discourage a search for news by denying it in response to a planted question, or by giving a premature and partial account if the full account is not deemed desirable.

If conferences were as simple as some think they are this would not be so easy — the give and take of question and answer as originally practiced by Harding would inevitably result, even in the case of an alert and highly intelligent politician, in the divulging of much unfavorable or unwanted news. Some of the correspondents are closely related in their methods to the trial lawyer, and it is an alert official who always comes out of the ordeal unscathed. Not even Mr. Roosevelt is without his flesh wounds.

But over the years an effective method of controlling the conferences has been developed and refined. This consists of dividing information into categories, so that no matter what the question, the man being interviewed is able to say whether his reply shall or shall not be published, and in what form. Clearly the system is far from perfect, but by and large it works. The correspondents accept it as reasonable and the prerogative of the President or subordinate official, even though they frequently realize that they are being "taken for a ride."

This is how it operates: There are four main categories of press conference revelations — material for direct quotation; material for attribution to the speaker but which must be paraphrased without direct quotation; material for "background," which may be used but on the reporter's own responsibility, without attribution to anyone; material for the reporter's information but not to be published under any circumstances. The extent to which each of these categories is employed depends on the individual speaking and the type of news with which he is concerned.

In general, Presidents are not directly quoted in accounts of press conferences, and it is assumed that they are not to be unless they so specify. For the most part they prefer to have their direct quotations prepared in advance and reduced to writing, to make sure that no unstatesmanlike utterances or grammatical errors will go down in history as coming from their lips. There is also, to be sure, the even more important factor of off-hand replies to questions which may inadvertently be so worded that they will be subject to misinterpretation by the newspaper reader.

But there come occasions when the President will answer a question and add: "And you may quote that."

These have a way of being times when, in the case of FDR, he is angry and wants to give special emphasis to his denunciation of, say, an opposition Senator.

At other times he will by chance make a striking statement, not necessarily of utmost importance, but which would lose something in paraphrasing. Then the reporters will ask permission to quote, and it is normally granted.

The great bulk of the President's press conference remarks are for attribution but not for direct quotation, but some of the White House correspondents have learned that in most cases they can get by with use of the President's actual words so long as they are put in the third person and there are no quotation marks. The trouble with this device, however, is that sometimes a copyreader with an itching pencil will insert quotation marks and thus violate the White House rule. And again, when the correspondent has scrupulously observed the restriction, the copyreader may use quotation marks in the headline. But the writer can recall few reprimands from the White House as a result of such a slip.

"For background" is the way the President or other official prefaces statements which the reporter may use but not attribute. The stated purpose of such material is to "enrich" the correspondent's information, to augment his fund of knowledge with official utterances, which, for one reason or another, it is considered unwise to attribute directly to anyone. Here again it is difficult to avoid letting the public know who is speaking, although the written record does not literally put him on the spot.

Secretary of the Treasury Morgenthau is addicted to the

practice of saying things in conference which may be used
so long as he is not given as the source of the information.
But a story often will lead off with such a statement and
then follow immediately with a direct quotation from the
Secretary on the same general subject, and the significance
of the juxtaposition is inescapable.

There are many reasons for giving out background
material. It may be that the official wants the press to
understand all the reasons for a stroke of policy or an
administrative act, but cannot state them flatly without
causing complications. This is particularly true in the field
of foreign affairs, where punctilio plays a large and important part. So the Secretary of State will make a brief,
attributable statement and then, with the remark, "Here
is background," give a full and detailed account of what
led up to the announcement. His account may contain
references to foreign governments or their representatives
which would cause embarrassment if coming directly from
the American Secretary of State, so when they are published they are prefaced by some such expression as "it was
learned in diplomatic quarters," or "high officials believe,"
or "it was reliably understood."

In the spring of 1941 Secretary Morgenthau made a flat
statement regarding Anglo-American policy but asked that
it be not attributed to him. A day or two later it was
formally announced by Jesse Jones, Federal Loan Administrator. The reason Mr. Morgenthau preferred not to be
known as the authority for the statement was that the
matter was one for the Federal Loan Agency to adjust and
announce, and the Secretary, though willing when asked to

give out information on a subject in which he had had a hand, desired to avoid appearance of muscling in on another Cabinet officer's special province.

These are the obvious and entirely legitimate reasons for the use of "background." A collateral and not so legitimate reason is a desire to pad the news accounts with material for which no government official accepts direct responsibility, but which will tend to color the dispatches the way the administration wants them colored — to give them the correct "slant."

And there have been not infrequent occasions when an official would publicly repudiate something he had said in this manner if the reaction of the newspaper readers was unfavorable. Theodore Roosevelt, who never held general press conferences, was particularly culpable in this respect, not hesitating to call a correspondent a liar by name if the news proved to be unpopular. Calvin Coolidge, too, often repudiated his own statements, an easy matter for him, since he never spoke for attribution anyway. Franklin Roosevelt has seldom directly repudiated any press conference statement — there have been rare instances of it — but he has frequently branded as false something attributed to him second-hand and of whose truth there was credible evidence.

There appears to be no valid excuse whatever for the disclosure of "off-the-record" or confidential information, and its possession is in most cases positively detrimental to the correspondent's objectivity. Two reasons occur why officials persist in off-the-record remarks. One is that some men can't keep a secret, and petty men in big jobs get so full of important information that they are in danger of bursting if they don't tell someone. Also they experience a pleasant inflation of the ego by reason of their ability to shock, surprise, or merely inform a group of men who do not have normal access to such secrets.

The other reason is that an official, having made a statement for publication, is then able by the use of the off-the-record device to create a distinct bias in the writing of the stories. Background material, as remarked, also has this dubious value, but when publication is forbidden and the reporter is required not even to take notes, then he is at the mercy of the speaker. The situation is precisely parallel to that in a courtroom where, after a piece of evidence has been heard, the judge orders it stricken from the record and admonishes the jury to pay no attention to it.

Clearly few minds are so dispassionate, so immune to suggestion, that they can wholly reject such material. Try as he may, a reporter who has been filled up to the neck with highly prejudicial statements in connection with something he is permitted to write is almost certain to be influenced in his writing by those statements.

From the point of view of the official himself there is every reason to avoid the utterance of any facts he does not want published. In categories such as that just mentioned, it is obvious that he desires publication, not directly but by inference, but in cases where he is really imparting information and not opinion, he himself is almost invariably the loser.

This is less the case when the official has been talking to an individual reporter in private; but when a President or a Cabinet member relieves himself of a few burdensome secrets in the presence of anywhere from twenty-five to two hundred correspondents, and then admonishes his auditors not to print them under any circumstances, he is being, to say the least, slightly naïve. For one thing, he is placing an unfair burden on the correspondent, who at some future time under pressure of work may inadvertently let slip some of this "confidential" stuff. Or he may, after the conference, make casual reference to it in conversation with an associate, not realizing that the other has not already heard it. The second man, not knowing the story is off the record or not considering himself bound to confidence, since no one told him so in so many words, then writes the story, and the cat is out of the bag. No statement to a large group is ever "off the record" for very long.

President Roosevelt, who indulges in relatively little off-the-record comment of any consequence, has gone to extraordinary lengths to safeguard what confidential information he does give out to the hundred or more men attending his conferences. He assures them that they are not to repeat what he has said to anyone, not even to their bosses.

Of course this is silly and is not observed. The White House reporter is the representative of the bureau chief, who in turn is the representative of the managing editor and the publisher. It is the reporter's duty to pass on, in equal confidence, to his immediate superior what he has been told in such circumstances. What he should not do, although it is too much to expect that he will not, is repeat confidential material to unauthorized persons, for that is the way it leaks out.

There is one Washington columnist who used to cover a department for an out-of-town newspaper. When the Secretary's press conference, in view of news developments, was fairly sure to include a large amount of off-the-record matter, this correspondent would not attend, but would remain behind in the press room. When the other reporters returned they would compare notes, reach full agreement on what was for publication and what not, and then write their stories. Our hero would sit quietly at his desk with his ears cocked and take it all in. Then, not having attended the conference and not being technically bound by any pledge of confidence, he would proceed to write at will what he had heard.

When President Roosevelt talks off the record it is entirely clear and unmistakable, but the same cannot be said of some of his subordinates. General Marshall, the Chief of Staff, is notable for the confusion resulting from his conferences, and it would require something approaching genius to separate the news from the confidences. The General will say a few sentences for publication and then a few in confidence, and so on until the conference has come to an end.

In consequence of this mingling of the printable and the unprintable, some of what he says off the record gets printed through sheer inability of the reporters to keep it segregated. If the General would make available a transcript of his remarks for purposes of checking he might save himself considerable grief.

If an official prefaces a remark by saying it is off the record, the reporter simply takes no notes and is usually successful in excluding what he hears from the account he later writes, but this is not always done. It is not at all common for a statement to be made and notes taken, and then for the great one to add hastily that it is in confidence. Often enough not everyone present hears the codicil, especially when the speaker is a feeble old man with a weak voice.

At the State and Interior Departments full transcripts of the conferences are available later in the day, with the result that there is no excuse for the reporters for the morning papers to print the unprintable. But also present are correspondents of afternoon papers and press associations, whose deadlines will not permit them to wait for the transcript. They simply have to rely on their own memories and offer up a prayer to Saint Simeon Stylites.

Many correspondents refuse to accept information in confidence when they are on the trail of a story along the same lines, but again, such refusal is difficult if not impossible in a formal press conference. Perhaps they have heard the confidential statement before the restriction was appended; at any rate, it is extremely awkward, when an official says "Now this is off the record," to make a break for the door before he continues. And from the practical point of view, the conference might be only beginning, with much important on-the-record stuff to follow.

When it comes to the President's conferences it is impossible to reject such confidences. The meetings with the press are carefully guarded; only those with proper credentials from daily papers, press associations or the radio are admitted, and after they are all in the doors are locked. It would be interesting to see what would happen if one individual, having decided that he didn't want to hear something off the record, tried to flee the presence.

There was one spectacular occasion, in the last year of the Hoover administration, when an entire press conference evaporated and came to naught because the man conducting it insisted on talking in confidence.

It was in the days when Bolivia and Paraguay were fighting their bloody little war in the Gran Chaco, the "Green Hell" which both claimed and neither could possess. The State Department was moving heaven and earth to get the thing settled, and there was a great deal of pressure being put on the ministers of the two countries by one Francis White, assistant secretary in charge of Latin American affairs.

One day White had been closeted alternately with two fiery diplomats for many hours. The State Department correspondents, to whom it was highly important news, asked White, through Michael J. McDermott, the able departmental press chief, if he would not vouchsafe them some publishable information after the secret sessions were over. White said he would. At about 6 P.M. he admitted the press to his office and said, in his pseudo-British accent:

"Gentlemen, I have some news for you, but it is all off the record."

Louis Jay Heath, correspondent for Latin America of the United Press, to whom the story was especially urgent, spoke up and in his suavest manner replied:

"I'm sorry, Mr. Secretary, but in that case I beg leave to be excused."

As he went out the door, one by one the other correspondents present repeated his formula, until there remained in the room only White, with his mouth hanging open, and McDermott, with fire in his eye. A friend of the reporters, McDermott without delay proceeded to give the assistant secretary an elementary lesson in the ethics of press relations.

The point of the story is not primarily that the correspondents were annoyed at being thus tricked, but that every one of them hoped to get some authentic news about the Chaco situation. If they let White tell all about it in confidence, they would be automatically barred from publishing it if they did get it elsewhere. It is all very well, as some reporters have done when accused of breaking confidence, to protest that they obtained the information from another source, but at best it is a fishy-sounding alibi even if true, and most of the corps will simply drop a story rather than incur such suspicion.

Once in a long while, in a large bureau, it happens that a reporter will come in with a story which another man has had, from another source, in confidence. It is entirely permissible to use the story as the first man received it, but it is embarrassing to get news in this way. A favorite device in such cases is to be sure that the writer's name is signed to the story, to make it clear that it was not written by the one who heard it off the record.

There are, naturally, always a few correspondents who will not hesitate to break an off-the-record story from a press conference if they feel sure they can do so without incurring reprisals, and for this reason if for no other public officials should never indulge in confidences with a large group. It embarrasses the source of the information when it leaks out, and it is highly unfair to those others who have faithfully observed the rule of silence.

Several years ago, in the earlier days of FDR, he confided a very important story to those attending his press conference. For perhaps a week the silence was unbroken, even though every correspondent and bureau chief in town knew about it. Then the correspondent of a large New York paper could stand the strain no longer, and broke the story. He did not pin it on the President, and he approached it in roundabout fashion, but he unmistakably broke confidence.

Naturally, correspondents of all the competing papers were called on the carpet by their managing editors for missing so important an announcement of policy, and they were forced to explain that they too had had the story but, unlike their rival, had respected the pledge of confidence. Then, because the news was out, they wrote it too.

A similar incident, though not involving a press conference, occurred in March, 1941, to the intense embarrassment of Lord Halifax, the British Ambassador, and perhaps to the eventual detriment of the press corps as a whole in its relations with the embassy. Halifax had been calling on Sumner Welles, Undersecretary of State, and the reporters, as usual, asked him afterward what it was all about.

It appeared that the Ambassador had been assured, before coming to this country, that the American press was of a different breed from the British, that he could talk freely to the Washington correspondents and be sure they would be discreet, and not rush to press with everything he might happen to tell them. So Halifax, in response to their questions, replied with utmost frankness, that, among other things, he had informed Mr. Welles that German submarines were understood to be preying on British shipping in the western part of the North Atlantic, inside the United States sphere of influence. He made it quite clear that he was not speaking for publication. That evening the International News Service carried the story on all its wires.

The United Press and Associated Press received immediate inquiries from their home offices, as did the bureaus of the New York papers. They all replied that Halifax had been clearly understood to be speaking in confidence, but the Associated Press sent out a "service message" to all its clients, telling the whole story but adding that it was not to be used! Thus the AP, apparently, considered that it was not breaking the rule.

By now, of course, the news was all over the place. INS client papers had printed it, and every editor of every AP paper knew of it. It was about as confidential as a Hitler broadcast. So the UP finally broke down and sent the story too. Next day it was made officially public by Winston Churchill and Mr. Welles.

If a confidence such as this, given to a few individuals who ought to be worthy of the most implicit trust, cannot be kept for more than a few hours, then how much more foolish is one given to a hundred or more heterogeneous reporters in a large room! Most government press officers, indeed, are strongly opposed to off-the-record statements in or out of press conference. Such statements usually prove most embarrassing to them, and they are inclined to agree, when pinned down, that no sound purpose is served.

Yet the policy-making officers of government continue to give such unsolicited confidences, and they find good reasons for it, from their point of view: the opportunity to create an unconscious bias in the mind of the reporter, and the further opportunity to cut short an independent search for facts by telling the story off the record.

This device can be most effective. The official knows that one or more reporters are on the trail of an important story which he believes should not be published, and he is morally certain that sooner or later they will get it. So in response, often, to a planted question from an innocent or complaisant bystander among the correspondents, he tells it all — "off the record, gentlemen!"

In 1931 President Roosevelt, then Governor of New York, was engaged in a sharp controversy with President Hoover over the development of the St. Lawrence seaway. Henry L. Stimson, now Secretary of War, was then Secretary of State, and one morning emissaries of Governor Roosevelt were closeted with him for two or three hours. When they emerged they told the correspondents waiting outside that any news of their mission must come from Stimson.

Within an hour the Secretary's daily conference convened, and the first question had to do with the St. Lawrence argument. Stimson immediately launched into a detailed account of his meeting with the men from Albany, all off the record. At his earliest pause for breath Pierce Miller of the INS asked:

"But Mr. Secretary, won't it be possible for you to give us something we can print?"

Stimson replied:

"If you'll just hold your horses, Mr. Miller, I'll get around to that presently."

So he resumed his off-the-record discussion, continuing for a half-hour or so, and then terminated the conference before another question could be asked, and without giving one word of information that could be used. All we could write about this matter of greatest importance to the United States and Canada was the fact that a meeting took place, followed by some vague generalities and sheer speculation. The Secretary of State, by full use of his control over the conference, had effectively cut us all off from a search for the truth.

A negative aspect of the same thing is the premature denial, a denial issued before a story has been written or printed or, perhaps, even obtained. It often happens that a rumor will go flitting about town and several correspondents will be trying to confirm it. If they are wise they will not bring the matter up in open press conference for two reasons: one, that it then becomes the property of the entire corps, and two, that if it is a story the administration would rather not see published, it affords an opportunity to issue a technical denial. These denials, like the off-the-record explanations, sometimes issue in response to planted questions from reporters who either know nothing about the story or who are willing stooges.

These stooges are the bane of the existence of all self-respecting newspapermen. Virtually every department has at least one, and the White House is no exception. They can usually be relied upon to ask a question given them in advance by the press officer, and they often assist in terminating the conference when the going is becoming heavy for the official holding it.

At just the right moment one of them will chirp "Thank you, Mr. President," or "Thank you, Mr. Secretary," and the Great Man says "Thank you," and that's all there is. Sometimes they are not precisely stooges, but have become bored or convinced that they have all the news their minds can absorb in one day; at any rate, the effect is the same.

Recently, since the radio news commentators have achieved the status of correspondents and are admitted to press conferences along with the newspapermen, one who regularly covers the White House has developed into almost an official terminator of conferences. He comes in with a little budget of questions, enough to fill his fifteen minutes on the air if he gets them all answered, and plants himself as close as possible to the President. Then he says:

"Mr. President, what the people would like to know today is — " and proceeds to ask his questions seriatim. As soon as they are all disposed of he smiles benevolently and pronounces the customary benediction. It is difficult to recall any President or other official who responded to that "Thank you, Mr. President," with "Just a minute, Mr. Smithers, I have something more I'd like to say," or "Hold on there — Paul has been trying to ask me something." Generally they welcome the closing line.

Secretary of the Interior Ickes appears to enjoy his press conferences about as well as any member of the Cabinet. He is an old campaigner, full of vinegar, who loves nothing better than a rousing debate with no holds barred, and who spends his leisure thinking up tart epigrams — and epithets. His entire adult life before entering the Cabinet was devoted to battling for righteous causes as a member of hopeless minorities, and it has been interesting to observe his conduct during these more than eight years in which he has been the spokesman for a very large majority. However he may have changed, it has not resulted in dull press conferences at the Interior Department.

Ickes is one who always provides a full stenographic record of the conference for the reporters to consult, and it was this transcript which once helped Winifred Mallon write a detailed and accurate account of her debate with him right after the 1940 election.

The Secretary, who for several years had been saying sharp things about the press in general (he once worked for a newspaper himself), had intensified his criticism during the 1940 campaign. The burden of his complaint was that the newspapers, by their opposition to President Roosevelt's policies, were doing the people a disservice and were not "free." The great majority of the voters had endorsed the New Deal in 1932, 1934, 1936 and 1938, yet except for the first and possibly the second of those four elections the majority of the metropolitan press had been in the opposition. They should have been with the majority, said Ickes.

In his first press conference after the election he reopened the subject along the now familiar lines, but this was the first time he had developed his theme in the presence of reporters who were in a position to question him. One did.

Miss Mallon, who has been covering Washington for a good many years and who fears no man, took immediate issue, raising the point that if the press went blindly with the majority it could hardly be termed free; that the very fact of its being in the opposition was evidence of its freedom in the meaning of the Constitution. In friendly but determined fashion the discussion continued for several minutes until one of the press officers, sensing that the Secretary was running into difficulties with his curbstone logic, signaled one of the faithful to change the subject.

But it was all recorded in the transcript, and Miss Mallon, as well as all the other correspondents present if they desired, was thus able to write a true account of the affair with direct quotations.

Secretary Morgenthau enjoys his conferences, but is cautious, sometimes to an extreme, partly because he is not entirely sure of himself, and partly because of the extreme delicacy of governmental finance. Yet when he does have something to say it has a way of being in extremely vigorous language, particularly when he is paying his respects to some proposal of Marriner S. Eccles, Chairman of the Board of Governors of the Federal Reserve System. And he dearly loves an exchange of mild badinage with the reporters. One time, after such an encounter, he returned a few days later from his New York State farm with a little boutonnière of raspberry for each of the Treasury correspondents, which he presented to them individually with elaborate ceremony.

One of the favorite Cabinet officers with the correspondents is Jesse Jones, the tall, plain-spoken Texan who has held important office in the government ever since the tag end of the Hoover administration. Now he is Secretary of Commerce and Federal Loan Administrator — head of the world's biggest and most powerful bank and simultaneously director of all the far-flung business-aid services of the government. His conferences are highly informal, usually opening with a salty joke, and are customarily full of information.

Vice President Wallace's conferences, when he was Secretary of Agriculture, used to be extremely popular because of the frankness and informality of his remarks and the fact that there was a minimum of off-the-record discussion. Perhaps because of his habit of blurting out impolitic statements, his conferences were usually attended by Jerome N. Frank, who was then General Counsel of the Agricultural Adjustment Administration.

Once, in the earlier part of the Roosevelt administration, there occurred an off-the-record exchange which there is no longer any reason to keep secret, that chapter in New Deal history having long since been closed. The New York State Supreme Court had just ruled that the State milk control law was unconstitutional, and Mr. Wallace, who was having an appalling amount of trouble enforcing the similar federal law, was asked for comment. Specifically, did he think the decision would affect the operations of the federal law?

"The Supreme Court can invalidate the federal milk law too for all I care," he replied, irritably.

All the reporters started furiously scribbling notes, and Frank, his eyes popping and his mouth hanging open, half rose and said:

"Of course you mean that to be off the record, Mr. Secretary."

"Off the record or on the record, it's all the same to me!" Wallace retorted.

Deliberately and with great emphasis Frank then said:

"It is the opinion of the legal division that it is off the record!"

And sure enough, it was!

The Secretaries of War and the Navy are always flanked by military and naval aides, quick to prompt or correct them if their tongues slip. Sometimes, especially in the case of the Navy, it is a little difficult to know who is conducting the conference, the Secretary or his sideboys, particularly since in a majority of cases the Navy Secretaries have been men who knew little about naval affairs. There have been instances when the War or Navy Department has considered it necessary, after a bad slip by the Secretary, to put out a formal press release making it clear that the head of the department was misunderstood — that he didn't really say what the reporters heard him say!

Of all the Executive agencies, there are only three which still have regularly scheduled and regularly observed conference dates. These are the White House, the State Department, and the Treasury Department, and of these the State Department is most punctilious of all. White House

conferences are held on Tuesdays at 4 P.M. and Fridays at
10:30, but sometimes they are canceled if the President is
ill or traveling. State Department conferences are held six
days a week, and if the Secretary is ill or absent, the Undersecretary fills in for him. Secretary Morgenthau meets the
press regularly on Mondays and Thursdays when he is in
Washington.

At the beginning of the New Deal nearly every Cabinet
officer had one or more regular conferences a week, and so
did the heads of important independent agencies such as
RFC and WPA. Secretary Ickes met the press without fail
on Tuesdays and Thursdays. The Attorney General did
likewise, and the Secretaries of Commerce, Agriculture and
the Navy held weekly conferences. The Secretaries of War
and Labor were less frequent, but only the Postmaster
General had no fixed dates.

In later years, however, the executives have become a bit
too bored or too busy to stick to their former schedules,
and the only Cabinet press conferences that can be definitely relied upon are those of the Secretaries of State and
the Treasury. And one other: Once a month, without fail,
Frances Perkins, Secretary of Labor, calls the reporters together to hand them a mimeographed press release from
the Bureau of Labor Statistics on the trend of industrial
employment and payrolls.

The press conference system, in fact, has been waning
for some time. It has received a new lease on life in the
Navy and War Departments with the advent of Frank
Knox and Henry L. Stimson, who resumed conferences on
a fairly regular schedule late in 1940, but Justice Robert H.

Jackson, who as Attorney General was one of the most popular men with the correspondents, seldom met them en masse; Secretary of Agriculture Wickard has very few conferences; Secretary Ickes has cut his schedule to one a week and often breaks that date, and Secretary Jones may see the press not more than once a month, although he is usually quite accessible to individuals he knows and trusts.

Gradually the handout has been substituting for the press conference, and except for State and Treasury, only the semi-weekly seminars of President Roosevelt continue without impairment.

IX

Congress — Uncensored

WHEN THE LATE JAMES COUZENS OF
Michigan was a member of the Senate he severely tried the
patience of his more orthodox colleagues by his habit of
revealing the secret proceedings of Senate committees.
Couzens, an old-school liberal, hard-boiled as any but with
an almost fanatical sense of public honor and private
decency, simply refused to be bound by any self-imposed
secrecy rules of committees of which he was a member, and
when he considered it advisable made it a point to report
to the newspaper correspondents what had taken place.

There were then — and are now — plenty of others who
see to it that unwarranted secrecy in Congressional proceedings is not permitted to be wholly effective; some, like
Couzens, from a sense of duty, others because they like to
do little favors for their friends the reporters and expect
similar favors in return, and still others because they can't
keep a secret. Whatever the motive, these men forcefully
illustrate the fact that so long as there is a free representative assembly there can never be an effective censorship of
the press. Congress has no press agent (other than its 531
members) but it always has been and probably always will
be the best source of uncanned news in Washington.

A President may develop delusions of grandeur — or

persecution — and with them dictatorial tendencies, and administrative underlings may become intolerably bureaucratic, but the members of Congress, elected by the people, responsible to the people, are acutely sensitive to anything that smacks of suppression. They also make outstanding asses of themselves from time to time, but in the main their collective influence has been on the side of free government and hence of a free press, if only because it is good politics. Individual quarrels occur, and there have been rare occasions when one House or the other stood on its dubious dignity and sought to penalize a particular correspondent, but most of the time they stand up for their good friends and involuntary publicists, the reporters, and give them priceless aid in their search for news.

Couzens' outstanding exploit was his daily revelation, early in the Hoover administration, of what went on behind the closed doors of the Finance Committee when it was revising the House version of the infamous Smoot-Hawley tariff bill. At those sessions everything went, including the regular attendance of a representative of a manufacturers' association in the guise of a Senator's secretary. Shamelessly the committee jacked up one schedule after another, from motives which in many cases were not at all above suspicion, and Couzens determined that the public should know about it. So, having warned his colleagues in advance, he reported each afternoon to the Capitol correspondents, with the result that the newspapers printed a running account of all the disgusting log-rolling and back-scratching which culminated in probably the worst tariff law ever adopted by Congress.

But a few months earlier the Senate had worked itself up into a fearful lather over the publication of two secret rollcalls on questionable presidential nominations, one of Roy O. West to be Secretary of the Interior (by President Coolidge), and the other of Irvine L. Lenroot to be a judge of the Court of Customs and Patent Appeals (by President Hoover). The Senate had the pleasant habit of going into secret session whenever a controversial nomination was to be voted upon, in order that whatever horse-trading took place would be just among the members of the club. These nominations were in that category, but Paul R. Mallon of the United Press obtained both rollcalls and they were widely published.

After the second leak, the Senate decided to make an issue of it, launched a half-hearted investigation to find out who was the Senator who had broken the club rules, had Mallon up on the carpet to no avail, and finally changed its procedure so that such secret sessions could be held only if a majority so ordered. Such a proposal had been pigeonholed in committee for a long-time, but Mallon and his public-spirited Senator provided the impulse which brought it out and got it adopted. Correspondents, as a collateral outcome of the same episode, were barred from the floor of the Senate, a privilege accorded to press association men theretofore, but since there was no valid reason why they should be so favored, only the Associated Press objected.

Since Congress is technically one third and for all practical purposes nearer one half of the federal government, the news it produces is of tremendous importance to the correspondents, but it is not only accounts of legislative proceedings which are obtained from its members. In their official capacity they learn a large amount of news about the activities of the Executive Branch as well, which they are seldom averse to divulging to a friendly reporter. One discreet correspondent with good connections recently found out all about certain highly confidential plans of the Reconstruction Finance Corporation involving our foreign policy from a prominent Senator, with no restrictions other than the usual one — that the Senator be not mentioned as the source. The story, however, had an ironic conclusion: the reporter decided that to reveal these secret plans would be detrimental to the public welfare and so they were not printed.

The most spectacular members of Congress have not as a rule been the best sources of news: they make plenty of it by their speeches and the legislation credited to them, but they are likely to be too preoccupied with their own affairs to bother with doing the reporters favors, and they don't have to in order to get publicity. Unquestionably the most consistently publicized member of Congress of this generation was the late William E. Borah, who came to the Senate term after term from the provincial State of Idaho, yet devoted all his public attention to national and international affairs having little direct interest to his constituents. He became a great public figure chiefly because of his oratorical ability, and his name is associated with few if any major legislative acts. But he possessed an acute sense of timing in making his pronouncements and profited throughout the greater part of his career by constant and favorable press notices. He used to wait until an important debate in the Senate had reached its peak of fervor and the galleries were crowded, then make his big speech, not to the Senate but to the world, and his rare visits to the hearings of committees of which he was a member were similarly timed. It was he who is credited with discovering that newspapers have least news to fill their columns on Monday, and with having applied this knowledge by releasing most of his big stories for Monday morning. And he was wont to remain in Washington for a few weeks after the summer recess had begun and feed apparently casual but really carefully prepared statements to the news-hungry correspondents.

After he became Vice President in 1933 John N. Garner was not noted for his loquacity, although as a member and Speaker of the House he had been one of the best of behind-the-scenes news sources. He appeared to feel that as Vice President he should have no visible connection with legislation other than to preside over the Senate, and no public opinions at all on pending policy decisions. Yet he was constantly in the news, and privately, with those reporters who were his trusted, old-time friends, he talked frankly and at length. Chief among these confidants was Henry M. Hyde of the *Baltimore Evening Sun*, a highly respected and able old-school journalist who looks like a backslidden Episcopal rector and has a nose for news like a bloodhound's. No doubt most of Henry Hyde's conversations with Garner were of the "background" variety — information and opinion which could be used only on condition that the source was not revealed — but every now and then a real news beat would appear in the *Evening*

Sun which all of Hyde's friends knew perfectly well came from Garner and no other.

There is a considerable collection of stories about Garner's behind-the-scenes direction of the legislative opposition to the New Deal after 1936, when he had fallen out with President Roosevelt; in fact, most of the tales told of him had to do more with his extraordinary parliamentary cunning and the salty quality of his commentaries than with any genuine statesmanship he ever displayed. Yet there was something about him that fascinated presumably unromantic newspapermen from the time in 1931 when it became apparent that he would become Speaker, and there is little doubt that his later reputation as a mighty statesman was largely their creation. He was a veteran legislator and extremely shrewd, with all the bold devices and clever tricks of a Texas politician, but it is unlikely that very many of his volunteer press agents really believed half what they wrote about him, if they took the trouble to study him dispassionately. Thomas L. Stokes, then of the United Press and as discriminating a reporter as ever covered Washington, was one of those who beat the drum for Garner in those days, and there were many others of equal rank who similarly helped publicize this pair of angry eyebrows as God's gift to Government.

Men like Borah, Garner, and other romantic figures on Capitol Hill are of great value in a general way to the correspondents and particularly to their close friends, but the ones who produce from day to day and who really help to crack any censorship-at-source in the Executive Branch are the hardworking gentlemen who spend less time in the limelight but who do most of the important committee work. Most of the work in the House and a great deal of the Senate's is done in committee, and it is the responsible committee member who really has news for the reporters before it is ready for general announcement.

With a membership of 531, it is clearly out of the question for correspondents to keep in touch with every Senator and every Representative and it would be silly to do so if they could, for most of the members as individuals contribute little of importance either in legislation or in news. But each correspondent makes a point of working up friendships with the men who can do him the most good, depending upon his needs. Assuming he represents a paper of general circulation, he will try to have one reliable informant in the House Ways and Means Committee, which has to do with raising revenue; one in the Appropriations Committee, which spends it; one in the Senate Finance Committee, which corresponds to the Ways and Means Committee in the House, and one in the Senate Foreign Relations Committee.

These friendships have resulted in some spectacular beats. The day after Secretary of the Treasury Morgenthau had told the House Ways and Means Committee in secret how he thought the Congress ought to proceed to raise defense funds, the New York daily news magazine, *PM*, published the full substance of the Treasury proposals, with schedules of tax rates for various income groups as well as the recommendations for luxury taxes and other special levies. It was an outstanding beat for Nathan Robertson, a former Associated Press correspondent who became one of *PM*'s real reporters, and this is in all probability how he did it:

When Morgenthau and his Assistant Secretary, John L. Sullivan, appeared before the committee they brought with them a number of mimeographed copies of their plan for distribution among the members. After the hearing some particular friend of Robertson's on the committee slipped him a copy. At any rate, a correspondent of the *New York Times* got one that way — the following day.

Sometimes the member cultivated is chairman of the committee, but as frequently he is not, because the chairman is a sort of liaison man with the White House and may not be so communicative. Often the choice will be a responsible member of the minority party, one who is sufficiently opposed to administration policy to want to tell secrets. But if the correspondent is fortunate he will have a source in both the majority and the minority. One canny reporter covering the House assiduously cultivated Representative Clifton Woodrum of Virginia, ranking Democrat on the Appropriations Committee, during the succession of short-lived economy waves that passed over Congress in the 1930's. Woodrum, a member of the majority, was at the same time with the minority in spirit, being an advocate of stern economy at a time when the New Deal trend was all the other way. Also, being in the running for the majority leadership — or even the Speakership — he was not averse to the personal publicity he received in return for his news tips.

Another correspondent, although working for a New York paper, obtains much important exclusive news from an important Senate committee chairman who comes from the Deep South and is affected little, if at all, by what this paper's readers say or think about him. But the reporter is a native of his State and the sectional bond bred a strong personal friendship which is the source of the majority of exclusive stories. This same paper has on its staff several Southerners who find that accident of birth most valuable in obtaining news from Congressmen. In a Democratic administration many of the most important committee chairmen are Southerners and they instinctively favor correspondents who "speak the same language," employ the same accent and know the same people.

A Southern newspaper would find such connections doubly valuable because sectional papers find it necessary to make friends with the members of Congress from their own regions. They can get the big national stories from the press associations, but what they particularly desire is to have a full quota of news of special interest to the folks at home. It is a common practice for a Senator from, say, Missouri to be consulted by the President before he appoints someone to be a federal judge in that State, and members of the House make it one of their principal duties to keep abreast of federal activities affecting their districts. Thus a Congressman frequently is able to tell the correspondent of his home-town paper that the War Department has approved the construction of an arsenal there before the Department gets around to make the news generally public. And he can tell in advance who is going to be nominated to be postmaster, or who is going to be collector of customs at Accotink.

If the particular delegations cultivated by a particular paper happen to include one or more members of national importance, so much the better, and it often happens that correspondents of a big city journal will get important news beats or, at least, "hot" tips, from their friends of the smaller, more localized papers. Such exchanges are sometimes on a fairly regular basis. The representative of a large Eastern morning paper with a nationwide circulation will have an informal understanding with a Middle Western colleague whose interest is principally in agriculture and who has become a genuine expert on the subject. Inevitably he obtains much important news ahead of the pack, and is able to share it with his friend from the East. Or the exclusive stories may be in the nature of gifts from correspondents of trade journals, the very specialization of whose interests enable them to get further with important Congressmen than otherwise.

Correspondents of big papers have occasionally found that friendships with obscure members of important committees can be as valuable as any other. Congressman Chaparejo or Senator Blowse from the Gila monster belt may have little influence on the ebb and flow of legislation, but he knows what is going on, is as hungry for publicity as his better-known colleagues, and inclines to be flattered at the attention paid him by the representative of a big paper two thousand miles from his district.

Of great value in an emergency is the ability of members of Congress, by reason of their official status, to obtain from the Executive Branch information which has been denied the press, either because some bureaucrat chooses

to keep it secret for obscure reasons of his own, or because
its publication might cause a controversy or cast an unfavorable light on the manner in which this agency conducts its affairs. A correspondent who gets wind of such a
story can usually, as a last resort, persuade one of his friends
on the Hill to requisition the information and let him have
it. Such a device has its reciprocal aspects; in most cases
the Congressman so solicited is happy to have the story
himself, since it may give him ammunition for a debate
or an investigation.

Petty rivalries between committee chairman sometimes
lead them to disclose news to reporters. It may sound silly
— and probably is — but career politicians are thoroughly
convinced of the value to them of being identified with
an important piece of legislation, and will go to great
lengths to attain this happy consummation. When a big,
administration-sponsored bill is introduced simultaneously
in the House and in the Senate, the chairmen of the committees to which it is referred get their names on it, but
that is not enough for them — each wants to have his name
first, so that the public will think he actually wrote the bill
instead of merely introducing it at the behest of the President. This is accomplished by having the bill passed first,
by the House or Senate as the case may be. More subtle
stratagems are devised, more valuable time wasted, by pub-
licity-crazed committee chairmen trying to outmaneuver
their opposite numbers in the other House than their
constituents would believe possible. Senator Carter Glass
of Virginia and Representative Henry B. Steagall of Alabama used to indulge in all manner of tricks to get their

names first on the various banking acts fathered by the New Deal, and their rivalry not infrequently resulted in one of them handing out an exclusive story just to get the jump on the other.

The personal equation cannot be too heavily stressed in appraising the ability of correspondents to get news from Congressmen. Accurate forecasts of Supreme Court and other appointments have resulted from friendships with Senators, and even when there is no spot news involved, such relationships enable the newspapermen to enrich his fund of background information against the time when he will be able to make use of what he has been told. A State Department reporter and a die-hard isolationist on the House Foreign Affairs Committee engage in protracted conversations after meetings of the committee, for the principal reason that they come from the same New England State and see eye-to-eye on foreign policy. The Congressman rarely tells the correspondent anything he can print at the time, but what he does tell in confidence serves the latter well as a check on what he may hear elsewhere.

Personal relationships, too, help to break news of presidential policy after conferences of legislative leaders at the White House, and it is in such cases that friendship with a high administration leader is invaluable. When the President calls legislative leaders to the White House there is usually little important news given out on the spot — at best it will be a brief, perfunctory statement lacking all the amplifying detail needed to make a good story. After one of these conferences, the novice among the correspondents lingers around the White House door, catching such crumbs as fall, but the adept has other methods. He will have found out in advance just who is going to be present — and he can find out at the Capitol even though the White House does not release the list — and will have selected from that list the one or two who are his friends. If possible, he makes an appointment in advance; at the least he tries to follow his source away from the White House for a private chat, and such chats produce news. Members of Congress, like most other men in public life, are reluctant to discuss developments in detail in the midst of a crowd, but are fairly co-operative — with the inevitable exceptions — when alone with someone they know.

While a sense of public responsibility such as motivated James Couzens to so great a degree is the cause of many important news breaks, the understandable desire to remain as long as possible on the public payroll is the cause of many more. This desire manifests itself in many ways, such as always playing safe on controversial bills, never doing or saying anything that will lose votes, and the like. But one of its principal manifestations is the desire for personal publicity mentioned earlier in this chapter. If a member can get his name in the papers often enough and in a not unfavorable light, he feels that it is worth many votes to him. Even if the story is in a paper which does not reach his remote district he can have it inserted in the Congressional Record as an "extension of remarks," and then mail it broadcast without paying postage.

Sometimes this publicity mania breaks out in strange ways; sometimes it overreaches itself to the extent that the correspondents become disgusted and stop writing about the Congressman unless he makes real news. The late William I. Sirovich of New York made such a nuisance of himself as a self-constituted authority on the drama and, by extension, on all the other fine arts, that he became the laughing stock of his own colleagues as well as of the press, particularly since his claim to authority rested on the authorship of one unsuccessful play. The late Royal S. Copeland, Senator from New York, got a very indifferent press despite his personal kindliness, because he would never let anyone forget that he had been a physician and Health Commissioner of New York City.

Sol Bloom of New York, Chairman of the House Foreign Affairs Committee, has always provided the press with considerable innocent amusement by reason of his unconscious buffoonery. Bloom was in the show business in Chicago before he ever thought of becoming a statesman, and the Little Egypt technique has carried into his life in Washington. In 1931 and 1932, as sole member of the George Washington Bicentennial Commission, the Republican chairman having resigned, Bloom did a magnificent job of publicizing himself, and not long after that the Sesquicentennial of the Constitution offered him a similar opportunity. The papers were full of comical tales about Bloom and his methods of introducing the Father of His Country to his children, but it was all taken in the best of humor, evidently on the theory that all publicity is good publicity, and the worst thing that can happen is not to be noticed at all! Since he became chairman of the Foreign Affairs Committee, however, Bloom has comported himself with a dignity more nearly befitting his high office,

and asks the reporters to refer to him NOT as Congressman Bloom, or just Bloom, but as Congressman Sol Bloom
(don't forget the "Sol").

One of his fellow members from New York City carried
to the ultimate extreme the theory that all publicity is
good publicity. Reporters noticed that from time to time
this man would vote against a bill which he had supported
in debate, but only when there was an overwhelming
majority for it. One of them questioned him and his answer in substance was this:

"Haven't you ever noticed that while the papers don't
often print complete House rollcalls, they do print the
names of those who voted 'No'? I vote the way that will
get my name printed in the New York Times and the
Herald Tribune."

Martin Dies of Texas, founder of the Demagogues Club,
is one of the most persistent and skilful publicity seekers
in Congress, but he attains his ends in an entirely unorthodox fashion. Evidently proceeding on the theory that a
front-page story in a few papers is better than an inside-
page spot in all of them, Dies, as chairman of the Dies
Committee, has a way of giving out statements and interviews to only the handful of correspondents regularly assigned to cover him. If any other reporter gets wind of
the story and asks about it, the Chairman makes no effort
to keep it secret, but neither does he attempt to give it
wide publicity. The system appears to work very well,
probably because of the passion of newspapers for exclusive
stories — and the pain they experience when a rival has
such a beat. The paper getting the tidbit from Dies gives

it prominence on page one, the rival paper gets excited at being thus scooped, and its correspondent in Washington is told to get on the job. So the wily Texan is always being called on the phone and begged for news of no particular importance. Part of his technique is to cast a cloak of mystery about the most routine facts such as the date on which he will begin a series of hearings. He will let it be known that he is going to expose the sinister Trojan Horse activities of the Patagonians, for example, but will not say when other than "next week." The favored few learn the exact day — the rest have to guess at it, and probably give the story more attention than it merits simply because of the additional effort they have devoted to it.

A few years ago there occurred a serious epidemic of what might be termed regional publicity campaigns, in which an entire delegation would seek to publicize the products of its State. Huey Long of Louisiana probably gave them the idea with his insistence that "corn pone and pot likker" be served in the Senate restaurant, but several years after his death Washington was intermittently deluged with Idaho potatoes, Maine potatoes, Rhode Island oysters, New York and Wisconsin cheese, and even New Jersey "champagne." All these commodities were served for a day in the House and Senate restaurants, and correspondents received quantities of them as gifts. Regional reporters, of course, sent out columns for home consumption, but by and large this sporadic exhibitionism became the laughing stock of the galleries, and suggestions began to be advanced that Senator Vandenberg ought to give away several hundred motor cars to publicize Michigan, or that the California delegation might well curry favor with the press by importing and distributing a few platoons of movie actresses.

All these antics, all these cheap political tricks to which even the best of the legislators at times resort, do not greatly elevate them in the esteem of the correspondents who see them from day to day and know what motivates them. Despite the general atmosphere of chumminess between Congressmen and reporters, an atmosphere compounded largely out of self-interest, the private opinion held by the latter of some of the former is far from flattering. Yet little of this attitude ever appears in the papers because of the difficulty of legal proof. The laws of libel are a great and constant source of protection to anyone who has done a good job of covering his tracks.

Nevertheless the dislike — or even contempt — of the press for an individual member does sometimes boil over and then the war is on. Magnus Johnson, a typical comic-strip Swede, blew into the Senate in the 1920's and immediately became a goldmine of highly entertaining news for the gallery correspondents, bored with the trivialities of the Coolidge administration. Johnson's brand of low comedy, which he appeared to mistake for cleverness, gave many a newspaper reader a hearty laugh at breakfast when it was most needed, but eventually it dawned on the Senator that he was being ridiculed, and mistaking the effect for the cause, he stormed into the press gallery and delivered a violent lecture to the correspondents. After that many of them boycotted him, a rather shortsighted procedure, since they were only depriving themselves of good comic relief for their papers.

J. Thomas Heflin of Alabama, a blowsy demagogue cordially disliked by Senators and press alike, engaged in frequent and amusing feuds with individual correspondents, denouncing them from the floor in his most picturesque terminology. His particular enemy was Frank R. Kent of the *Baltimore Sun,* whom he characterized as "that contemptible little pinwheeler," but Carlisle Bargeron of the *Washington Post* also got his name in the Congressional Record as "one of Ned McLean's gallery squirrels." Some of the papers started boycotting Heflin as they had Johnson but at least one, the *Baltimore Sun,* chose the reverse procedure of giving him the run of the paper, on the theory that nothing makes a charlatan appear so ridiculous as to print all he says the way he says it. Most of the Senators left the Chamber whenever Heflin began one of his long-winded orations, but one, a former college professor, always remained seated, listening attentively. Finally one other member asked him:

"Why do you always stay here and listen to that insufferable windbag?"

"He fascinates me," replied the professor. "I have yet to hear him make a grammatical error!"

Congressmen and correspondents customarily treat one another with an elaborate display of respect however they may feel in private, since it is so clearly to their mutual advantage to maintain friendly relations — the one getting news, the other, free publicity. This is an attitude of long standing, dating back to the early days of the Republic when the national leaders realized that freedom of the press would mean little unless news was made reasonably accessible, and it has resulted in lavish accommodations for the newspapermen in both House and Senate. A commodious separate gallery and workroom has been set aside in each, with free telephones, free stationery, typewriters, desks, sofas and all the other equipment a journalist requires, including batteries of telegraph wires which can be hooked up on a moment's notice to any desired point.

No one is permitted in these working galleries but accredited correspondents of daily papers or press associations, although they may entertain guests who are also working newspapermen. To enforce this and other rules of the press galleries there is a Standing Committee of Correspondents, elected every two years, which works in close co-operation with Congressional officials. They draft amendments to the rules when required, arrange for press accommodations at national conventions, and supervise the paid gallery attendants. The attendants keep a general eye on the conduct of the correspondents, attempt to bar all unauthorized visitors, take messages for men temporarily absent, and let them know when a rollcall is about to be taken so they can get out into the gallery in time.

Before L'affaire Mallon in 1929 a handful of correspondents, by reason of their employment by press associations, were permitted to walk into the Senate chamber at will and interview members at their desks, but now, when any correspondent wants to discuss anything at all with a member of Senate or House during a session, he must employ roundabout means to do so. If the member is on the floor, the correspondent sends in word by a page, asking him to step out for a few minutes, and unless something momentous is in progress on the floor the member usually complies, because the reporters are generally careful not to abuse the courtesy. At other times the Senators and Representatives may usually be found in their offices or cornered in a corridor.

Surprisingly little pomposity is encountered by the press in either House or Senate, the members evidently appreciating to the full the personal advantage accruing to them from being friendly with the correspondents. Probably the hardest thing to make the run-of-mine Congressman understand is objective reporting; if you give him good publicity in connection with one bill and bad in connection with another, he concludes that you have turned against him, and many members of Congress as well as officials in the Executive Branch appear to feel that if your paper approves of a policy it should avoid printing any news, however legitimate, on the other side.

Correspondents accredited to the Capitol press galleries enjoy many small perquisites in addition to the working facilities. Their names and addresses appear in the Congressional Directory, with symbols to indicate whether they have wives, daughters, or "other ladies" accompanying them, and it is from this list that invitations to many official and unofficial social functions are made up. Each correspondent receives a copy of this directory with his name printed on it in return for his one-dollar registration fee. Until recently, too, the gallery membership card was sufficient identification for a correspondent in any govern-

ment office including the White House — it was the police
pass of the political reporter, signed by the Speaker of the
House and the Chairman of the Senate Rules Committee.

Whether because of changing personnel in Congress,
or because the members have more important matters on
their minds, there has been less entertaining of correspondents by individual Congressmen in the Roosevelt administration than in earlier years, although there is no evidence
that the fundamentally friendly attitude has altered. But
some of the Congressional parties were rather famous.
Fred Britten, an Illinois Republican and former prize-
fighter, used to have a New Year's morning affair at his
home, with liquor flowing copiously. Britten adhered to
the informal manner and passed out the cocktails himself,
but he also had expensive rugs, so that if he happened to
pour a glass too full, he would take a sip from it before
handing it to his guest, lest any drop of alcohol damage
the furnishings.

And an old Southern Democrat, who was re-elected year
after year despite his intermittent insanity, gave an annual
oyster roast for his friends among the correspondents. One
day this aberrant statesman was on his way into the Chamber while the House was in session, and a colleague said
to him:

"Do you know what they're doing in there? They're just
about to pass a bill grading members on the basis of their
efficiency, and scaling their salaries accordingly. They have
Grades A, B, C, and D, and you've been put in Grade D."

The poor old fellow waited to hear no more but rushed
into the chamber, got the floor, and launched into a pas-

sionate address defending his legislative reputation and vigorously objecting to his classification. Right in the middle of his oration he pointed a trembling finger toward a press association man in the gallery and shouted:

"There — right there — is a man who attended my oyster roast last year!"

X

Syndicated Oracles

THE OPINIONS OF THE SYNDICATED
columnists have to a considerable extent displaced the
traditional editorial views of the newspapers which publish
them. This is not particularly surprising, in view of the
natural preference of the average reader for a personal expression by a journalist whose name he knows to the
anonymous outgivings of a hired editorial writer representing such an impersonal entity as most newspapers have
become. When the *New York Tribune* published an editorial in the 1860's, its readers knew Horace Greeley was
speaking; James Gordon Bennett was the *New York Herald* and Charles A. Dana the *New York Sun*. But nowadays
the big city newspapers (except for the Hearst chain)
which are identified in the public mind with a single man
can be counted on the fingers of one hand. Something of
popular appeal has been lost in the process of becoming a
big business, and it probably was inevitable that the columnists should rise up to fill that lack.

Thus you do not often hear the average citizen say "The
editor of the *Saugatuck Sentinel* says . . ."; but you do
hear him remark "Dorothy Thompson says" or "Walter
Lippmann says" or "Raymond Clapper says." The odd
circumstance is that these newspapers continue to write

and print staff editorials as if nothing had happened: they have yet to realize that they are, in fact, buying syndicated editorials which their customers read instead, and that they have no control over the opinions expressed in these canned soothsayings. And because they pay well by the year for the columns, they tend to continue to print them whether they like them or not, so long as their readers appear to be pleased.

What all this boils down to is that the political columnists today are the most important force, by and large, in American journalism, and there is a very serious question how many of them comprehend the heavy responsibility they have incurred. Most of them, certainly, give little evidence of such comprehension. They go on dashing off their columns from day to day as if they were just another variety of reporter, getting more money and having a larger number of readers, but otherwise just specialized reporters. Too often are their columns used to grind private axes; too often do they express half-developed opinions one day and reverse them a week later; too often they offer as the "low down" on news developments their own deductive reasoning, a reasoning not always entirely sound. And because there are no rules of evidence to govern them such as govern and restrict the ordinary reporter, those who purport to give news as well as opinion frequently present unconfirmed rumor as fact, the wishful thinking of one government official as established policy.

The columnists accomplish daily what nearly every newspaperman has from time to time wished he were able to do — write not only the news but also what he personally thinks about it, without regard for his paper's editorial position or the inhibitions of style or subject matter. Most of the columnists were once newspapermen themselves, and that first fine sense of freedom they experienced when they wrote their first column must have been very enjoyable indeed. But it carries with it such a burden of public trust as ought to make the writer extremely humble, extraordinarily careful, about everything he puts on paper.

There is room for considerable doubt whether many of these writers fully appreciate how implicitly they are relied upon by their readers, particularly in small towns in the interior of the country where no great variety of journalistic conjecture and opinion is available. The knowing air with which tidbits of alleged news are written, the "I'll let you in on a secret" manner affected by most of the columnists, is terribly impressive to the old ladies in Philadelphia, Miss., or Eureka, Mich., convincing them that their favorite columnist surely has access to news hidden from the other Washington correspondents, and no amount of persuasion or proof will make them think otherwise. They know the editor of the village paper; they know his faults and foibles and prejudices, but Mallon or Clapper or Pearson & Allen are so many names to them, names which eventually take on a bit of the infallibility of an oracle.

The astonishing thing about the development of the political columnists' craft is that few of them by training or education are any more qualified to be leaders of public thought than any other good newspaper reporter. Their chief stock in trade is an ability to write plausibly at least, brilliantly in the case of some, but always with a pontifical air about current affairs. The earlier ones, as a matter of fact, engaged more in the dissemination of news than of opinion: they scouted around the city looking for odd bits of important or merely interesting information and wrote them in an informal, racy style. They were one up on the regular reporter because they were not bound to quote any authority for what they said — their signature on the column was their authority — and this gave them far greater latitude. Because of it they could publish rumor as well as news items for which they would not have been able to adduce acceptable proof, and by the same token could get such items from perfectly responsible persons who for one reason or another desired to avoid identification.

But as time went on it was only natural that these first columnists should inject a little opinion into their recital of undercover news; after a while in most cases the opinion began to outweigh the news in volume, and eventually most of them were writing only opinion, and had become full-fledged editorial writers on a free-lance basis. Washington today boasts a dozen or more syndicated columnists of whom not more than three can be said to publish news in their columns, and those three not on any full-time basis. The rest are editorial writers pure and simple, writers of editorials printed daily all over the country in papers whose views may or may not coincide with the very positive ones expressed by the columnists.

Their editorials began to change in tone, too. At first they were expressions of opinion for its own sake, but it was not long before some of them, like Dorothy Thompson and Hugh Johnson, had graduated into the category of elder statesmen, whose function it was not merely to comment, but to instruct the government in the way it should go. This trend reached its apogee in 1940 when Miss Thompson advised the Democratic National Convention to nominate Roosevelt for President and Wendell L. Willkie for Vice President. They did not take her advice. The loftier of the columnists, too, fall into the habit of writing about one another: General Johnson and Miss Thompson particularly have been addicted to this practice, having at one another with great vehemence for the sin of being on the other side of the fence.

The Washington columnist is a sort of neo-Winchell, with some of the characteristics of the Nineteenth Century letter writers who were the first Washington correspondents. These old-timers came to the Capital as observers and their news and comment thereon were published in the form of long letters to their papers. At the same time many of them represented more than one paper, thus foreshadowing the syndicated column of today. But the difference was that whereas the modern column is sold to anyone who will buy it and may continually controvert the individual paper's editorial policy, the old letter writers would represent a few papers with coinciding editorial views, so that the Washington correspondence never violated the publisher's own opinions.

There are a few Washington columnists, some of them of considerable distinction, who are on the staff of a single out-of-town paper and who write for that paper alone. These are not columnists in the orthodox sense, inasmuch as they write in accordance with their paper's policies and are responsible members of its staff. Their columns are more in the category of signed editorials. Some of them, like Arthur Krock of the *New York Times*, whose austere observations have an international audience, are chiefs of their paper's news bureaus. In fact, many of the newspapers with regional circulation and one-man offices in Washington require their correspondents to write a column of commentary once or twice a week. And the *New York Times* has a Sunday news review supplement to its editorial section, in which members of its staff from all over the world write, on specific assignment, signed interpretative articles on the week's developments. While these have more or less of an editorial flavor, they fall outside the columnist classification because they are written to order and not on a free-lance basis.

Frank R. Kent of the *Baltimore Sun* writes a daily column of acid commentary and opinion on the front page of his paper, and by long accepted practice says what he wishes regardless of how it may conflict with the editorial views of the *Sun*, of which he was formerly managing editor. This journalistic freedom for Mr. Kent caused the editors considerable pain in 1928, when his columns on the presidential campaign were all pro-Hoover, although the paper, as well as the *Evening Sun*, had gone overboard for Alfred E. Smith. In recent years the *Sun* has syndicated Mr. Kent's column to a few other newspapers, but he still falls within the category of representatives of a single paper, inasmuch as he continues to be a regular member of its staff.

Those column writers who do not merely pass personal

judgment on published news, but who attempt to offer authoritative background information designed to improve the newspaper reader's knowledge of the "why" of things, have to work as hard and as intelligently as any reporter, and with very similar methods. They cannot, if they are honest, offer their own hunches in disguise, but are compelled to interview privately large numbers of public men on a large number of subjects, men whose friendship and confidence they have taken pains to cultivate. The difference between such as these and those who dish up their own views and prejudices unseasoned by current research, can be illustrated by comparing the columns of Joseph Alsop and Robert Kintner on the one hand and General Johnson or Dorothy Thompson on the other. On May 14, 1941, for example, "The Capital Parade," discontinued a month later, was primarily a news feature about the problem of providing ships to carry supplies to Britain. It was full of purported facts, statistics and names. On the same day Miss Thompson's "On the Record" was a reply to a speech by Herbert Hoover, in which she endeavored to show by force of argument that Hoover was wrong and she right about convoying cargoes. The one was a factual discussion of an important issue, the other a polemic.

The news-plus-background columnists soon become identified by those thoroughly familiar with the scene with certain individual or group news sources. It becomes known that one has the particular confidence of, say, the Undersecretary of State; another is in the good books of Thomas G. Corcoran, and a third learns much from the Chairman of the Securities and Exchange Commission.

What must always be remembered is that while these sources are extremely valuable for direct news tips and background information, they do at the same time use the columnist as an agent for trying out new ideas, or for the promotion of some pet scheme which has yet to win the full approval of their superiors. In other words, the column is a favorite medium for sending up trial balloons, and when a columnist whispers to the world that "the administration" is planning to do so and so, it is well to bear in mind that "the administration" may be only one fairly important public official with an idea he would like to see put into effect. It is also well to note carefully the phraseology employed in publicizing these anonymous stories, for the President may be "considering" some action only to the extent that someone has just recommended it to him, with only the remotest likelihood that anything will ever come of it.

As the art of column-conducting develops and matures, a tendency also appears for particular columnists to be identified with particular points of view. Few of them any longer remain above the political battle, appraising it dispassionately and delivering commentary of as mature a quality as they are able regardless of who is right and who wrong. Instead they become known as pro-administration and anti-administration, and their readers know what to look for. This is inevitable because the writer who gets most of his material from one ideological clique is bound sooner or later to become its journalistic spokesman.

A few years ago, when most of the top-rank columnists were inclined to be opposed to the New Deal, the *Wash-*

ington Post, itself generally of the conservative opposition but desiring to be fair, engaged Ernest K. Lindley, chief of the Washington Bureau of *News Week,* to write a daily column representing the New Deal point of view. And John Franklin Carter, a former government employee and writer for *Vanity Fair,* who writes daily under the pseudonym of Jay Franklin, appeared about the same time to wage total war on all critics of the Roosevelt administration. His column is syndicated by the *Des Moines Register and Tribune,* which also picked up Lindley's column from the *Post.* It is common practice in Washington to refer to Lindley and Franklin as "captive" columnists of the New Deal, but there are as many who are "captive" of anti-New Deal interests.

Lindley is a modest, highly intelligent, scholarly young man, son of a University president, who came to Washington with the New Deal as a member of the *New York Herald Tribune* bureau. He covered the White House, was frankly pro-Roosevelt, and has written several books about the New Deal. Eventually he became dissatisfied with having to work for as strongly anti-New Deal a paper as the *Herald Tribune,* and gave up his job. He became Washington representative of *News Week,* and writes his column for the *Washington Post* on the side. Generally he has been strongly pro-New Deal on matters of domestic policy, but less so in the foreign field. It is only natural that a columnist of Lindley's ability and intellectual integrity who is also a partisan of the New Deal should find himself the recipient of exclusive news tips from New Deal sources: if you have a secret to tell you tell it to your friend, not your enemy. But to call Lindley a "captive" columnist is distinctly unfair.

John Franklin Carter was a minor foreign service officer in the State Department at the time Roosevelt was elected, and whiled away the hours writing special articles for *Vanity Fair* under the Jay Franklin alias. Just prior to the inauguration of Roosevelt he left the State Department, preferring journalism to diplomacy, and there was some talk of his attempting to form a new political party. But his articles continued to appear in *Vanity Fair*, and after the Agricultural Adjustment Administration had conducted its first appalling experiment in crop reduction Franklin began to be highly critical, referring caustically to "the obscene slaughter of the little pigs." A short time later he reappeared in Washington as assistant to Rexford Guy Tugwell in the Resettlement Administration, where he had charge of press relations, and the critical tone disappeared from his writings. When Resettlement was absorbed into the Department of Agriculture, Franklin began writing his column, which concerns itself mainly with violent assaults on the critics of the administration.

The column conducted by Drew Pearson and Robert S. Allen, "The Washington Merry-go-Round," was a direct outgrowth of a book by the same name written anonymously in 1931 by these two with a third collaborator, George Abell of the *Washington News*, a Scripps-Howard paper. Pearson, son of Hoover's governor of the Virgin Islands, was covering the State Department for the *Baltimore Sun*, and Allen was correspondent of the *Christian Science Monitor*. The book caused a tremendous stir because of its forthright attacks on important public figures, and also within the press corps because of a chapter taking individual members over the jumps, notably Richard V. Oulahan of the *Times*.

When its authorship became known the *Monitor* discharged Allen, but Pearson kept his job with the *Sun* until after a second edition, called "More Merry-go-Round," was published, this time not anonymously. About this time Pearson too was discharged, for his criticism of public officials, according to his own version; although just prior to his dismissal the *Sun* had published a handsome front-page retraction of a story by Pearson about Secretary of War Patrick Hurley and former Secretary Newton D. Baker. Abell had dropped out of the team, which presently began writing a column in the *Washington Herald*. Soon this was widely syndicated, and now is probably the best-known of the Washington columns.

The "Merry-go-Round" is frankly a muckraking column, generally pro-New Deal, but concerning itself to a considerable extent with personalities and with factional struggles within the administration, wherein Pearson and Allen openly take sides. There was one occasion a few years ago when they engaged in a notable argument with Secretary of State Hull over a matter of foreign policy, they attacking in their column, he replying in formal statements and press conference remarks. The column appeared to be especially active in obliquely seeking an appointive job for Sherman Minton of Indiana, a lame-duck Senator who had lost out in 1940 after a single term despite his passionate espousal of all New Deal policies. After a brief waiting period Minton was made one of the President's "administrative assistants with a passion for anonymity," but before he had had an opportunity to do very much there he was appointed to be a federal circuit judge.

The Merry-go-Round has never changed its character from the time it was started. It continues to publish news items as well as comment, and its editors are entirely fearless in their methods. They are continually being sued, the most spectacular of such actions being that brought by Douglas MacArthur, then Chief of Staff of the Army. It was settled out of court. Pearson and Allen are extremely energetic, unlike some other columnists, who hire young reporters to be energetic for them and simply rewrite, comment upon and sign the material turned in by their anonymous assistants.

"The Capital Parade" was abruptly discontinued in June, 1941, when both its authors, at considerable financial sacrifice, took commissions in the armed service — Alsop in Naval Intelligence and Kintner in Military Intelligence — but in its relatively brief life-span it attracted so much attention and had so great an influence on official Washington that, even though dead, it merits special discussion.

Alsop and Kintner came to Washington as members of the staff of the *New York Herald Tribune*, Alsop covering Congress and Kintner the financial agencies. Alsop was a cub reporter with some experience on the New York staff, a Harvard degree, a capacity for omnivorous reading, and a good literary style. He collaborated in 1937 and 1938 with Turner Catledge of the *New York Times* on a series of magazine articles about President Roosevelt's efforts to

pack the Supreme Court and about various other aspects
and personalities of the political scene. The Supreme Court
articles were revised and amplified in a book called "The
168 Days," a work of historical significance which received
far too little attention. Then the inevitable occurred: Catledge and Alsop were offered a contract to write a joint
Washington column for the North American Newspaper
Alliance, a newspaper feature syndicate. Catledge rejected
the offer but Alsop accepted and Kintner took the second
place.

The column maintained unusually high standards of
literary merit and veracity. Always dignified, it never de-
scended to mud-slinging, and dealt relatively little in rumor.
If it attacked an individual politician it did so openly and
frontally, not by covert sniping. Like some other columnists,
Alsop and Kintner did all their own work. Their technique
generally was to select some controversial topic concerning
which there was considerable confusion in the public mind,
and attempt to clarify it. This involved not only the thumb-
sucking process so popular in Washington, but also a great
deal of exploration and interviewing of officials who know
what is going on. The facts these collaborators were able
to develop were intended to clear up misapprehensions and
give their readers an intelligible account of what was going
on, what was the matter, and who was responsible. Naturally
the column frequently indulged in rewarming of old hash;
naturally also it sometimes beat the drum for a pet idea of
one of its pet sources of tips, because official tipsters have to
be kept happy and co-operative. But on the whole its level
was higher than most, it was written in a consistently lit-

erate manner, and sometimes contained a generous amount of hitherto unpublished news.

One of the oldest of the Washington columns is that written daily by David Lawrence, who blends column-conducting with a weekly magazine, the *United States News*, and other collateral enterprises. Lawrence has largely inherited the mantle of the aging Mark Sullivan as the outstanding exponent of extreme conservatism in Washington columnar society, but his daily feature, blending what purports to be informed commentary on news developments with obvious personal opinion, is almost a side issue. For many years he has published a factual journal of governmental news, which started with a subsidy in the 1920's as the *United States Daily*, became a weekly newspaper a few years later, and recently changed over to the magazine format. In addition he maintains several widely marketed services of legal, labor and other news.

Lawrence's magazine and his information services always adhere strictly to the uncolored facts, but his column is his own personal medium and has been found at times to be at rather wide variance with what his other services were saying. The National Labor Relations Board, in a circular letter to the papers publishing his column, once proved beyond cavil that critical assertions in his column about the operations of the Wagner Act were based on assumptions contradictory to the factual statements made in his labor news service. In some ways Lawrence is the most skilful of all the Washington columnists: he has the ability to appear sweetly reasonable while making the most highly prejudicial statements of opinion, unlike those others who never attack any person or policy without advertising the fact.

Paul R. Mallon was a star reporter for the United Press up to 1932, and had distinguished himself by a number of first-class news beats, but he fell victim to an acute attack of office politics and was relegated to relatively unimportant duties. About that time he received an offer to start a column to be syndicated by the McClure Syndicate and took the plunge. Later he transferred, first to the North American Newspaper Alliance and then to the sponsorship of the Hearst syndicate. Mallon's column, "The News Behind the News," is forthright and vigorous, and is frequently embroiled with some government officials, notably Lowell Mellett, Director of the Office of Government Reports, and Secretary of the Interior Ickes. He comes closer to the Pearson-Allen pattern than any other in Washington (although his column is older than theirs), and remains primarily a reporter rather than an editor. Over the years he has built up a staff of silent assistants who do much of his leg work for him.

Of all the strictly Washington syndicated columns now being written, that of Raymond Clapper in the Scripps-Howard papers probably attains and maintains the highest journalistic standards. Clapper also had had a long career in the United Press and was manager of its Washington Bureau when Mallon was on the reporting staff, but he too fell afoul of office politics and presently started writing a daily column for the *Washington Post* at the time when Eugene Meyer, wealthy financier and former Republican government official, was trying to make of it a national organ. Meyer, however, never succeeded in his attempts to syndicate the work of the group of journalists he assembled at the outset, and among those who presently deserted him was Clapper. It was a good move for him, because his column now appears all over the country and enjoys great and increasing prestige.

Clapper, who gives evidence of being at once temperamentally conservative and intellectually liberal, concerns himself solely with commentary, never pretending to purvey news as such. He writes better than most, is eminently fair in his judgments, and devotes much constructive thought to what he says before he says it. Somehow he contrives to convey the impression that he is fully cognizant of the responsibilities of a writer with as wide an audience as is his.

Of the others, Dorothy Thompson, Walter Lippmann and Westbrook Pegler are not properly classed as Washington columnists, since they merely moved in on the Capital after becoming fully established in their fields. A word, however, should be said about those who are columnists, not because of any journalistic prestige, but because of reputations they have made in totally foreign activities. There are two of these of any consequence — Eleanor Roosevelt and Hugh S. Johnson.

Mrs. Roosevelt is a columnist solely because she is the very active wife of a very active President, plus the fact that she is deeply interested in everything and loves to talk about it. Of late her "My Day" has been more carefully read by Washington newspapermen than before because of the suspicion that it sometimes foreshadows important decisions on policy by the President himself.

General Johnson, author of "One Man's Opinion," was snatched up by the Scripps-Howard Newspaper Alliance for no other reason than that he had been National Recovery Administrator and had demonstrated that he could write with a vocabulary of a sort which had become almost obsolete in American letters. The world is his backyard, and he lays about him indiscriminately, often denouncing someone on general principles one day and praising him with equal fervor a few weeks later. His pet peeves are Secretary Ickes and Dorothy Thompson, and there are those who have got the impression that his dissatisfaction with the conduct of the federal government dated from his resignation as NRA chief.

Washington of course is swarming with strictly local columnists, and the vernacular press is so full of their comment and opinions that sometimes there is little room left for what is commonly known as news. One paper will publish as many as eight or ten such, not counting the chatter of the society editors. The Scripps-Howard Newspaper Alliance, represented here by the *Washington News*, is the happy hunting ground of those who believe their personal views are of daily value to the public, for not only does it syndicate a large number of them, but also every correspondent on the staff of the Alliance is at least half a columnist, since all are encouraged and expected to flavor their news stories with comment and opinion. The Alliance sponsors Clapper, General Johnson and Mrs. Roosevelt, and syndicated Heywood Broun's column for years up to the time of his death. And the United Feature Service, a close cousin of the Alliance, handles Pearson and Allen. Evidence that the Scripps-Howard people became aware early in the game of the tendency of columnists to usurp the prestige of the editorial page was seen in the frequent tiffs between Broun and Roy W. Howard, when Howard would write chiding open letters to Broun and Broun would reply.

A strange offshoot of the columnist's craft is the institution of confidential letter writers, former newspapermen most of them, who send out to paying clients by mail a weekly report on Washington affairs, purporting to be absolutely inside stuff, but more often than not a synthesis of the news with corollary observations and advice. Many of these were started for a highly specialized set of subscribers interested in a particular phase of governmental activity, but most of them will not turn down a new subscriber regardless of how far removed from this group he may be.

Chief among them is *Kiplinger's Weekly Newsletter*, designed primarily for businessmen, and a highly reliable, conservative institution. Kiplinger, with a sizable staff, composes his letter in the tone that will best suit his readers, but he strives honestly to give them a fair appraisal of Washington news and as intelligent a forecast of developments affecting business as is possible. He always hedges his predictions, and is seldom caught far off base. His letter is dignified and stimulating. Many of the others are of a distinctly fly-by-night character, written by men of slight qualifications or by others who are pandering to special and none too savory interests. And still others, such as *American Aviation Daily*, serve very limited groups and make no pretense of covering the world or knowing what everything is all about.

XI

The Submerged Tenth

THERE OUGHT TO BE NO EXCUSE FOR A separate discussion of women correspondents. The women in the press gallery should be accepted on their merits as are the men, but so long as they are excluded from membership in the National Press Club, and so long as the President's wife excludes men from her press conferences, there is no choice but to proceed on the established fact of sex segregation.

About one-tenth of the correspondents listed in the Congressional Directory as having regular gallery privileges are women, and the same proportion holds in the radio correspondents' gallery. In addition, as with the men, there are many who are loosely classed as newspaper workers but who do not have the connection with a daily telegraphic service to make them eligible for gallery membership.

If women had not been discriminated against from the beginning in this as in many other fields where men were the pioneers they probably would make up a much larger fraction of the correspondents than is the case, for they have as a whole, if it is possible to generalize by sexes, more of the natural equipment of a reporter than men. Their native curiosity, their minute attention to detail, their implacability when a-hunt, and their readiness to employ any device, however unorthodox, to gain their ends, all are traits which any first-rate reporter should have. But since most managing editors and city editors have been men, incapable of comprehending the peculiar merits of women as reporters, most of them have had to begin their journalistic careers on the society page, and most of them have stayed there.

It has been asserted that the reason women do not get along better as reporters is that they cannot go everywhere, do everything, that a man can do, and to a degree this is so. But it is not true in the case of the Washington correspondents, where for the past eight years there has been at least one story the men could never cover, and none from which women would be barred for any reason whatever. In addition to Mrs. Roosevelt's press conferences, which have taken on some of the aspects of a Monday Morning Culture Club, there are numerous other assignments peculiar to Washington where women feel far more at home than men. The first woman reporter in Washington, as a matter of cold historical fact, was one who capitalized her sex not at all, and who went after her stories with the grim fixity of purpose of a bloodhound. She was Anne Royall, who sat on President John Quincy Adams' clothes on the bank of the Potomac until he gave her the interview she desired. No man has ever been able to do that to a President — or at least no man has ever had the nerve to try.

Anne Royall was not only a reporter — she was editor and publisher as well, and for five years from 1831 to 1836 she got out a venomous, Winchellesque sheet called *Paul Pry.* She never had to start on the society page, but late in life used her widow's inheritance and the education her husband had given her to launch upon a journalistic career. Like many newspapermen of today, she was wild and illiterate. She was a member of a vagrant Maryland family, wandering from place to place like gypsies, unwashed, unkempt, uneducated except in the simple lore of the Indians.

Eventually Anne's family straggled down into Virginia, where they settled down on the periphery of the ménage of William Royall, a Revolutionary War general and a wealthy planter. Royall saw something in the raggedy woods colt and presently married her, making her in that act the lady of the manor and mistress of broad acres and many slaves. A scholar of sorts himself, he compelled her to learn to read and write, pounded the classics into her obstinate head, and goaded her into studying Jefferson and Voltaire, as well as the mystic symbolism of the Free Masons.

All this took some sixteen years, whereupon General Royall died of exhaustion and Anne became a wealthy woman in her own right. Like many others, she erroneously concluded that having learned the alphabet and the multiplication table she was now fully equipped for a literary career, so instead of taking her ease as a planter in the Old Dominion she set out on a tour of the South, in a coach with three slaves for company. She was probably the first American journalist, of whom there have been many since, to visit a strange land and chronicle her impressions. She wrote about everything and everybody, her pen dipped in the deadliest venom, and eventually, at the age of sixty, she was arrested in Washington and fined as a common scold.

Thus she qualified as the first gossip columnist in America, and two years later started publishing *Paul Pry*, undoubtedly the only newspaper of the time which was not actively devoted to the interests of one or another political clique. She exposed the sins of the world and particularly of the United States Government with a vicious glee; rejected bribes right and left and printed the news about them; campaigned for sound money and against the Bank of the United States, and in general pursued an editorial policy enlightened enough to have had a sponsor who was less of a crackpot.

Suddenly she became a respectable journalist; why, nobody knows. But after five years of *Paul Pry* sensationalism she suspended publication and immediately started another paper — *The Huntress* — vigorous as its predecessor, but saner, better balanced and more literate. Her two papers had a national circulation and exercised considerable influence in the National Capital at a time when most newspapers lived on party subsidies. She was a lifelong friend of John Quincy Adams despite the advantage she took of him, and he had her for dinner at the White House, describing her, rather romantically, as "the virago errant in enchanted armor." Perhaps it is journalism's loss that she never visited Europe to analyze for the newspapers the misdeeds of the autocrats of her day.

The first woman to have professional access to the press gallery was Mrs. Jane Grey Swisshelm, who was in Washington on a brief assignment for the *New York Tribune* and wanted to find out how it felt to sit in the gallery on a basis of equality with the male correspondents. That was in 1850, when there were perhaps fifty accredited correspondents in the Capital, and Mrs. Swisshelm had to enlist the personal intercession of President Millard Fillmore to crash the sacred gate for a single day. But from then on women began to creep mousily into the gallery from time to time, with an occasional exception who was decidedly not a mouse, such as Mary J. Windle, who was imprisoned by Lincoln as a Confederate spy.

The first bona fide woman correspondent — who used the telegraph to send out spot news instead of confining herself to flowery tidbits from the feminine point of view — was Emily Edson Briggs, who wrote for the *Washington Chronicle* and the *Philadelphia Press* under the pseudonym of "Olivia." By that time there were eleven women listed in the gallery, or about the same ten percent as today. Of one of Olivia's contemporaries — Gail Hamilton — it was written:

"A lady, at whose mention stalwart men have been known to tremble, and hide in corners; who 'keeps a private graveyard' for the burial of those whom she has mercilessly slain; who respects neither the spectacles of the judge, nor the surplice of the priest; who holds the mirror of men's failings till they hate their wives because they belong to her sex."

Today the women correspondents are no novelty in Washington and there are among them as many of high caliber in proportion to the whole as among the men. Several run their own news bureaus, corresponding for a number of papers at once, while others do regular assignment work for the press associations and the big city papers. One — Cora Rigby — was for seven years, from 1918 to 1925, chief of the *Christian Science Monitor* bureau.

Because of the traditional prejudice against women in what has been mistakenly termed "man's work," the women correspondents are not admitted to membership in the National Press Club, and many of them resent its all-inclusive title. Any bona fide newspaperwoman or member of one or other of the two women's press organizations has limited privileges in the men's club — she may cash checks or buy cigarettes at the counter, and a small but superior air-conditioned dining-room has been set aside for her use. From noon on Sundays and holidays, too, ladies accompanied by members are admitted to the main dining-room, otherwise a private preserve. In the spring of 1941, for the first time in the Club's history, the working newspaperwomen were invited to a special off-the-record forum on censorship in the Press Club, and one of them was a member of the questioning panel.

For many years the women correspondents in Washington struggled along as best they could, with a relative few able, through sheer merit, to rise above society news and the D.A.R. But in 1933 all that was altered. Mrs. Roosevelt came to the White House, observed that "the newspaper girls" were being discriminated against, and promptly, in her warm-hearted, impulsive way, set about to remedy matters. Many of the women thus brought in out of the cold are not at all sure that their professional standing has been improved by reason of Mrs. Roosevelt's kindly attentions, but most of them luxuriate in the warm glow of her beneficence and only pause to remark, on cloudy days, that the reportorial experience they get from attending the First Lady's conferences could be put in your eye. Sometimes there is reason to wonder whether Mrs. Roosevelt herself consistently enjoys these weekly meetings with "the girls"; whether, having rashly seized a bull by the tail in 1933, she is simply unable to let go gracefully. She herself is too great a lady ever to admit it in any event, and none of her protégés would hear of such heresy.

Her predecessors received the newspaperwomen on the rarest of occasions and then only socially. Mrs. Harding, an ambitious woman who knew the value of publicity, was particularly gracious. Otherwise, each society editor received without fail invitations to all the White House receptions, and before each State dinner was permitted with her sisters to have a look at the table decorations, which were usually pink roses, buddleia and maidenhair fern. The table was always laid with "the gold table service, plateau and epergne dating from the administrations of Madison and Monroe." Then they went back to their desks and wrote gentle but effusive stories about who attended and where they sat, and what sort of entertainment they had afterward in the East Room. Few of them ever had an opportunity to report any of this first-hand.

Between State dinners and receptions there were occasional secondary activities of the President's wife which it was their privilege to report — the annual visit of "Big Buffalo" to the Girl Scouts headquarters, and similar uncontroversial events. Otherwise they wrote Capital society in dreary reams, unless their bosses were enlightened, or shorthanded, enough to give them some honest reporting to do.

Mrs. Roosevelt changed that. As soon as she was established in the White House she invited to lunch all the women reporters who had come down from New York for the inauguration, and afterward took them on a personally conducted tour of the mansion, showing them where all the children slept, where the President kept his stamp album — all the little items that went to make up a composite picture of how this extremely unorthodox family lived in this extremely orthodox house. From then on weekly press conferences were the established custom whenever Mrs. Roosevelt was in town, with but one fixed rule — no men allowed.

The first such was a remarkable affair, judging from available accounts. Virtually any woman who could claim the remotest connection with a newspaper was admitted, with the result that some seventy-five, from authentic reporters to aged, rheumatic society writers swarmed through the front door and into the Green Parlor on the main floor. There stood the ancient butler, his hand on a red velvet rope which barred the uninvited from the private apartments on the second floor. At a given signal he unhooked the rope and the ladies of the press hurriedly mounted the stairs, arriving out of breath and awestruck in the Monroe Parlor, where they dived for the chairs nearest the sofa on which their hostess was to sit.

There weren't enough chairs to go around, so two of the veteran news reporters in this impromptu game of Going to Jerusalem found themselves standing in the middle. Mrs. Roosevelt, seeing their embarrassing plight, invited them to sit at her feet on the floor, and there they have sat, off and on, ever since, their admiring gaze winning for them from their colleagues the sobriquet of "the incense burners."

Mrs. Roosevelt shook hands all around, had a kind and reassuring word for each, rustled up a box of candy, and the party was on.

That, in substance, is the scene at any of Mrs. Roosevelt's conferences. It does not do justice in its condensation to the individual aspects of the newspaperwomen, from the feminist Ruby Black in her simple working clothes to the elegant Hope Ridings Miller of the *Post* in her best tea-party costume complete with gardenias, but it suffices. Mrs. Roosevelt herself is always dressed as simply as possible, usually in a becoming morning frock, at other times in riding habit, and she is grace and affability incarnate no matter how trying the circumstances.

And they are trying. If the men who make up the vast majority of those attending the President's semi-weekly conferences asked half the leading, personal questions regularly put to his wife the conferences probably would be discontinued. She has been asked how it feels to outstrip her husband in a popularity poll, what she thinks of son Elliott's radio criticism of the New Deal, whether she intends to curtsey to the King and Queen of England, and virtually every other pointed or naïve inquiry that pops into the heads of the women correspondents. She takes it all in good part, only occasionally turning on the refrigeration.

The wonder of it is that since so little news worth printing comes out of these meetings they continue to be held with such unfailing regularity, or to attract so large an attendance. Since that first mob scene the eligibility list has been somewhat curtailed, so that only twenty or thirty now regularly show up, but the faithful platoon is always there to listen to the First Lady's casual observations, observations not greatly unlike those everyone may read in print in her column, "My Day." Whenever possible she varies the diet by inviting as guest artist some woman of special interests or accomplishments — a painter, a sculptor, a social worker, or a labor leader. Once it was Catherine Lewis, daughter of John L., assistant to her father and as beetle-browed and generously proportioned as he, except for the voice. Her voice is very small, and all through her remarks the ladies of the press kept calling out "louder, louder!", as they frequently do.

Mrs. Roosevelt herself is extremely hard of hearing, and her secretary, Mrs. Malvina Thompson Scheider, has been known to indicate by a touch on the knee where a voice is coming from in the crowd, so that she may turn in that direction and watch the lips of the questioner.

The big day for the newspaperwomen came early in the summer of 1939 when the King and Queen visited Washington. Days were spent in preparation for covering this unprecedented event, and Mrs. Roosevelt went minutely over the ground with "the girls" to make sure they got everything straight. They wrote thousands of words in advance — what Mrs. Roosevelt would wear on each State occasion, what the visiting monarchs would be fed, where they would sleep, where their equerries and ladies-in-waiting would sleep, when they would be routed out for breakfast, how many personal maids the Queen would have with her and why, etcetera, etcetera.

The reader will recall that Their Majesties slept one night at the White House. Next morning they received — or rather were received by — the ladies of the press. Mrs. Roosevelt had promised in advance, in response to great pressure from the ladies, that if she could arrange it the Queen would have a press conference. At any rate she advised them all to be on hand at a certain hour on the morning after the royal arrival and they would see what they would see.

"Now off the record — off the record, mind you! — if any of you ladies asks the Queen about the Duke of Windsor I shall personally slay you!" admonished Mrs. Roosevelt, shaking a warning finger.

Her admonition was unnecessary, as it turned out. The Queen evidently balked at the unaccustomed and unscheduled ordeal, and when the newspaperwomen — eighty-five of them — arrived that morning they were lined up on each side of the main hall of the White House, leaving a lane down to the door. As the bashful young King and his self-possessed consort came into view on their way to the next function of the crowded day, Mrs. Roosevelt headed them gently but firmly toward the formidable avenue of eager reporters, decked out in their Sunday best. Down the line they walked, the Queen rapidly regaining her self-possession and smiling sweetly at each of them, the King, who shied noticeably when he first saw what was coming, making the best of it in his superheated uniform. He ran a nervous finger around his collar and murmured:

"My word, I didn't know there were so many of you!"

Afterward one of the newspaperwomen wrote:

"She (the Queen) stopped in front of me, looking up with an expression in her blue eyes that seemed to say: 'How sweet of you to call!' and smiled. I felt a lump in my throat, and a rush of such heroine worship as I had not experienced since my teens. It was all I could do to keep from dropping to one knee and murmuring 'Your Majesty!' I almost felt like swearing allegiance to the British Crown just to have her smile at me like that."

Occasionally — only occasionally — there is genuine spot news in one of Mrs. Roosevelt's conferences. Frequently she passes opinions on affairs of the moment which make publishable stories, but they are nevertheless just opinions. But there were, early in her tenure at the White House, two news breaks for the women, and those who still believe the conferences are journalistically valuable will always cite you those two to prove it. Both came within the first year. The first was after the legalization of beer in 1933, when Mrs. Roosevelt announced that the beverage would be available to White House guests. The second was similar — after prohibition repeal. Mrs. Roosevelt, discussing the problem posed by this development in a ménage which had been officially non-alcoholic for more than fifteen years, said that American table wines would be served, but no distillates.

This second announcement was made in the form of a brief typewritten statement handed out to the correspondents as they entered the building, and elaborated upon later. They were expected to hold the release until after the conference, but one of them made a mad, immediate dash for the nearest telephone and gave the news to her paper. The others, thus scooped, were in a considerable dither, but "Queen Eleanor," with her usual capacity for quick thinking, hustled Bess Furman of the Associated Press, Ruby

Black of the United Press, and Marie Manning (Beatrice Fairfax) of the International News Service to private phones so that no daily newspaper would have the news ahead of any other. Then she held up the conference until calm had been restored.

There is reason for grave doubt whether the ultimate professional stature of women as newspaper writers has not been retarded rather than advanced by Mrs. Roosevelt's kindliness. If, as they argue, all they desire is to have an equal opportunity with their male colleagues, then it is open to question whether this compulsion to attend weekly meetings which provide little or no news, and in which there is none of the stimulus of competition with the men, is of any value whatever. Rather there is considerable room for the belief that Mrs. Roosevelt, in thus coddling "the girls," is doing them a genuine disservice in their chosen careers. The impression cannot be avoided of a great and good lady taking a bevy of forlorn little ones by the hand and saying:

"There now, don't you fret. You just let those men be reporters if they want to — we can play at newspapers too!"

There is no good reason why the President's wife — even one as active and as interested in as many topics as is Mrs. Roosevelt — should be expected to have news for the correspondents every week. She is not a policy-making officer of the government, and in fact has found it necessary to keep a close watch on her tongue to avoid comment on pending decisions of State, since her remarks would inevitably carry greater weight than they ought; consequently there is really little news for her to dispense. If the women correspondents are to compete on equal terms with the men, they will not be able to do it through the medium of chit-chat press conferences for ladies only.

This is not to say that none of "the girls" find the conferences profitable. There are in the Capital many women correspondents of small, back-country papers — some daily, some weekly — to whom these sessions are a godsend. Their papers cannot afford to buy "My Day," and so Mrs. Roosevelt's periodic seminar in current events fills a great deal of space. And it must be remembered, also, that Mrs. Roosevelt herself is enough of a public figure to command such space in any but the biggest journals.

Once a year, in the early winter, Mrs. Roosevelt entertains the "widows" of those attending the Gridiron Dinner, a pleasant fancy of hers which because of her kindliness has grown into a sort of mass meeting. At these sessions the "widows" and the working newspaper women alternate in putting on a program in imitation of that provided at the Willard Hotel by the Gridiron Club itself. Supper follows, and afterward there are "after-dinner speeches" by a dozen or so women invited by Mrs. Roosevelt for the purpose.

The guest list at these White House parties has been expanded each year just to make sure that no one conceivably eligible is omitted. It includes, first, the wives of members of the Gridiron Club; second, their house guests, if any, which would be the wives, sisters, cousins, aunts or daughters of Gridiron Club guests; third, active members of the Women's National Press Club and the Newspaper Women's Club of Washington; fourth, any other newspaper women Mrs. Roosevelt chooses to invite, and she invites more and more each year; fifth, an assortment of other women friends of hers; sixth, women members of Congress, women holding office in the Executive Branch of the government, and Secretary of Labor Perkins; seventh, the women members of the White House staff, from Miss Marguerite LeHand, the President's confidential secretary, down to the housekeeper. So long as Sir Ronald Lindsay was the British Ambassador, American-born Lady Lindsay was a regular guest, but she was the only diplomatic wife so honored. Her after-dinner talk was the hit of the evening, and she has been sorely missed.

On their own account the women of the press in Washington have two professional organizations — the Women's National Press Club and the Newspaper Women's Club. The former, established in 1919, is the only one with a valid claim to being a truly representative professional group. Its active membership is limited to writers, and they must have had not less than two years' experience in newspaper work to be eligible, even though as members they may be magazine writers or government press agents.

Once a year, in the spring, the Women's Press Club has a "Stunt Night" for women only — the female counterpart of the Gridiron Dinner. Elaborate preparations are made, the program is prepared and acted by club members, and Mrs. Roosevelt is the guest of honor, along with a very pretentious list of other non-Club members who have distinguished themselves in a variety of professional fields. And during the season the Club has regular Tuesday luncheons to which outstanding women — or sometimes men — are invited to speak off the record and submit to questioning. In 1940 President Roosevelt consented to attend one of these affairs, the first Chief Executive so to dignify the club.

XII

Champagne Punch

THERE IS A QUAINT SUPERSTITION THAT the way to get favorable attention from the Washington correspondent is to entertain them frequently with plenty of food and fine liquor. If some of the embassies and others realized the skimpiness of the results obtained by this petty bribery they might be able to prune their inflated budgets by a few dollars.

The news sent out about the diplomats, government officials and lobbyists is in direct ratio to their importance, their activity, or their talkativeness, and has little if any relation to the amount of mass entertaining they do. The correspondents usually accept invitations to receptions and teas, drink as much champagne punch and Scotch as they can stand, partake generously of the food on the long table, and gossip with the friends they encounter in the mob. But they don't rush back to their offices and send out dispatches about the statecraft of Ambassador So-and-so, or the purity of Mr. Such-and-Such's search for his peculiar political Grail.

Every year, early in November, Ambassador Oumansky used to give a big *de rigeur* reception in celebration of the Great October Revolution. A huge frozen sturgeon or a brace of frozen salmon adorned the table in the great hall;

a bewildering array of hors d'œuvres and salads and pressed duck and sandwiches and bonbons and cakes and ice cream surrounded these delectable centerpieces, while at improvised bars in the corners bowls of punch and shakers of cocktails and bottles of Scotch were emptied with great rapidity, and as rapidly replenished. The same scene was reproduced in miniature on the second and third floors. Aromatic Russian cigarettes burdened the air with their fumes.

From five o'clock to seven the guests poured in. Diplomats on speaking terms with the Russians, State Department officials who found absence impolitic, members of "resident society," well-known barflies and a large number of newspaper men and women drifted through the front door, checked their wraps, walked upstairs, and shook hands with the Ambassador and Mrs. Oumansky with vague smiles. Then with as little delay as possible they headed straight for the liquor, where a milling mob crept and climbed and pushed to get to the bar and make off with a drink or two.

Here one saw a few old timers, men and women, lapping up the liquor — old timers who were not identifiable as diplomats, government officials or newspaper correspondents — who seemed to appear at every catch-all diplomatic party where there was plenty of food and drink. The women always seemed to be wearing the same dowdy old gowns, and the voracity of their appetites seemed never to abate. After lingering as long as possible at the bar, they moved on systematically to the buffet table and heaped their plates with the most substantial items in view.

These are the Capital society barflies, who have somehow managed at some time or other to get on the invitation lists of a few strategic embassies, and appear to save the price of many a meal, many a highball, by responding to all invitations received. They are not sources of news.

Each embassy where entertaining is on a large scale feels that it is necessary and politic to include in the regular invitation list a large number of reporters, with the impression that great benefits will flow from such condescension. The reporters behave as well or as badly as the other guests, eat and drink what they want, and presently go home. What they may write thereafter about His Excellency the Ambassador of the Soviet Union or the Japanese Empire or the Cuban Republic is in no wise colored or conditioned by the fact of having been invited to a party.

The attitude of the press toward these parties, after the first few invitations, is singularly blasé. They know precisely what it will be like — a crush of people, all struggling to get to the liquor and food — and the only question to be answered is, how good will the food be? Even this imponderable is to a considerable extent eliminated after a few visits, because each embassy has a characteristic reception menu which varies little.

There is one veteran diplomatic correspondent who religiously accepts all such invitations, from the mob scenes to the intimate affairs, and he gets on most lists because of his known position. But in the course of his work he pays but little attention to any of the embassies or legations but the big fellows, although never missing a chance to eat a plate of food, sip a glass of punch, and smoke a Havana, wherever he is invited. It is his "duty," part of his job. But all the attention lavished upon him by the Argentines and the Cubans and the Mexicans might as well be spared — he seldom visits their embassies except socially.

In 1939 when the Russians were celebrating the Great October Revolution, a swarm of newspapermen attended, and spent their time there, when their mouths were not full of food, explaining to their friends that they came simply out of curiosity — they wanted to see who would be there, in view of the Russian assault on Finland, you know! By 1940, when it had become apparent that it was the policy of the government to keep the Russians happy, they felt better about going, and didn't have excuses for their friends at the tips of their tongues.

A great deal of this mass entertaining, to be sure, is for the purpose, at least in part, of letting the Americans know what nice people, and how important, are the representatives of the country concerned. When the Russians first reopened their ornate plush-and-gold embassy they threw a party apparently designed to end all parties. They imported a sturgeon so big it had to be shipped in two sections and stitched together again on its arrival. They opened virtually every room in the place and all but threw food and drink at their guests, apparently to prove that Communists were people and as civilized as the next fellow.

Some of the embassy parties on the other hand are of a very special and very enjoyable nature, and the impression gets out that the Ambassador really wants his guests to enjoy themselves. When the Cuban embassy celebrated the anniversary of the nation's independence it hired two native orchestras, one for the ballroom and one for the garden, and the guests danced and had a wonderful time. And when they showed off their dictator, Batista, they again outdid themselves. Nothing perfunctory about it.

But again, all this has little effect on the output of the correspondents. What does have some effect, sometimes, is the series of relatively intimate parties to which only a carefully selected few are invited. They may be stag drinking parties or small dinners or luncheons; they may be tête-à-tête affairs with the ambassador or the counsellor of the embassy, and with much carefully directed conversation. The correspondent, until he becomes inured, is likely to feel a bit flattered at being thus singled out, and if he is in a position to do so, may unconsciously reflect some of his pleasure in the way he handles the next story involving that country.

Much of this entertaining has been greatly curtailed with the outbreak and spread of the war, but it used to abound. Kurt Sell, veteran correspondent of D. N. B., the official German news agency, who was here long before Hitler reached Berlin, used to give a party regularly, once a year, for a large group of correspondents, men only, in a private dining-room at a leading hotel. Vast quantities of German food were served, and oceans of fine German beer. And for several years the former Ambassador, Dr. Hans Luther, gave a regular bock beer party at the embassy (under Kurt's direction), also for newspapermen, plus a few strategic Senators and officials.

At these parties, financed by the German government, the American correspondents rubbed elbows with the embassy attaches and found them very *gemütlich*. The food was good, a Bavarian troupe performed native folk dances, and there was much singing of German and American songs to the accompaniment of the little Bavarian orchestra.

It was all propaganda of the very best and most effective variety until, after Hitler was firmly established by his plebiscites, microphones were set up, a dictatorial song leader "organized" the party, and hired photographers took pictures of Senators and newspapermen in their cups to send back to the Fuehrer. And Dr. Luther, all his roly-poly geniality gone, delivered himself of a passionate speech about the glories of the Reich and the misunderstood policies of National Socialism.

Thus the propaganda overreached itself. The next party was extensively boycotted and according to all reports from the faithful few was a dismal affair. But the writer recalls with pleasure a little, amiable Prussian attache with whom he once drank many steins of bock and sang "Die Lorelei," a friendly little man who certainly was no Nazi at heart, if at all. I wonder where he is now.

The Japanese are notorious for overreaching themselves. They haven't been entertaining so much in recent years, but when they do they are all smiles, and all but say "See how nice we are!" They are great lovers of alcohol, and their Scotch is of the finest, but it is liberally fortified with pointed propaganda and equally pointed questions about American policy which give the show away.

The writer well remembers one such occasion, when the first secretary gave a party for the new counsellor, or something of the sort — a party for some hundred or more news-paper correspondents, where Scotch and saki and Japanese beer flowed like water, and the food was good and varied.

It all appeared like another of those times when the party-loving Japanese had found themselves another excuse to drink Scotch, until your correspondent found himself hemmed in by a couple of the little fellows, who kept re-placing his glass each time it was empty, meanwhile plying him with that same pointed propaganda and those same pointed and slightly plaintive questions.

A casual glance around the room revealed that two other guests were getting the same treatment — both of them specialists in foreign affairs — so it was obvious what was on the program: a large amount of priming followed by a large amount of pumping. What in the world these little men expected to find out, or what influence they thought we three had at the State Department or the White House heaven only knows, but they worked hard and faithfully for the Emperor, so faithfully that they got very drunk. One of them, in fact, wound up virtually speechless, thus losing his value as a secret agent.

Needless to say, this sort of bold effrontery goes very badly with the vast majority of the correspondents and re-coils violently on its perpetrator. Needless to say, also, most of the attempts to influence the press socially are far more subtle, involving the small dinner, the luncheon for two, the prized invitation to a state affair at the White House or an embassy whose invitations are rare and exclusive.

The annual party for the press at the White House, instituted in 1934 by the Roosevelts, has been bluntly set down as an attempt to cultivate goodwill, but it is not so easy as all that, because the Roosevelts are an extremely genial and hospitable family. Undoubtedly it is, fundamentally, "one of those things," but it has overtones of genuine good fellowship which cannot in fairness be overlooked.

Yet it brings once a year a large number of correspondents into direct contact with one of the most magnetic personalities that has ever occupied the White House; correspondents who may not have been face to face with the President all year. And this is important. It may not have any direct and obvious influence on their attitude, but it certainly does in many cases have a slightly softening effect: reporters go about for twelve months cussing the President and his policies, and then on the last day of the twelve put on their dinner jackets or white linens and meet him informally, and dance to the music he has provided, and warm to Mrs. Roosevelt's smile, and watch the Great Man emitting personality in great, warm waves. For a little while, at least, he must seem not quite all bad even to his most consistent journalistic foes.

The veterans in the press corps for the most part take the "social lobby" in their stride. They go where they think it politic, and stay away if possible when they don't feel like going. One press association reporter who specializes in the affairs of Europe and the Far East, frequently flips a coin with his wife to decide whether to accept an invitation and save the price of a dinner, or stay at home and avoid boredom and a wasted evening.

It ought not to be assumed that all these parties are onesided, that the dinners and teas and the like are of value only to the host for propaganda purposes. At the smaller, less formal affairs the seasoned reporter makes many valuable news contacts and picks up many legitimate news tips. It is not always logical, but it is entirely natural that officials will talk most freely to news men with whom they have become well acquainted, so it is to the best interest of the correspondent not to neglect the social aspects of his work. All that he ought to bear in mind is that it's all part of the day's work.

The late Louis Jay Heath, a distinguished United Press correspondent for that organization's Latin American clients, moved constantly among the Latins, drank extensively of their rum concoctions and ate with gusto of their fiery foods, making more valuable friends than he drank Daiquiris, absorbing more information than he ate enchiladas. At the time of his death a few years ago the Latins would tell him more "secrets" than they would confide to anyone else, unless it was his friend and associate, Harry W. Frantz.

Not all the "propaganda parties" in Washington are given by government officials or diplomats. There abound in this strange city hundreds of lobbyists and "legislative representatives," many of whom seem to think a reporter can be bought with a meal or subsidized with a highball.

Out of a clear sky the Washington representative of a public utility lobby asked the writer to lunch at his club a few years ago, talked amiably about nothing in particular, and in general played the affable host. But for many months thereafter this lobbyist considered that it had become his privilege, by reason of the expenditure of a dollar and a half or so, to call up the writer at any hour and ask, somewhat insistently, for information of any description whatever. Perhaps Senator Norris had just seen the President: our friend was on the phone asking for full details before the White House correspondent had had an opportunity to report. Or an important and controversial report had been issued by the S. E. C. about some phase of the utility business. Copies were scarce and it would have been obvious to anyone that we would be using our copy to prepare a story, but the man who had bought my lunch never hesitated to call up and ask me to send it over to him for his bosses to read, or even mail out of town.

That was really a very expensive lunch for the Committee of Public Utility Executives, because it turned an attitude of calm indifference into one of active distaste. Normal co-operation with a friend in perfectly harmless ways became out of the question because the would-be friend was constantly trying to get back the price of the meal with ten thousand percent interest.

There was another mildly amusing episode when the dictator of Venezuela died after a reign of many years, and his successor, one Lopez-Contreras, was not at all sure how long he would be able to remain in office. The diplomatic representatives in Washington, too, found it to their interest to make Señor Lopez look as big as possible, so one day the secretary of the legation called me up and invited me to a club for a cocktail. I had never met him and had no idea what it was all about, but went.

After a cocktail or two the young man gave me a little

lecture on the high order of the new president's statesmanship, and said he would like to have me come to one of the
minister's literary luncheons. Next morning I received from
him a biographical sketch of Señor Lopez for publication
in the *Times*. I managed to make, legitimately, a brief story
out of it, but there was a lot of news that day and it never
got in the paper. Needless to say, I never again heard from
the first secretary, and never was invited to luncheon with
the minister.

What the diplomats never seem to comprehend, a failing shared to a lesser extent by officials and private citizens
of our own country, is that the Washington correspondents, even though they be bureau managers, have little or
nothing to say ultimately about what does or does not
appear in print. They report the news as they receive it,
exercising selective judgment the while, but once it is on
the wire it is beyond their control. The bosses in the home
office are then the arbiters of its destiny.

Even at this point a certain element of chance enters into
the fate of secondary items. As almost everyone knows, the
day-to-day size of a newspaper is determined in part by the
amount of advertising that has been sold. Some days the
paper will be light, sometimes "wide open," but always
there is a rough ratio maintained between news and advertising. So it may be that one day the home office will be
clamoring for more stories to fill space, while the next day
they are telling us to "hold down," and many lesser stories
just don't have a chance.

It would be lovely if a newspaper every day could print
everything it considered newsworthy, but since it lives by

advertising, and since neither the forms nor the type are made of rubber, the mechanical and financial problem involved in such a policy would be virtually insoluble.

Consequently, though far be it from me to help lobbyists and special pleaders to make life hard for Washington correspondents, the ones they should cultivate if they wish to get big results are the responsible executives in the home office. If the big boss is convinced that a story is of prime interest, it is pretty likely to get printed, relations between bosses and subordinates being what they are.

XIII

The Party Line

No ONE FOR A MOMENT SHOULD entertain the notion that all the social life in Washington which involves the press is at the expense of those who want to get something into the papers. The correspondents are as anxious to get news as officials, diplomats and lobbyists are to dispense propaganda, and they resort to a large amount of entertaining to "cultivate sources." They are probably at least as successful as the other half.

Social activities here are probably as artificial as in any other world capital — more so than in the rest of the country — and the reporter with the most hay in his hair on arrival for the Washington assignment doesn't take very long to learn the ropes. Soon, if he is ambitious, he begins to cultivate personal friendships in the circle in which he moves as correspondent. He invites officials to his home, or to the annual dinner of the White House Correspondents Association; he buys better and more liquor than he can afford, and serves it without stint.

The chief reason is his knowledge that personal friendships breed confidence, and confidence leads to the disclosure of news which he could not possibly get in the orthodox fashion. But there are other collateral reasons, and more than likely there is a blend of them all. The artificiality of Washington society is somehow contagious: men brought up on the wrong side of the tracks in jerk-water towns soon learn how to wear tails, and their wives learn how to drink tea without crooking their little fingers. They reconstruct their budgets to hire inferior servants to prepare indifferent food; they give formal dinners in two-room apartments; they give grandiose cocktail parties with by-the-hour butlers and check girls.

All this makes them feel very inflated. If they ever stopped to analyze their conduct they might put it somewhat along this line:

"Look at me! Before I came to Washington I never owned a tail coat and white vest; when I had to wear a dinner jacket (once in a while), I rented it. I never was served by a butler outside a hotel. Now I can put up as good a front as the next one."

Not that all the new correspondents in Washington are as socially inexperienced as all that, for there are many who know just what to do with the finger bowl and the doily on the dessert plate. With these latter the entertaining may be a bit colder, a bit more calculating: they are here to get news; the way to get news is to know sources of news; the way to attract sources of news is to put on an impressive front.

And there is yet another reason. Correspondents who get invited out not infrequently feel it necessary to repay in kind, up to a point, in order to avoid any suggestion of being under obligations to a man whose motives are not at all obscure. This costs them a lot of money if they take it too seriously, money they usually can't well afford. A few newspapers, whose publishers or managing editors are aware of this situation, provide their Washington correspondents with entertainment allowances, or at least allow them liberal expense accounts. But most of them do not, so that the correspondent who throws a party strictly for business reasons, or who invites a news source to lunch for the same reason, has to foot the bill himself or disguise it on his expense account as "taxicabs."

The Washington correspondent who is really wise eventually learns which invitations have to be repaid and which not. If he is invited to tea at the White House or the British Embassy, he knows the President and the Ambassador don't expect a return engagement, but if a second-class embassy official invites him out too often, then sooner or later he feels he ought to reciprocate just to keep the slate clean. Plus the fact that it makes him happy to hobnob with this glamorous group and plus, also, the fact that he hopes to get some news that way, eventually.

Some correspondents become so socially active that they can barely spare time for their work, and here the cocktail party masquerades as work by way of easing the reportorial conscience. When they are not attending parties they are giving them, or are having some of the younger set in for a round of drinks after a diplomatic affair.

Many a correspondent who has made the grade socially in Washington or who has gone bankrupt in the attempt can truthfully say, "I owe it all to the little woman," for not the least by far of the forces which drive erstwhile bohemian or bucolic reporters into cocktail society is that exerted by their ambitious wives. The virus appears to attack the female first, and by her is communicated to the male.

This is one city where in what passes for "society" no one is ever accepted at his face value; where the wives who know the ropes always put the newcomer through a sort of silent third-degree to find out whether she is a potential rival. Or rather whether her husband is a potential rival of the other husband, with her as his propulsive force.

In this the newspapermen and their wives are little if any different from the aspiring government officials and diplomats whom many of them try to ape; it is a competitive field, and your social acceptability is in direct ratio to the importance of your job, with but slight relationship to your personal qualities. Even when there is no possible rivalry the same attitude is likely to be in evidence, and gossip is corrosively vicious. Wives who for one reason or another get about socially are the envy and the target of those who don't, and the husbands are drawn into it whether they like it or not. Those who are not often seen at parties are patronized.

It would almost seem as though social advancement were the aim and end of a Washington newspaper career; certainly if he was sufficiently observant Lord Northcliffe had more in mind than political gossip when he characterized Washington as "one great whispering gallery."

As a group the correspondents entertain extensively. If it were not for this social phase it is extremely doubtful how many members the National Press Club and the various other associations of reporters would be able to retain. They give many parties, and their principal guests are usually government officials or diplomats.

Best known among these is the Gridiron Club, formed originally as a small social group with an annual dinner at which public men and their affairs were put "on the gridiron" of journalistic wit, but now an extremely pretentious affair. There is probably no other affair in the country today to which so many important persons consider it a distinction to be invited; the dinners are held twice a year, in April and December, and the guest list reads like a catalogue of all the big names in the country, leading off with the President of the United States.

It is no secret that substantial bribes have been offered for invitations to this dinner, though if any ever was accepted it is a secret. The Club itself invites the President, the Cabinet, the Supreme Court and other outstandingly important politicians and business and professional men. In addition, each individual member is entitled to invite, at his own expense, a limited number of guests, and it is here that the journalists have their annual opportunity to pay off social debts, inflate their egos, or both.

The active membership in the club is limited to fifty bona fide correspondents, but there is a large associate membership, including men who sing or lead bands or are good actors or who in some other way can improve the quality of the amateur show which is part of the dinner. The Marine Band orchestra plays, and the director is an associate member, paying well in hard work for the privilege, since he not only conducts his band but also helps in the rehearsals.

The President if he attends (sometimes he plays hookey) delivers an off-the-record address in response to one from some member of the political opposition — a Senator, a defeated presidential candidate or the like. This semi-annual dinner is the outstanding example of how the power of the press has been translated into social prestige, when men of wealth and high public standing will miss no opportunity to attend, or even privately degrade themselves to get invited.

For years it was the custom of Club members and their guests, after the dinner, to repair to the suburban home of a wealthy and genial old baker, who loved to bask in the pale periphery of the light shed by the brighter stars among the Washington correspondents. Here in the private auditorium the late Nicholas Longworth, Speaker of the House, used to play by the hour on the pipe organ, while those not musically inclined found their pleasure in Mr. Corby's private bar.

The White House Correspondents Association, a huge, amorphous organization composed of any Washington newspapermen who can spare a dollar as membership fee, has a blowout once a year to which the President is also invited, though here he does not ordinarily make a speech. Anyone who pays his dollar and can afford the high price of a ticket is welcome to this party, a sort of brummagem version of the Gridiron Dinner. The correspondents do little in the way of putting on comedy skits, contrary to the Gridiron custom, but they persuade one of the big broadcasting companies to bring a lot of talent down from New York and stage a free show. President Roosevelt is said to consider this to be more representative of the working newspaperman than the Gridiron Club, and in 1941, for the first time, used the dinner as the occasion for a major address on international affairs.

The National Press Club, part of whose membership consists of working journalists and part of press agents, lobbyists, lawyers, bankers and the like, gives a series of parties in the course of the year, topped by the annual dinner. But unlike the other two just described, this dinner is open to members only and a few distinguished guests of the Club, headed by the President of the United States.

At the other and less formal parties Senator Capper and many other members of Congress and minor government officials are much in evidence, and at least once a year the Club has a Congressional night, when the legislators are the guests and help with the entertainment. It is a beautiful and awesome thing to see a Congressman remove his toga, let down his hair, and be one of the gang. Since members of Congress are such valuable sources of news it is entirely obvious why the Press Club makes a point of entertaining them with unfailing regularity. It is by way of slight repayment for the many little favors they have done for the newspapermen in the pursuit of their daily tasks; of showing the legislators, in an offhand, friendly way, that the correspondents appreciate their co-operation. There's no honor attached to such an invitation, but everybody has a big time and drinks a lot of beer.

Once a year, also, the Club organizes a baseball game between correspondents and members of Congress, in which both groups shed their dignity and play hard for an interminable afternoon. It is a bit difficult to establish whether one of these games was ever finished. And the annual outing of the Club, for members, wives and guests, is one of the other rare occasions when correspondents really cut loose and forget all about social prestige and professional throat-cutting. They hire a river boat or charter a special train, and spend a long Saturday eating and drinking and enjoying all the childish delights of a country fair.

The Press Club, in fact, is the proletarian among the correspondents' organizations despite its imposing building, with twelve floors of office space for rent and a floor and a half at the top for the Club. How that building happened to be agreed upon, and how the money was raised, is another story entirely, a story which even today, more than fifteen years later, makes many an old-time member see red. But within the confines of the Club itself the members take their ease, with a bar and a billiard-room and card-rooms and a "library" where they can stretch out on a sofa for a nap. In the grandiose dining-room they can strip off their coats in Summer, knowing that the ladies have been safely detoured into their own room adjacent to the bar. In the lounge opening out of the dining-room they can loll about and read the papers or play the radio, with no alien note to intrude.

Several times during the winter they have a dance, and the ballroom is overflowing with members and their wives and guests, in dinner coats and evening gowns, having a big time on a small amount of money. The only thing formal about these parties is the costuming; in fact, the Club usually has some difficulty being really formal, as was demonstrated in the spring of 1940 when an elaborate affair was planned in honor of Pan-American Day, the anniversary of the founding of the Pan-American Union. The committee labored long and hard. They gently shook down Latin American ambassadors and ministers for such gratuities as Mexican orchids and Chilean wine, and Pan-American Airways brought the orchids up free for the publicity. They invited all the heads of the Latin American missions and some of the secretaries and counsellors, with their wives and daughters, and they planned a unique dinner of Latin American dishes — arroz con pollo, a whipped avocado dessert, and Chilean white wine. They had an elaborate schedule of entertainment intended to give off a Latin aroma.

The guests of honor, seated on a platform running the length of the room, were most polite, but the pollo was broiled chicken, instead of the appropriate stewed fowl, the arroz was sticky, and the special dessert was something to forget as quickly as possible. The entertainment, by non-Latins, didn't go over so well either, and there wasn't enough of the good wine. The committees had worked hard, but they were short-circuited by the hired management, which didn't know any better, and by their own limited ideas of how Spanish Americans amused themselves.

Most members of the Gridiron Club and the Overseas Writers and the White House Correspondents Association are also members of the Press Club, and many of them attend all the functions of all four, but only at the Press

Club can they unbend at will. If they could only keep the Club for such purposes all would be well enough, but its infrequent attempts to be magnificent have a way of falling flat.

The Press Club's one bid for intellectual distinction is the weekly luncheons during the winter, when more or less distinguished officials and visiting journalists are invited to speak and answer questions. Some of these affairs are very much worthwhile, although the large attendance, and the heterogeneous character of the club's membership, tend to discourage the guests from saying anything out of the ordinary. In contrast are the periodic luncheons of the Overseas Writers Club, composed only of bona fide journalists who have been foreign correspondents. The Club exists only for these meetings, and the most cagey diplomat will usually loosen up there, knowing that when he speaks off the record his remarks will be held in confidence. By the same token, the questions asked are likely to be more pointed and more intelligent, on the whole, than those at the huge Press Club luncheons.

It ought not to be concluded that all Washington correspondents are gauche or cold-blooded social climbers, that they don't know how to behave themselves and that their private lives are an occasion for shuddering, but it is invariably true that in any group the ones who shrewdly court publicity are the ones who get most. Behind this false front there are very many who have relatively little to do with the artificialities of a political society. They go to parties, certainly, and they enjoy them more, perhaps, because they are not all the time thinking about whether they are being seen by the right people, or whether their names will appear in the next day's society columns. They go to the Press Club to dance and within the limitations of such parties they have a good time. And they do their share of entertaining at home, but they usually forget to invite the "right" people, choosing instead the ones they like. These correspondents and their wives really ought to know better; they ought to know that unless they follow the Washington party line they will have to rely entirely upon their own merits to get ahead as newspapermen.

The New Deal, to be sure, caused some amusing complications in Washington society, for some of us found ourselves enduring the conversation of outlandish creatures merely because they held important government jobs, creatures whose manners were a trifle off-hand, whose trousers were sometimes unpressed and who didn't bow from the waist. All they had to contribute was intelligence.

Many who had become thoroughly depressed with the Hoover regime found this a welcome change. A new and startling and stimulating force invaded the Capital, and because the New Deal emergency agencies fell into no particular rank, those who worked for them cut straight across society, temporarily breaking down the stratification that had come to be accepted. But as the temporary agencies became permanent and the New Dealers who smelled revolution just around the corner settled down into harmless bureaucrats whose chief interest was in preserving their jobs, the old order reasserted itself. Nowadays if you want to shock your politer guests with an "intellectual" about the best you can do is to invite Leon Henderson, and Mr. Henderson is very, very busy.

XIV

Tabloid News

Within the past two decades there have arisen to plague the newspaper publishers three new vehicles for the distribution of news — the weekly news magazine, the radio, and the news reel. The publishers recognized the radio as a powerful competitor too late to do much about it other than gnash their teeth; they have yet to comprehend the potentialities of the controlled news reel. The news magazines, on the other hand, perhaps because, like newspapers, they consist of type and pictures, have already had a profound effect upon the form and content of the daily press.

Immediately after the first World War, when radio was just beginning to develop as a medium of entertainment and instruction, and there was no federal law governing its operation, the publishers, had they then realized its possibilities, might well have effected almost a monopoly over it. Many of the original broadcasting stations were the property of big newspapers, and many others could have been had for a song in those formative days, had the publishers looked upon radio as little more than a toy. A few did foresee the development of broadcasting into a major industry, financially profitable and with illimitable potentialities for influencing the public, but many more got rid of the stations they had started, or permitted opportunities to buy into the business to slip through their fingers. Now there is a law, and a federal commission which casts a fishy eye upon efforts of newspapers to enter the broadcasting field. The golden opportunity is gone, probably forever.

In the early 1920's two young fellows with a million-dollar idea obtained the interest of sufficient capital to start the first weekly news magazine. One of its founders is dead, but under the resplendent leadership of Henry Luce *Time* has grown beyond Briton Hadden's fondest dreams, and has acquired two astonishing sisters — *Life* and *Fortune* — and a thoroughly respectable imitator — *News Week*. There had been one news magazine of sorts — the *Literary Digest* — as long as most readers of this book will be able to remember, but it bore no more resemblance to *Time* and *News Week* than an old lady in hoopskirt and pantalets does to a 1941 edition jitterbug. The *Literary Digest*, before its bad guess as to the result of the 1932 election pushed it into the ashcan, was content to give a staid, departmentalized review of the news, with cartoons reprinted from the papers, and a wit and humor page. *Time* brought romance into the retelling of the week's events; it concerned itself with the little items as well as the big, and if they were not intrinsically jazzy, its editors gave them a shot in the arm. It has a very large circulation. *News Week*, by reason of its very unwillingness to live for romance alone, has not been able to duplicate the astonishing success of *Time*.

Fortune, at a dollar a copy, boxed, presumably has a millionaire circulation, and it gives its readers long, scholarly articles on serious topics of the day, articles which in many instances tend to be positively subversive of the traditional millionaire philosophy. Its writers are well paid but anonymous. *Fortune* is distinctly not a rival of the newspapers.

Life, on the other hand, is decidedly a potential rival. A complete picture magazine using the name of a dead comic weekly, it appeals to that great class of citizens who appreciate a pictorial presentation of the news as a supplement to the printed page, and even to those who are willing to substitute pictures for words. It is the successor to a long line of picture magazines, from the *Police Gazette* and *Leslie's Weekly* to *Pictorial Review*; and the inspiration, save the mark, of a perfect pestilence of others with monosyllabic names such as *Look* and *Pic* and *Gaze* and *Gawp*, some of which are devoted exclusively to news photos with the necessary brief captions, and others, like *Look*, hazarding an occasional signed article on a current topic. It is said of the proprietors of *Look* — newspaper publishers to whom it is a sideline — that they wish they could somehow dispose of their papers and just spend the money they make on this cheaply printed, lower-middle-class contribution to visual education.

The motion picture news reel, a medium not particularly new, has in recent years been expanded and refined to the point where it has become a strong, positive influence on the national life, and when one considers the impossibility of producing a news film without great selection of detail, it becomes readily apparent what an instrument for propaganda it can be. It is the only one of the three media which, in the case of governmental news, is entirely dependent upon official sanction and official approval for its existence.

Henry Luce saw its possibilities several years ago when, more as an advertisement for *Time* than anything else, he began the production of a long, carefully planned, carefully edited, news-reel a month, each developing a particular topic. Obviously relatively little of the material so used could be spontaneous pictures of spontaneous events: co-operation of the principals and the use of plenty of extras were required. Each "March of Time" movie has a scenario as meticulously worked out as that of a feature film, a process culminating in Luce's full-length feature on World War I, made by hired amateur actors, skilfully pieced out with bits of old newsreel, and graphically illustrating in its entirety the propagandist possibilities of the motion picture.

In Washington those who work for the radio, the news reel and the news magazine enjoy a peculiarly favored position in relation to the correspondents of the daily newspapers. Their number grows each year, and the government evidently realizes to the full their value as channels of propaganda.

The combined bureau of *Time, Life* and *Fortune* employs some twenty-four people, of whom about two-thirds are on the staff of *Time. News Week* has a staff of seven. As of January 1, 1941, there were forty-eight news cameramen — other than the "locals" — claiming membership in the White House News Photographers' Association, of whom thirteen, or more than one fourth, represented five news reel companies. The total does not include the photographers on the staff of *Time* and *Life,* since the association has the same rules as the press gallery — membership only for those whose work appears daily. The President and Secretary-Treasurer and two members of the Executive Committee were news reel representatives — four officers out of a total of seven. There were on the same date forty-four full-time radio news gatherers or broadcasters entitled to membership in the Radio Correspondents' Gallery at the Capitol, in addition to those part-time broadcasters who are employed primarily by newspapers or syndicates.

Thus the total of all these collateral news gatherers in the National Capital amounts to about twenty percent of the number representing the daily press. Clearly so large a number of representatives of three such valuable means of propagating ideas merits respectful attention — and gets it. Of late they have had so much that old-line newspaper correspondents have found reason to complain, fairly or unfairly, of favoritism. Part of this "favoritism" stems from the peculiar problems of the news broadcaster, the news reel photographer, and the weekly news magazine. There is a different sort of deadline, and the necessity for anticipating events which does not as a rule greatly concern the reporter for a daily paper.

At any rate, when President Roosevelt, in May of 1941, delivered his long-heralded broadcast of defiance to disturbers of world peace, the radio and the news reel were unmistakably favored at the expense of the newspapers. The address, it will be recalled, was delivered in the East Room of the White House, a large ballroom occupying one whole end of the building, before an audience of Latin American diplomats and State Department officials. It had been announced that it would be a message of the utmost gravity, to be broadcast to all foreign countries; consequently all four of the big networks were permitted — or requested—to set up their apparatus in the East Room in advance. Also it was considered fit material for newsreels, to bring to the American public a visual image of the President defying the dictators, so the newsreel companies dragged in their ponderous equipment as well. The regular news photo services were invited to send their cameramen for still pictures of the scene.

But what of the correspondents of the daily press? After some pressure had been brought to bear, with some intimations of discrimination, the White House decided to admit one each from the three press associations — the Associated Press, the United Press and International News Service. The White House correspondent of the *New York Times* thereupon applied a little single-handed pressure, and eventually was told that if a *Times* man should happen to appear in dinner clothes at just the right time and the right entrance, he might be admitted. He was.

The scene he witnessed was startling. President Roosevelt, serious and careworn, sitting at a desk at the end of the room, faced a brilliant diplomatic audience from behind a battery of microphones. To the right and to the left were news cameramen and news reel men with their big machines grinding out film while the Klieg lights glared. The President posed repeatedly for the photographers, patiently complying with their instructions, while the diplomats sat waiting for the preliminaries to be over and the main event to start.

The prepared text of the speech was not ready until after seven o'clock, which meant that correspondents having to write stories about it in time for their first editions — many of them with the added factor of daylight-saving time operating against them — were hard put to make the deadlines. In this particular case they were not as bad off as the writers for the news magazines, which are distributed on Thursday and for whom Tuesday is the deadline. The address was delivered on a Tuesday, and they used all manner of persuasion to obtain from Stephen Early, the President's Secretary, some inkling of the trend of the speech, so that they would not be left holding the bag. But they were not successful. Early, who had co-operated with them on other occasions, flatly refused in this instance to give any suggestion of the precise content, with the result that there were some bad guesses.

But there have been other times when the news magazines received advance official tips, or the actual texts of documents, so that they might make a good showing that week. A notable instance, a few weeks after the big broadcast, came when President Roosevelt, in compliance with the terms of the Lease-Lend Act, reported to Congress on operations under the Act to date. This report, like the broadcast, was issued too late in the week for the news magazines to get a look at it if they were treated in the same manner as the representatives of the press, so they were provided with advance copies, to be held in confidence, for the purpose of writing their stories.

Similarly, when the President delivered his famous "knife-in-the-back" speech at the University of Virginia on the occasion of Mussolini's declaration of war against France, the radio news men were advised to listen carefully at a particular point in the broadcast, and not to rely too heavily upon the advance text with which they had been supplied. It was at this point that the President had interpolated a passage — the sensational passage of the whole speech — after the original copies had been distributed.

Actually the news magazine correspondents are not yet in the favored position occupied by the radio and news reel representatives, but they are getting along. There was the election night scene at Hyde Park in November, 1940, when all the correspondents, including the Washington manager for *Time*, were advised in advance that they would not be permitted at Hyde Park House. But the *Time* correspondent discovered that the news reel and radio men were enjoying the presidential hospitality and getting their fill of pictures and atmosphere, so he organized a mass protest on the part of the news correspondents and obtained permission for them to have a look, too.

The New Deal has long recognized the outstanding publicity value of the visual and the aural outlets for news, but the weekly news magazines have had to work for what they obtained in the way of special concessions, probably because they look too much like newspapers and the bureaucrats have failed to understand their special importance. But more recently it has begun to be recognized, as is witnessed by the fact that these journals are more closely scrutinized by officials each week than is any daily newspaper.

There is nothing surprising about this preoccupation

with sound and sight on the part of an administration with a program to sell to the people, and a President with a golden voice and a photogenic smile to sell it. Mr. Roosevelt simply had the good fortune, considering his personal attributes, to come on the national scene at a time when the radio and the news reel were reaching a high point of efficiency. Herbert Hoover could have had the same facilities at his disposal, but anyone who has heard him speak or observed him in the act of delivery will understand why it was not feasible for him to make use of them.

The news magazines, occupying a position somewhere between the pictorial and the aural on the one hand and the prosaic news record on the other, perform a highly specialized function for at least two main groups of readers. For one thing, with one weekly deadline instead of from four to eight daily, they are able to study the news, synthesize it, and devote more time to the attempt to place each item in its true position with relation to the whole. Thus, intelligently and honestly edited, a news magazine becomes highly valuable collateral reading for citizens otherwise dependent upon the daily press, with its ever-present requirement of speed.

Again, there is a large mass of intelligent readers in the interior of the country, lacking prompt access to those great daily newspapers which attempt to give a full and intelligible account of national and international events, to whom a good weekly news magazine is indispensable. It is a matter of common knowledge that while the newspapers in the hinterland — save for a few in well-established cities — are extremely efficient in the publication of local and regional news, they are sadly lacking in the broader fields. To citizens in these communities the news magazine fills a great gap.

Add to these two main factors the practice of the news magazines of writing in a provocative, entertaining style, with none of the inhibitions of the daily press against opinion or "interpretation" in the news columns, and the fact that they consistently devote special attention to news of science, music, literature and the drama, and you have the reason why they are so popular. There is evidence that this is beginning to dawn on the New Deal publicists, and the time might well come, should we ever have an administration desirous of controlling the channels of information, when the news magazines would find themselves being dictated to even more than the daily papers.

There is an atmosphere of superiority in the vicinity of the *Time* office which arises from the apparent belief that news magazines, or at least *Time*, are the superiors of the daily papers in every way, far more important to the nation, and even destined, perhaps, to supplant them. This does not entirely jibe with Mr. Luce's reported efforts to buy into the New York newspaper business, but it does jibe with his understandable tendency to endow with major importance anything for which he is responsible. And it does lend to the Washington office of *Time* an *esprit de corps* which makes its staff a formidable rival of any of the major newspaper bureaus. Headed by Felix Belair, Jr., one of the best Washington correspondents of his generation, the *Time* staff scores frequent news beats over the daily press, the result of incessant alertness and creative imagination.

Allowing for the difference in proportions, the same is true of *News Week's* Washington Bureau, with Ernest K. Lindley as its chief correspondent. Indeed, the Washington newspaper correspondents are coming more and more to watch the columns of these two magazines for news tips, tips which, when run down and developed in traditional newspaper style, are not always recognized by newspaper readers as the same stories they saw a day earlier in *Time* or *News Week.* Lindley, by reason of the contacts developed in connection with his daily newspaper column, is in a particularly favorable position, and both magazines, since they waive the rule that a source of information must be given or at least indicated in any news story, are able to state facts and make forecasts as they never could if they had such a rule.

Yet there is little likelihood, if any, that the news magazines, the radio and the news reel will ever supplant in the public favor the daily newspaper reports from Washington. They will, and do, supplement them, but a nation as highly literate as ours is not likely to be willing to accept fifteen minutes of news summary as a substitute for columns of detailed description of the same events; it is not likely to take a few minutes of obviously staged, obviously edited news via the motion picture in place of an expertly written account of the same event; and it cannot be expected, having been educated to news reported twice daily, to wait for the same thing in capsule form once a week. Not even all three, expertly co-ordinated, could displace the daily newspaper, for at best they would still be purveying tabloid news, no matter in how many forms it appeared.

Certain it is, however, that the newspapers, and their Washington correspondents, have much to learn from these tabloid news media. They have developed the art of selection as have few newspapermen, and they have learned at the same time how to present news with full regard to its dramatic content. Newspapers and newspapermen can do the same thing, but they will have to work harder than many of them now do, and they will have to learn the story teller's art.

XV

OGR — School for Censors

IF YOU WERE TO CANVASS WASHINGTON for the agency most on the defensive you probably would wind up in the Office of Government Reports. Its Director, Lowell Mellett, has somewhat the appearance of a man bracing himself for a blow, and when a new employee starts work, he is likely to be asked what sort of things he has been hearing about the OGR, and to be assured that there's no truth in them. It is unlikely that very many people have ever heard of this peculiar agency, yet in Washington, among members of Congress and the press, its very existence has given rise to the most bitter controversy.

If war comes — and it may be here any time now — and if we have some form of censorship — as we most certainly shall — there is every reason to believe that the Office of Government Reports, with Mellett directing its activities, will constitute our nearest approach to a Ministry of Propaganda. Such statements as this have in the past inspired more than a little resentment in Mellett's mind for reasons which are somewhat difficult to assign, and he has taken pains to point out that the act under which his Office operates does not mention censorship or newspapers in any way. What, then, is the Office of Government Reports, and why is there this conviction among journalists that it is, in a manner of speaking, a school for censors?

In November of 1933 President Roosevelt created what he called the National Emergency Council, a misleading title for an agency whose functions were to assemble and dispense information, and devise and disseminate New Deal propaganda. It was, in short, a combination of question-and-answer service and publicity office by which the Roosevelt administration learned what the people were thinking and then ground out material to "sell" them the New Deal. It was very useful.

Some six years later, under the authority of the Reorganization Act of 1939, President Roosevelt abolished the Council and transferred its functions to a new Office of Government Reports, which operated as an immediate adjunct of the White House. The Executive Order and subsequent validating act of Congress under which it operates say that its purposes are:

"(a) to provide a central clearing house through which individual citizens, organizations of citizens, and State or local governmental bodies may transmit inquiries and complaints and receive advice and information; (b) assist the President in dealing with special problems requiring the clearance of information between the Federal Government and State and local governments and private institutions; (c) collect and distribute information concerning the purposes and activities of executive departments and agencies for the use of the Congress, administrative officials, and the public; and (d) keep the President currently informed of the opinions, desires and complaints of citizens and groups of citizens and of State and local governments with respect to the work of Federal agencies."

As organized the Office has three divisions — Field Operations, Press Intelligence and Information Service. The Division of Field Operations, according to Mellett, "serves as a contact between the Federal and State Governments, local governments, and citizens" and "as an information service to the President on the functioning of Federal programs in the States." The Division of Press Intelligence "makes available to Government officials — executive, legislative, and judicial — a day-to-day and permanent record of newspaper information and newspaper opinion on matters of public importance." All the "more important" newspaper columns are filed by date, says Mellett, under the name of the columnist, and "are easily accessible for reference." The United States Information Service is designed "to make available to the public factual information regarding Government departments, agencies, and functions." It "limits its dissemination of information to the strictly factual," and "does not undertake to interpret regulations, orders, reports or other data, but refers inquirers to the sources from which interpretations may be obtained."

This, officially and in brief, is the Office of Government Reports. But the process of distributing "information" to the public naturally involves putting that information in the best possible light, particularly when it has to do with any controversial matter. There are various ways of doing this, among which are the preparation of educational films and radio programs, and Mellett's office fought and lobbied very hard to prevent prohibitions against such activity from being attached to the bill making the OGR permanent. A subordinate of Mellett's was present on the floor of the Senate when the bill was debated there in May, 1941, coaching the Senator in charge of the legislation. He succeeded in eliminating the prohibitions against radio programs and motion pictures, the latter a relatively meaningless restriction, since the Interior Department, in addition to producing radio programs, has a well-developed service for the production of "educational" movies.

The Office of Government Reports goes out among the citizens and listens; it reports "to the President" what they are saying, and attempts to restore their equanimity if they are unhappy or dissatisfied about anything their government is doing. To this end it gives them large doses of factual material, sometimes in answer to direct questions, but also in the form of educational movie shorts and local radio programs. And it is a source of supply for politicians seeking material for radio speeches. It is the sort of agency that Haroun-al-Raschid might well have created had he been too busy with the affairs of state to prowl about in person among his subjects.

But this is not all there is to the Office of Government Reports — or rather to the duties of Lowell Mellett. There is another side which was not mentioned in the somewhat rancorous debate, in committee and on the floors of Congress, over the bill to make the office permanent. Mellett, to the best of this writer's knowledge, has never referred to it in public and has inferentially denied its existence. It is the one other phase of his work which, in the minds of many newspaper correspondents who have nothing personal against him, rounds out the OGR as a potential censorship bureau and propaganda office.

When Stephen Early became secretary to the President in 1933, one of his duties was to organize and administer the entire press relations system of the Executive Branch. He worked out a general pattern for the departments to follow, personally selected their chief press officers, kept an eye on them to be sure they did their work efficiently, and made replacements when a man was discharged or resigned. By the end of four years Early's burdens had increased to the point where he no longer found it possible to give the press bureaus the close supervision he felt they required, and he cast about for a man to relieve him. He found that man in Lowell Mellett, a zealot in defense of all New Deal policies and projects, who had resigned as a Scripps-Howard editor rather than oppose President Roosevelt's court-packing plan.

Just why Mellett is so cagey about this extra-legal aspect of his work is a mystery to his friends as well as his enemies. Even in private discussions at the Press Club early in 1941, when he was questioned politely but extensively about the functions of his office and his views on press relations, he never once referred to it. Of course there is a fiction that all press relations officers of the government are entirely autonomous, subject only to the will of their respective superiors, but any Washington correspondent knows this is not true. Early set up the system after the disintegration of press relations in the Hoover administration, and made a particular duty of keeping it in order, with especial attention to personnel. That duty he later shifted to Mellett, but for some reason Mellett doesn't like to discuss it. Strictly speaking, it is not part of his work as Director of the OGR, but as Administrative Assistant to the President, for he is one of the "six assistants with a passion for anonymity" whose salaries were authorized by the Reorganization Act of 1939.

One correspondent who discussed the matter personally with him was told that he really had no supervision over the press agents — that if a Cabinet member or other administrative officer asked his advice on whom to hire, he naturally did his best to recommend a man, but that was all. That is far from all. When a vacancy occurs in the top job in a press bureau, Mellett very often supplies a man to fill it, generally from among his closer journalistic friends. While not all of them received their appointments through his good offices, the government is full of press officers who were his associates when he was editor of the *Washington News,* and many of them come to him regularly for advice.

Harold Jacobs, whose attempt to censor a list of correspondents to be invited on a War Department junket is described elsewhere, used to be a Scripps-Howard editor, and before Mellett sent him to the War Department with instructions to make a "survey," he was in charge of press relations for the Wage-Hour Division of the Labor Department, where he has since returned. Principally, the Mellett associates are to be found in the strictly New Deal agencies rather than in the old-line departments. When the big national defense effort was begun in 1940, Mellett was told to take care of press relations for the Defense Commission (later the Office of Production Management), and he appointed Robert W. Horton, a former employee, to be his legate. Horton at that time was "Director of the Division of Maritime Promotion and Information" of the Maritime Commission, but he moved over to the Defense Commission as a simple "Director of Information."

But why should Mellett be so modest about admitting any administrative connection with the New Deal press agents? One who knows him intimately has suggested that it is because he delights to move in an atmosphere of mystery, but a more specific explanation is that he is perfectly conscious of the growing criticism of the OGR as a possible instrument for press control, and so insists, all facts to the contrary notwithstanding, that his sole function is to collect and disseminate factual information for inquiring citizens.

His activities, however, belie this. As part of the authorized duties for which he draws his $10,000 a year he reads the newspapers and magazines with great care, and when he sees something therein which he considers to be unfair to the Administration he takes it upon himself to complain, personally or by letter. He thus complained to the publisher of *Time* about an eye-witness account of the scene at Hyde Park on election night, 1940, and he has been reported to have telephoned radio news broadcasters to reprimand them for their remarks on the air. Obviously, the Director of the OGR has functions quite other than the assembling and redistribution of factual information.

Early in 1941 a man from the staff of a national magazine came to Washington, interviewed Mellett, assembled some data on the OGR, and wrote an article detailing what was supposed to be the official plan for news censorship in the event of war. The control point, he said, would be the OGR and Mellett would be the censor. No doubt he made the same mistake as many visitors to Washington — of leaping to the conclusion that whatever blueprint he saw was the last word on the subject — for at this writing there are several plans, advocated by several influential members of the government, and all differing materially. Mellett in any event did not like the article, although it involved no personal criticism of him, and when, before a House committee, he was asked if the writer were a friend of his he replied:

"Well, he was up to a few weeks ago."

Nevertheless it is true that, according to present indications, Mellett will play an important part in whatever emergency press relations scheme is devised in the event of war. It was not for nothing that President Roosevelt selected this newspaper editor to be head of the National Emergency Council and its successor. And certainly OGR by its very structure and the very nature of its work is an instrument made to order for centralized press control. Mellett has said many times that he is opposed to censorship — censorship of the sort we see in European countries — but no record is at hand of his expressing opposition to that other type of censorship, call it what you will, which edits and selects the news of government to be made available to the press, and which obtains from the press "voluntary" pledges not to print this, that and the other.

An examination of the avowed purposes of the OGR,

in the light of its other activities and those of its Director as Assistant to the President, readily reveals how admirably it is adapted to the needs of a censorship-minded government.

One of its purposes, as stated in the act, is "to collect and distribute information concerning the purposes and activities of executive departments and agencies for the use of the Congress, administrative officials, and the public." While this function, narrowly construed, is that of a simple question-and-answer bureau, in reality even now it is far more than that, and is the framework if need be for an even broader structure — a public information bureau which, considering Mellett's general supervision of the government press agents, could well be the sole source of news in time of war, news which would then be doled out to the departmental publicity men and through them to the newspapers. Through its employment of the radio and the educational newsreel it could simultaneously distribute an unlimited supply of propaganda to "supplement" the news, and regardless of what Mellett or anyone else may say, it is impossible to produce an educational radio program or newsreel which is not propagandist in its essence.

A second purpose is "to keep the President currently informed of the opinions, desires and complaints of citizens and groups of citizens . . ." This laudable function, again, is so broadly stated that it is open to complete perversion into a sort of informer service, by which dissenters could be dealt with if need be.

Within its own framework as it implements these instructions, the OGR's "Division of Press Intelligence" keeps a complete newspaper and magazine clipping service. If the agency should by any chance be compelled to administer wartime press relations, what more natural than that the press intelligence division should be employed to keep check on the press and enable the government to apply pressure where needed, in the event a bit of news or an editorial was considered to be "unpatriotic"? Stephen Early, the President's secretary, once in an irritable moment told the White House correspondents that it was unpatriotic for them to send out any news which he had denied; an astonishing dictum, since it made Early the fount of all wisdom and the paragon of accuracy. But it is an attitude not uncommon in this Administration, and it is not difficult to see how it could be applied in time of national emergency. Many examples already have been given of the extreme pressure put upon correspondents and their employers to prevent the publication of undesired news, or to discredit the correspondent after publication. And that has been in time of peace, when "the Four Freedoms" were the objects of repeated genuflections.

It is not intended to imply that all this is going to happen, or that Lowell Mellett is the frightening individual the initials of his organization might indicate. It is intended, rather, to point out how readily, under Mellett or anyone else as zealous in defense of the New Deal and all its acts, the OGR could be perverted to the ends of press control and censorship. While Mellett's frequent protestations that he is anti-censorship, that he was once a newspaper man himself, must be taken at their face value, what of his character is ascertainable in so silent a man raises the serious question whether he is not, indeed, exactly the type that would be chosen for the job.

His experience before entering government service is such as to give him a profound practical knowledge of what newspaper work is all about, for he is the son and brother of journalists, and his own entire career up to 1937 was in that field. His father, Jesse Mellett, was editor of the *Free Press* in Elwood, Ind., a town later to be vaguely associated with a presidential candidate. The *Free Press* was generally Democratic in politics, but when Jesse Mellett opposed Grover Cleveland for the Presidency he became the 1892 equivalent of a "Red."

Lowell Mellett's brother, Don, was editor of the *Canton* (Ohio) *News*, and was murdered in 1926, as a direct result of his courageous exposure of the affiliations between gangsters and the city government. He had been repeatedly threatened, and his persistence resulted in his being killed from ambush.

Lowell Mellett himself was for one year managing editor of *Collier's Magazine*, and had a long and honorable career as a Scripps-Howard editor. Editors in this newspaper syndicate are shifted about from city to city like Army officers, and Mellett had his share of transfers, winding up as editor of the *Washington News*. Here for four years he championed the policies of the New Deal, but when the owners of the chain decided to turn against President Roosevelt he abruptly resigned. Very soon he became Director of the National Emergency Council, and when the Reorganization Act allotted Mr. Roosevelt six $10,000-a-year assistants, Mellett was one of the first to be chosen. He stands high in the regard of the White House and of all the more wholehearted New Dealers in Washington, both in and out of the government.

Whether or not the OGR was created, and Mellett appointed to direct it, with a view to press control plus propaganda, most Washington correspondents will agree that rumors to this effect, from the ridiculous to the plausible, arise in considerable part from Mellett's own secretive attitude. His own friends and associates from his newspaper days admit that they never have been able to fathom him; that he always kept his ideas and projects to himself; that he seldom let anyone know what was going on in his mind. One former newspaper correspondent who worked with Mr. Mellett for five years in the Scripps-Howard organization has said that he never gave the staff in general the slightest inkling of his instructions to any one of its members; that each man worked independently of the others; and that when Mellett finally broke with Scripps-Howard, his employees and associates received their first intimation that there was trouble brewing when his resignation was announced, a week before it took effect.

In brief his attitude, not only within the government but during his newspaper days, has been decidedly lacking in candor, an interesting commentary on a man whose principal avowed function is the "dissemination of information" regarding the government to the public. His refusal to admit any jurisdiction over the press agents — a well-established fact — is a striking illustration of this secretiveness, not to say deviousness. So likewise are his repeated and categorical denials that there exists anywhere in the

Roosevelt administration a plan for regulation of press relations in war time. Obviously, from the point of view of the government, the absence of such a plan would constitute a tragic oversight, as the experience of Britain proved, yet Mellett has reiterated in public and in private that such is the case.

Yet what are the apparent facts? The magazine writer who in February aroused Mellett's ire for his forecast of a war-time censorship spent some time in Washington preparing his article, and told several of his friends that he had actually seen such a plan and that he had seen it in Mellett's office. About that time, too, I myself was discussing government press relations with a man who subsequently became one of the highest-ranking publicity directors, and he brought up the subject of the "master plan," with the comment that he considered it unworkable. I asked him directly if it was Mellett's plan and he said it was. I have no reason to doubt his testimony, for he is an honorable man, regardless of any argument over his efficiency as a publicity director. Presumably the job of a publicity man is to publicize, while that of a censor is to create and maintain an atmosphere of secrecy. Mellett is essentially a secretive man. It may be that his denials of the existence of a press-control plan hinge upon his highly technical definition of censorship, discussed elsewhere in this chapter, but as has been pointed out, not all censors wield blue pencils.

Temperamentally he would appear to have many of the attributes which in a free society should disqualify him from the job of directing press relations in war time or any other time. In addition to his lack of candor he is emotionally intense, strongly partisan, and a meticulous critic — in private — of the press and the magazines. To the best of my information such criticism, unlike that of Secretary Ickes, has never been voiced in public; instead it takes the form of letters of complaint to editors and publishers, of veiled hints to the writers themselves. His complaint to the publisher of Time about the Hyde Park story was characteristic — he wrote a detailed bill of particulars, some of which were merely that items in the description "gave a wrong impression," but omitted mention of the fact that he himself was not there. The correspondent of Time was there.

Mellett is a "100-percenter": that is, he appears to feel that anyone who opposes any part of a program he favors is "on the other side." In this he is like many other New Dealers who have demonstrated their blindness to the possibility of constructive criticism. President Roosevelt himself has said many times that he has no objection to constructive criticism, but it becomes abundantly clear that what he and some of his aides really mean is that there is no objection to criticism of details of administration so long as the policy itself is accepted. ("No doubt but ye are the people, and wisdom shall die with you.") This is not dissimilar to the avowed method of the government of the USSR, which encourages the exposure of internal corruption and mismanagement, but requires complete obedience to the party line. If this is the official attitude of the New Deal, then it is treading on dangerous ground for a defender of democracy, and if one so subjective in his point of view as Mellett is to be at the controls of its relations with the public, then the first amendment to the Constitution is in peril.

There is no purpose here to compare the New Deal with Communism — I have been and still am a strong supporter of most of its objectives, and I am as strong an opponent of Marxism and its Twentieth Century perversion — but the tendency to brand critics as unpatriotic is far removed from the spirit of Thomas Jefferson, and no man who feels that way has the right to any place of importance in the government's publicity machine. It must be remembered in this connection that not only the newspapers, not only the magazines, but also the motion pictures and the radio are subject to this same influence. The radio reporters have to go through the same procedure to get their news as do the newspaper correspondents, and news reels of official events are made only with the consent and co-operation of the government.

Stephen Early at the outset of the Roosevelt administration constructed almost from the ground up an efficient, wide-open system of press relations which won the delighted acclaim of the Washington correspondents. Details of it have been discussed earlier in this book; it was manned in the main by diligent, public-spirited journalists who were New Deal partisans but who at the same time were fully aware of the necessity and value of honest criticism, of revelation of flaws and incompetence. That system has wilted considerably since Mr. Early delegated its administration to Lowell Mellett. Mellett without doubt has the best of intentions, but his temperamental peculiarities flavoring an organization whose *potentialities* at best are open to suspicion, completely disqualify him, in the minds of many patriotic newspapermen, for the job which has been assigned him.

XVI

Press Control in the Making

Early in 1941 the chief of the War Department's press section had compiled a list of leading newspaper correspondents, some from Washington and some from other cities, who were to be invited on a conducted airplane tour of defense establishments. It was a representative list, providing a cross-section of the big city press. But temporarily assigned to the press section at that time was Harold Jacobs, former Scripps-Howard editor and a close friend and associate of Lowell Mellett, Director of the Office of Government Reports. Jacobs asked to see the list, and as he read it, drew lines through the names of several men.

"What's that for?" asked the Army officer.

"These papers are opposed to the Administration," Jacobs replied.

"Look here," said the officer. "This office has always operated on the principle that no favorites are played; news is news and we don't give it out on the basis of friendliness or hostility to the administration. That has been the policy and so long as I am here it will continue to be the policy, and you can make an issue of it if you like."

The names were restored, but the incident was alarm-

ing to all who believe in the credo summarized by the
Army press officer, a credo grounded in the first amendment to the Constitution. It brought home to those who
heard of it at the time the slenderness of the inhibition in
the Bill of Rights against abridgement of the right of free
press, free speech, free assembly, and free worship. The
first amendment does not forbid such abridgement — it
simply forbids Congress to pass any restrictive laws in these
fields. It does not prevent the Executive from indulging
in restrictive measures if he is able to do so without the
passage of a law.

No one in the government is on public record as advo-
cating any act which will inhibit the press in the discharge
of its accepted function of informing the people, yet there
is abundant evidence that administrative officials are continually, and with increasing efficiency, employing methods
which to a limited extent accomplish this end. Such methods have always been operative to a greater or less extent
— it is part of the traditional warfare between the press,
seeking news of official acts and projects, and the bureaucrats, desirous of withholding publicity until the most
favorable moment. But in the past year or two, up to the
middle of 1941, the volume of such attempts at restraint
has grown and the means employed have become more
obvious and more effective. Those who indulge in such
methods are usually the first to assert that they abhor the
very thought of censorship, but when they use the word
they are found to mean censorship in its most technical
and limited sense — the requirement that all copy be submitted to an acknowledged censor for editing.

Censorship — or its effects — can be accomplished in many other ways than one so crude and obviously contrary to the spirit of the Constitution as that. When any government official or agency closes or constricts the avenues of search for news to the point where the press is compelled to rely upon prepared statements to fill its columns; when direct pressure is put upon correspondents, editors and publishers to prevent the publication of news, then there is a censorship, whatever else you may wish to call it.

Every responsible Washington correspondent, every managing editor, is constantly engaged in a sort of self-censorship in the public interest, and it would be appalling if they were not, particularly in times as troubled as these. In the routine pursuit of their duties reporters keep digging up items involving national policy whose publication would seriously impair the legitimate activities of the government, and there is ever present the question of whether these shall be printed. Mostly they are not. There are those who insist that everything is news, that a paper has no right to suppress anything it learns, but no thoughtful newspaperman will subscribe to any such thesis. Officials are fully aware of this self-restraint on the part of the correspondents, yet many of them are unwilling to let matters rest there: they wish to go further and have the last word on what a paper shall print if it involves their particular administrative agency. This is censorship.

Clearly, in great national emergencies some restrains are necessary, but once they are imposed, co-operatively or otherwise, there follows always the temptation to restrict or conceal matters which are not military or diplomatic secrets but legitimate news which ought to be in the possession of the public. The newspapers are ready and willing to co-operate in any reasonable secrecy if publication would tend to give aid to the nation's enemies, but they are not, or ought not to be, willing to surrender their most sacred privilege in response to the whim of a bureaucrat who is afraid of criticism.

Soon after the United States government adopted a policy of armed non-belligerency instead of neutrality, both Army and Navy suddenly required the issuance of special passes to all their departmental employees as well as to anyone else habitually going in and out of the buildings. Of course any newspaperman covering these agencies had to have such a pass, which consisted of a hideous oblong badge with what purported to be his photograph on it. In the absence of such identification it was possible, though difficult, to get to see a particular individual by appointment, but many a correspondent, unexpectedly assigned to cover a press conference at War or Navy, has missed the conference entirely on account of the laborious unwinding of red tape that perforce preceded his admittance to the holy of holies. L. C. Speers of the *New York Times* returned to his run at the Navy — a run he had covered for many years — after a week's illness, and found that in the meantime the new regulation had been promulgated. Or rather he didn't find it out, for he marched in to the press room in his usual brisk manner without anyone stopping him. But once there, a full-dress investigation was set in motion to determine how he had got in, and for quite a while Speers was not at all sure they would let him out again, even though virtually everyone in the building knew him personally.

What appeared at first to be the last straw was an announcement at the White House that everyone entering the Executive Offices on business must have a special pass. Each one had to be "mugged" and fingerprinted and his record checked by the FBI and the Secret Service, and if he was found to be kosher and not a Trojan horse, he received a handsome pass with his picture on it. As it turned out, however, this pass was a godsend. At the suggestion of J. Fred Essary of the *Baltimore Sun* the President ruled that the White House card should be good for admittance to any government office, so that correspondents were enabled to go to the War Department, Navy Department, Defense Commission, or anywhere else without having to wear an array of silly badges on their lapels.

There was some talk of requiring special passes at the Defense Commission, but it finally narrowed down to employees of that agency. But here the bureaucrats, jealous of the nation's safety, ran into a snag, for William S. Knudsen, chairman, flatly refused to wear a badge. He said he had worn too many, punched too many time clocks, in his day to begin again at this late date. The problem was solved after a fashion by having him photographed and then giving a copy to every service employee in the building so that if they saw him enter without a badge they wouldn't seize him as a spy.

Late in 1940 Frank Knox, Secretary of the Navy, sent identical letters to newspaper publishers and Washington bureau chiefs asking them to refrain from publishing certain categories of news which he said would be detrimental to the public interest. These included the movements of naval vessels, descriptions of warships or naval planes, descriptions of "secret weapons" such as bombsights, and details of construction of naval shore establishments. Many of the recipients of this letter felt that it went further than was necessary, but the publishers hastened to assure Mr. Knox that they would comply to the fullest. The ship movements had been kept secret so far as official release was concerned for several months before this, but the other restrictions were new.

Some months later the British battleship *Malaya* steamed into New York harbor in broad daylight and in full view of the German consulate, for repairs at an American shipyard. The sailors from the ship strolled about the city in uniform with the name *H.M.S. Malaya* on their caps. Most newspapers refrained from publication of this obvious piece of news, but two or three saw no reason why, if the British themselves made no effort at secrecy, they should not cover the story. So they did, with pictures. The Navy and the British were greatly upset, the pilot of the plane from which the *New York Daily News* cameraman took his pictures was called on the carpet at Knox's instance for violation of Civil Aeronautics Board rules, and the Secretary hastily added movements of British warships to his category of forbidden topics. To his credit it must be said that he publicly criticized the British for entering the harbor in the daytime and permitting the sailors to be so readily identified.

A month or so later the Navy announced that it would

no longer make public the daily record of personnel transfers, and soon afterward the Maritime Commission requested newspapers not to publish news of the movement of ships carrying supplies to Britain or her allies. Since many of these ships also carry mail, the question immediately arose whether the routine notices of arrivals and departures and the time of closing of the mails should also be placed on the forbidden list. Within two weeks the Post Office Department, at the instance of the Commission, issued such an order. For a time newspapers in port cities had been printing on their ship news pages the statement that "a ship" was leaving at such-and-such a time for such-and-such a port and telling when the mails closed. The Post Office order made it impossible to print even this much, except in the case of voyages within the Western Hemisphere.

There was little resentment against the Navy and Maritime Commission requests for secrecy, because in general they appeared to be reasonable and inspired by a desire to promote the national safety, even though some of Knox's points appeared to go a trifle further than necessary. But some of the methods employed by the Navy in enforcing its restrictions upon news have been somewhat less than intelligent. As long ago as the autumn of 1940 a correspondent of the *Wall Street Journal*, who happened also to be a reserve officer, almost got into trouble with the Navy because of an article he rewrote from the *Encyclopædia Britannica*.

The correspondent, Vermont C. Royster, now on active duty in Puerto Rico, was assigned to write an informative story on the manufacture of armor plate, but when he inquired about it, officers at the Department informed him in considerable consternation that he was asking for military secrets, and when he discussed the matter further threatened him with disciplinary action. So he went to the Encyclopædia, where he found a perfectly good essay on armor plate without any military secrets at all. He wrote a story based upon this, whereupon the Department ordered an investigation of his source of information. Evidently the petty bureaucrats responsible for this comedy of errors didn't know a military secret when they saw one; they only knew that there were secrets involved in the manufacture of armor plate for the American Navy, hence anything at all about armor plate was a military secret.

The Army has made fewer egregious errors of this sort than the Navy, perhaps because the Army has always been a bit less addicted to secrecy than the Navy, and perhaps also because the Army developed a large and comprehensive public relations staff ahead of the Navy. In fact, the Army's policy of relative liberality in releasing news has brought it into some amusing conflicts with Navy policy. A short time before Secretary Knox's circular letter was sent out, there had been numerous stories in the press hinting that our secret bombsight had been released to the British for use on their planes. Much was made of this, since it had been stated rather definitely in previous months that while we were giving Britain many of our most modern weapons, the real military secrets were being kept at home. The bombsight mentioned was that manufactured by the Sperry Gyroscope Company.

Finally General George C. Marshall, Chief of Staff, called a press conference in which he admitted that the Sperry was on the big bombers sent to England, but minimized its importance, saying it was not "the" bombsight at all, but a secondary one. The Norden, said he, was the real secret weapon. It appeared fairly obvious to those in the know that the General was trying to cover up a bit for the unfortunate news leak by trying to give the impression that the Norden, which was not being released, was vastly more important than the poor old Sperry. But the joke was really on the Navy, which was generally understood to use the Norden whereas the Army was said to use the Sperry, and the Navy people, without referring to General Marshall, commented rather sourly that this publicity for the Norden bombsight had caused them all manner of trouble and had entailed the posting of extra guards around the Norden plant, as well as around the person of its proprietor.

Some time later the United Press carried on its wires a story from Honolulu that a large number of bombing planes had arrived in Hawaii to reenforce the garrison there. Numerous correspondents, at the insistence of their editors, telephoned the Navy Department to ask whether it was all right to print the story, and the Navy said it wasn't, that the Secretary's letter had requested that nothing be printed about the movement of ships, and these were ships. Next day it developed that the planes were Army planes and the commandant at Honolulu had given out the story himself!

Since these amusing incidents occurred, both Army and

Navy have greatly expanded their bureaus of information, the Army's under a Major General and the Navy's under a Rear Admiral. The Navy has as assistant to Admiral Hepburn Hal O'Flaherty, managing editor of Secretary Knox's *Chicago Daily News*, with a sizable staff of assistants both civilian and naval. General Robert C. Richardson, a cavalry expert, spent several months building up the Army's Public Relations Division, but in July of 1941 was shifted back to a field command. The division he headed embraces a very large staff, headed by Col. Stanley J. Grogan, a thoroughly competent and realistic officer who ran this press service with only two or three assistants for some time before the Army began to expand. Grogan has at his command not only a number of other line officers, but also a dozen or so reservists pulled in from the newspapers, the radio and the news reels, with temporary ranks from lieutenant to major. The *New York Times* alone was raided to the extent of six men.

General Richardson is a high-minded officer who conceived it to be his duty to keep the public as fully informed as is compatible with military safety. He has often said that not more than five percent of all the War Department's acts have any reason to be secret — that the other ninety-five percent should be made public fully and immediately. It has been the experience of the Washington correspondents that Colonel Grogan shares this view. General Richardson was opposed to off-the-record discussions in press conferences, believing that reporters should be at liberty to print whatever they are told. He considered it to be contrary to public policy — to public safety — for the nation to be kept in the dark about what its organized defenders are doing. In France, he has said, a large part of the press was utterly uninformed as to the course of events, and he desires that no such catastrophe shall befall the United States.

Under his guidance, and since, the War Department Division of Public Relations has poured out an ever increasing flood of prepared press releases on all manner of subjects, and the less important they are the longer the releases tend to be. This writer recalls receiving a formidable looking mimeographed document, fully 1500 words long, which developed on inspection to be a detailed feature story, very well written, about the Department's laboratory in Philadelphia where Army clothing is tested for quality. Some one of the reserve officers in the division must have been very proud of the essay, but there wasn't any news in it. The impression gains force that the War Department is striving mightily to keep the proportion of items released at ninety-five percent of the total, with only five percent withheld, but that in order to achieve this quota it has adopted the practice of putting out a great volume of handouts on subjects which heretofore would not have been considered worth the ink and paper. The number of handouts has multiplied, but not the net news content, which diminishes steadily in proportion.

But for all this, it must be kept in mind that the nation is preparing for war, a condition in which military secrecy is almost as important as under actual war conditions. Correspondents may chafe at the Navy's acknowledged censorship-at-source, at the Army's freshet of foolscap in lieu of what we used to call news, but they admit a certain validity in all this under the circumstances. In other agencies of the government, however, they are able to discern very little validity in methods which tend to make it increasingly difficult for the public to keep informed, methods whose evident aim is to force the reporter to rely upon formal official statements for the bulk of his news.

Very recently an active and resourceful correspondent of the *New York Times* was commenting on the volume of his copy on a particular day, and remarked that if he were paid by the word he would grow rich. The writer replied that he would gladly pay two cents a word for all stories which were not based on handouts, if the reporter would refund a like amount for the rest. A check-up revealed that the reporter had written 3700 words, or about four and a half columns, of news, of which only 800 words, or one column, did not involve rewriting a press release! Some of these stories were of a highly technical nature and the handout method was justified, but in general the exchange aptly illustrated the governmental trend away from confirmation of facts developed independently by the reporter, and toward formal release of carefully edited statements without the possibility of amplification. And it has become the practice in many agencies to put out these releases more or less in one batch late in the day, with the result that it is difficult if not impossible for the correspondent to do anything more than rewrite them without corollary research.

There is nothing very new in all this — it has always been the desire of administrators that the press use their prepared statements and no more — but only in the past year or two has the system been perfected to the point where independent research is actively discouraged. Indeed, the writer knows definitely of one newspaperman who became so active and so resourceful in obtaining non-handout news from the War Department that word was passed around there not to permit him to talk privately with any officer outside the public relations division! This was a striking example of the bureaucrat's deadly fear of what the policy-making officer of Cabinet rank or lower will say if permitted alone in the same room with an intelligent reporter, a fear generally justified, because the top men usually will talk with relative freedom to a friend. This particular correspondent obtained much exclusive news, frequently volunteered, from a junior Cabinet member, whose "indiscretions" were a source of acute sorrow to all his subordinates. This assistant secretary not infrequently gave his friend news which in all reason he should not have divulged; why he did so is one of those unsolved mysteries, since he himself was never quoted as the source and consequently he received no personal publicity, beloved of the politician.

As far back as 1935 Frank L. Kluckhohn of the *New York Times* was instrumental in getting the release of statistical information about Rexford G. Tugwell's utopian Resettlement Administration which most of the press corps had tried in vain to obtain, by publishing a story which made one of Dr. Tugwell's minions so angry that he spilled the whole thing, but in a manner designed to discredit Kluckhohn with his publisher and with the rank and file of newspaper readers. After the vast work relief program had been in operation a few months, Kluckhohn set out to get comparative statements of the number of unemployed each component was caring for, and the administrative cost in each case. WPA's Morton M. Milford and PWA's Michael W. Straus were entirely co-operative, providing him with the best they could give on the subject, but Resettlement was strangely reticent about telling how many relief workers were on its rolls, and how much the agency was costing to operate aside from relief wages. But from other official sources it was possible to obtain an accurate estimate, and the story as published showed Resettlement to have an extremely high "overhead" and an extremely low employment rate. Next day John Franklin Carter, now writing a daily column in defense of New Deal acts, telephoned this writer and said:

"We are releasing an open letter to your publishers; I just wanted you to know about it."

The open letter, given out as a piece of news to all the correspondents, denounced Kluckhohn's story without refuting it, and incidentally gave detailed statistics of the sort he had tried in vain to get two days earlier. The device of the open letter, of course, was particularly stupid, since it ought to have been obvious that no other correspondent would use it in that form if he could avoid doing so. Each would think, "This is what will happen to me if I run afoul of this agency." As a result only the Times printed it.

A few months earlier George Creel, famed as Director of the Bureau of Public Information and our nearest approach to a censor in the first World War, was working on a per diem basis for the Federal Emergency Relief Administration, predecessor of WPA, but no one could find out what he was supposed to be doing. It so happened that Creel simultaneously was Washington correspondent of *Collier's Magazine*, and thus was holding two jobs and drawing two salaries at once. Finally the *Times* printed the ascertainable facts — that he was working per diem for FERA but that it was all a great mystery. Creel telephoned me and said:

"This is George Creel. I want you to know that that story about me in today's *Times* is extremely embarrassing to me in my relationship with *Collier's*. I wish you to refrain from printing anything further about me."

I replied that I would be delighted to comply, but that so long as he made news I was afraid we would have to print stories about him. I do not recall that the occasion ever again arose.

Generally speaking, attempts to control what the newspapers shall print about governmental activities take one or all of five forms. These are (1) the practice, elsewhere discussed, of flooding the correspondents with handouts to the extent that they have little time or opportunity to seek news independently; (2) the device of making it very difficult to talk privately to the top men in an agency, thus forcing the reporter to get his news from a press agent; (3) the diminution in frequency and importance of Cabinet press conferences, with those which are held so carefully guarded that the Secretary has little chance of saying anything his subordinates think he ought not to say; (4) the practice of issuing technical or absolute denials of stories that have been published, in such a way as to reflect discredit upon the veracity of the reporter and his paper; (5)

the reprisal method, which takes on a variety of aspects ranging from scoldings personally administered to letters of complaint to the correspondent's superior.

The first method is most successful in the case of individual correspondents or very small bureaus with the whole town to cover: such as these dare not throw away the handouts, which may and often do contain news of some importance, and yet if they go through them conscientiously it takes an astonishing amount of their time. In the case of a large bureau with anywhere from ten to twenty reporters on its staff the device is not so successful, for while all the handouts are inspected, it is usually a desk man who does it while the reporters are out ranging for news which has not yet been sterilized and canned. And there is usually at least one reporter in such a bureau who has no particular agency to cover and thus is free to roam the city for exclusive stories having their source in no mimeograph machine.

It has been said elsewhere that the astonishing freedom given the press in the early days of the New Deal has in recent years become considerably constricted, and this applies with particular force to the difficulty correspondents now experience in getting to see the men who really formulate policy and execute it. Even when, a few years ago, it was hard to interview a busy Cabinet officer or other administrator in private, they all had frequent and regular press conferences at which questions were freely asked and as freely answered. Much of that has been changed. Not only are the top men not available, but their press officers take on more and more of the habits of the anchorite, presumably because they are so busy supervising the production of handouts that they have no time to talk to reporters. Several departments have a general rule that no official may be interviewed, even over the telephone, by a newspaperman without the permission of the press officer, but if the press officer himself is not to be found, the correspondent finds himself up against an impenetrable wall, a wall soft, spongy and resilient, but unyielding.

In May of 1941 the writer was trying to find out, in response to an inquiry from his New York office, an extremely simple and harmless bit of information. A second soft-coal strike threatened, and the reporter in New York, where the negotiations were in progress, wanted to know whether the Defense Mediation Board, which had settled the first, still had jurisdiction, and whether in any event the federal government contemplated any immediate intervention. It was three o'clock on a Friday afternoon, but the chief press officer of the Labor Department had left for the week-end, his office said. The call was shunted around to three other Labor Department offices in rapid succession, in each case the person interviewed being a secretary to an official, but the answer was not forthcoming. A call to the press officer for the Defense Mediation Board yielded a pleasant-voiced secretary, but the press officer himself was "out just now." More shunting about, with the polite secretary eventually volunteering her view in the matter, which turned out to be the reverse of correct. In this case not only was it impossible to get in touch with any responsible official: it was also out of the question, apparently, to obtain the simplest sort of information even from a long series of subordinates. The matter was of minor significance so far as the news went, but of major importance as an indication of the disintegration of a system in which the information officer becomes so preoccupied with other matters that he can't find time to talk for two minutes to a newspaperman. This may not be censorship — incompetence is probably the apter term — but the effect in the last analysis is the same: no news.

When Henry Morgenthau, Jr., became Acting Secretary of the Treasury in 1933 one of his first acts was to issue an order that all Treasury news must come from a press relations officer; that no other officer should talk to the correspondents. The Treasury Correspondents Association protested with great vigor not only to the Secretary but also by telegram to the President himself at Hyde Park, and the order was revoked, with the result that the press obtained an efficient aid it had not had before, without the semicensorship Morgenthau had intended to go with it. Nowadays such restrictions, written or de facto, are becoming the rule rather than the exception, and the correspondents, aware that they are confronted with an accomplished fact, endure the system in comparative silence.

Yet there is a point, still remote and which all Washington correspondents hope never will be reached, at which repressive methods in relation to the news will recoil upon themselves and create in press relations a state of anarchy which will be most detrimental to the government, the press itself, and the nation. The American press cannot be expected to waive completely or for any protracted period its hard-won freedom to find and print the news. If avenues of approach to official news are closed, or so constricted as

to make publication of important facts too difficult, then
the press may well be expected gradually to revert to the
old dog-eat-dog methods of a generation and more ago. No
confidences will be honored, no pledges of secrecy will be
given, no proof will be adduced for such news as is printed.
The newspapers will get what they can by whatever methods are necessary, without regard to the elaborate ethical
standards which have been developed parallel to their rise
to the status of public utilities. Every reporter then will
lapse into the category of a gossip columnist. Government
officials will see news in print that ought not to have been
published; the general public will read many stories which
are only half true or are totally unverifiable rumor, and the
press itself will have lost all the ground it has gained, all
the public esteem, of the past half-century.

The best and most prolific issuer of denials always has
been the President, regardless of who he is, because so many
of the stories which elicit such denials involve forecasts of
national policy. President Coolidge constantly denied his
own words; Roosevelt I did likewise, and Roosevelt II has
on a few spectacular occasions publicly repudiated correspondents who knew that what they had written was true.
FDR early in his administration went so far as to say, in a
formal release, that a reliable story by a reputable correspondent was "pure fabrication, with some doubt as to the
purity." Such a statement obviously was designed to discredit the writer of the story with all who had read it, and
it was issued only because the story itself prematurely revealed important plans.

More common is the informal and technical denial, of

the sort which, if closely inspected, is not really a denial of the substance of the story at all, but of a careless bit of phrasing. A story whose general content is perfectly true may say "the President is considering," and the President will deny that this is so, although it may well be that his subordinates have in preparation a project for his consideration of whose existence he is fully aware. Robert Jackson, as Attorney General, once formally and with great vigor denied a story which was perfectly true save for one such minor detail, then two days later issued a statement which confirmed the whole thing. The story had said that Jackson had written letters to certain people. He had not yet written the letters, so for public consumption the entire story was branded as false. Yet the author of the piece had tried in vain for two successive days to see some department official for confirmation.

Within four or five days of President Roosevelt's proclamation of an unlimited national emergency the same correspondent got wind that Jackson was investigating for the President the desirability of such a proclamation. He requested, and this time obtained, a private interview at which the Attorney General "took down his hair," discussed the entire subject with charming candor, and denied that Mr. Roosevelt would think of doing such a thing. The story was dropped, and within a week had come true. In fairness to Mr. Jackson, his close associates have since insisted that he really thought he was telling the truth this time — that he was opposed to the proclamation and believed he had convinced the President.

Occasionally a correspondent who is quite sure of his

ground but whose story has been denied in advance by a responsible official, will print the news and the denial in the same story. This gives his readers the news and the government's attitude toward it simultaneously, but it also has a way of making the denier angry, because the story can be construed as calling him a liar. Two outstanding examples come immediately to mind. In the first instance a South American correspondent ran across a bit of significant news involving our relations with the Latin countries which he was unable to send himself because of local censorship, so he contrived to transmit the tip to the Washington correspondent of his paper. The story was investigated from several angles and the Washington man found sufficient proof to convince him. But his ultimate and most authoritative source in the State Department then gave him a flat denial. What to do? On the advice of a superior he wrote the story but included prominently in it the official denial, which he was sure had its inspiration in a desire to avoid the appearance of friction with any South American government. The other case was a reliable report that Edward R. Stettinius, chief of the Division of Priorities of the Office of Production Management, was about to be shifted to an important assignment outside OPM. From a highly responsible official close to Stettinius the story was confirmed, but Stettinius himself said it was not true. Again the story was printed with the denial featured, although in this instance, perhaps because of some administrative decision, the story did not come true for several months.

In this instance there were no repercussions, but in the case of the other story the State Department official became rather upset and expressed his anger in a letter to the chief of the bureau. His action was representative of a trend in governmental policy toward the press, a trend which takes the form of personal letters to editors and publishers objecting to (a) their editorials or (b) the news they publish. Such letters may contain no more than friendly expostulation as man to man, but more often they contain sharp criticism, usually of a particular story or of a particular correspondent. They have their roots in a desire to discredit the correspondent with his employer, and there have been cases where they have been successful, notably the removal of Eugene Lyons from Moscow by the United Press at the request of the Soviet government, and the assignment there in his stead of a Washington correspondent who had favorably impressed Maxim Litvinoff and his entourage in 1933.

Complaints of this sort sometimes are based on the failure of a paper to print a particular story, rather than its publication of some undesired bit of news, and in this field private news sources and propagandists are fully as active as those working for the government. The first step is to try to obtain a promise from the correspondent that the story will be printed; when he is non-committal (he seldom refuses point blank to consider it) or replies that he has no control over his copy after it has been telegraphed to the home office, the author of the material may get in touch with the home office and "build a fire" under the correspondent. Or perhaps he just waits, grimly, and if the story is not published, complains not to the reporter but to his managing editor, who then is compelled to make inquiry. A series of such complaints can have one of two effects:

either the paper or the correspondent grows so thoroughly tired of the propagandist's insistence that he is virtually boycotted, or the correspondent takes the easy way out and makes a point of writing stories from this source thereafter just to avoid annoyance, regardless of their merit.

Benjamin Marsh, director of "the People's Lobby," which purports to be devoted to the defense in Washington of the interests of the inarticulate masses, is perhaps the most insistent lobbyist on the scene. He makes a point of requesting time to testify at every Congressional hearing in which he is at all interested, obtains two minutes or so along with a score of other minor witnesses, and then releases to the press a voluminous statement which purports to be the testimony he gave or would have given had he been permitted. Then, no matter how many other minor witnesses' names have been omitted with his from the stories for lack of space, Marsh makes a point of writing severe letters to the editor charging discrimination, letters which are referred back to the Washington bureaus for investigation. He is not the victim of discrimination, but of his own methods. Of course every Washington bureau must do a considerable amount of daily editing because only a fraction of the volume of news available can be printed. The victim of this editing, however rational it may be, nearly always considers that the press is corrupt and venal.

There always have been and always will be officers of the government itself who will thwart any ill-advised attempts to prevent the citizens of the Republic from knowing what is going on, officers of high enough rank to be able to do so with little fear of reprisal. Before the current war broke out, when a French military mission was secretly touring the country under government sponsorship, delving into what were supposed to be our darkest military aviation secrets, it was a high-ranking Army officer who gave a daily report of the subsequent investigation to one newspaper correspondent because he deemed it his patriotic duty to do so. He had been opposed to the administrative policy which had led to the revelation of secrets to a foreign power, and particularly to the atmosphere of secrecy which cloaked it, secrecy grounded in the fear of Congressional criticism. The only condition imposed upon the correspondent was that the informant should not be quoted. That was a sinister episode, not because the administration sought in those last months before the cataclysm to aid France in every way possible, but because a regime professedly devoted to the principles and defense of democracy had been unwilling to confide in the co-ordinate branch of government.

Secrecy per se does not necessarily involve censorship as we interpret it, for, as has been said, the government always has ample reason for keeping certain matters secret for the time being. A detailed diplomatic maneuver upon which the actual physical welfare of the nation may depend most certainly ought to be a secret until it has been accomplished or abandoned, and there are many other categories which are similarly inappropriate for publication. Most responsible Washington correspondents realize this and co-operate to the utmost with any official who in turn plays fair with them.

But how do these things leak out? Simply through the

inability of government employees, from Cabinet rank on
down to the lowliest clerks, to keep their mouths shut. And
the lowly clerks are not as a rule to blame because they
don't know about these departures in high policy: it is
more likely to be a high administrative officer who leaks.
If the responsible members of the government are unable
to maintain secrecy, then it is a bit difficult to comprehend
the line of reasoning which says to the press: "you ought
not to have printed that story because it is detrimental to
whatever we may have had in mind to do." News does not
come to us in a dream — someone has to tell it to us.

The parallel necessity for both secrecy and frankness in
times of national emergency poses an almost insoluble problem to both government and press. On the one hand an
important and highly laudable project may be ruined by
premature publicity; on the other hand if it is kept secret
and terminates disastrously, public resentment is justified.
And when Congressional authorization is required the problem is even more baffling, for the tendency of Congressmen
to talk is well known and the administrator testifying in a
secret committee session may wish to reveal as few of the
details of the scheme as possible. Yet if he doesn't tell the
whole story the members grow suspicious and put up a fight
against a bill which they might have supported had they
been informed of its true import.

In the spring of 1941 an extremely important bill grant-
ing vague but extensive powers to an existing agency was
subjected to a withering fire in both Houses of Congress
largely because the membership had no accurate knowledge
of its purpose and so feared the worst. Yet at least one cor-

respondent had obtained a detailed explanation of the bill from a responsible Senator before it ever came up for debate. This Senator knew about it because, in closed session of the committee of which he was a member, the hidden purport had been disclosed. The correspondent confirmed the details from the head of the agency but never wrote the story, in the belief that to reveal the plan would defeat its purpose. But no one had asked him not to, and all the while members of Congress were kept completely in the dark.

Episodes like this provide one of the greatest incentives to measures for control of the press, or at least for a variety of censorship which will make news hard to get, and the attitude is easy to understand. The trouble is that a bureaucrat with his first taste of censorship is like a sheep-killing dog — he gets a craving for it and doesn't know where to stop.

XVII

If War Comes

As this is written — August 1, 1941 — the nation is rapidly moving toward a state of undeclared war; some say this condition already exists as the result of numerous frankly unneutral acts on the part of the government. By the time this chapter is printed a "shooting war" may well have become a reality for the United States, and the title "If War Comes" may then seem rather superfluous. Nevertheless it is imperative, in times like these, to take into consideration what may be expected in the event of war, in writing a book on the Washington correspondents and their relationship with the government. The writer can only hope that the predictions to follow will not prove to have strayed too far from the facts.

Much has been said in the past twelve months about censorship. Newspaper editorials and magazine articles have elicited official disclaimers. National magazines such as *Collier's* and *Fortune* have published strong arguments against press control, and the Office of Government Reports has been "exposed" as a "Ministry of Propaganda" already functioning under cover. President Roosevelt has said that he is opposed to censorship — without a declaration of war — and has added this ringing precept:

"Representative democracy will never tolerate suppression of true news at the behest of the government."

And his secretary, quoting that statement in January, 1941, amplified it in these words:

"Thank God our editors are subject to no limitations except those imposed by the law of libel. . . . A free press is absolutely essential to the democratic way of life. Since democratic government is in the last analysis government by public opinion, our whole democratic structure falls if freedom in the expression of opinion is curtailed or suppressed in any way."

Lowell Mellett, Director of the Office of Government Reports, said on February 26 to a committee of Congress:

"If any censorship is contemplated by this administration, I believe our organization would not be a particularly useful one for that purpose. I do not believe we are organized in any way that would make us a good spot for any censor to operate from. *However, I do know that no censorship is contemplated.*"

Asked by a committee member whether a wartime censorship had been considered, Mr. Mellett replied:

"None that I know of. It is my belief — and I believe my information is as good as anybody else might have on the subject — that none is contemplated in wartime. If I might be permitted to explain, that does not mean, in case there should be war, that there will not be military censorship, as there has always been and I presume always will be. In other words, the Army and the Navy will have control over the information coming from the Army and the Navy. But censorship in the sense that I believe is feared, that is, the kind we see abroad, the actual censorship of newspapers or other publications, simply is not contemplated in any manner."

Asked a little later about "voluntary censorship," Mr. Mellett remarked:

"That would be a matter of the newspapers getting together on it, the purpose being to keep free the free press of America. The publishers certainly would be free to get together and agree not to publish things, *but that rests entirely with them.*"

When a friendly Congressman interposed:

"But it would come solely from the publishers and not from the government," Mr. Mellett rejoined:

"That is right."

There has never been a so-called voluntary censorship of the press in the United States which was not agreed upon at the urgent insistence of the government itself, regardless of what Mr. Mellett or any other government official may say to the contrary; the record is clear on that point. In World War I the government in writing asked the press to refrain from publishing certain types of information and they agreed, as George Creel, the censor in that war, puts it, "with one hand on the heart and the other on the flag." On December 31, 1940, Frank Knox, Secretary of the Navy, circularized 5,000 press, radio, and picture editors, requesting that they cease publication of any unauthorized news in four specific categories covering virtually all important aspects of naval news. Since then a fifth has been added.

In neither of these cases was there anything really voluntary about it. The publishers and editors in 1940 were requested as a patriotic duty to let the admirals, speaking through the Secretary, be the sole judge of what should constitute publishable news from the Navy — in time of peace. In 1917, with the nation physically at war, the voluntary aspect was even fainter. In each case there was the implicit threat of some form of censorship if the editors and publishers failed of their patriotic duty as the government saw that duty.

All the discussion, then, seems to boil down to a question of what constitutes censorship. This writer is convinced that Stephen Early, the President's Secretary, considers that any unnecessary or capricious withholding of news from the press or radio is censorship. He is equally convinced that Mr. Mellett of OGR and the admirals of the Navy employ a much narrower definition — the actual, physical editing of the entire content of a newspaper by government officials employed for the purpose.

Beyond that narrow definition is a limitless field in which unwarranted interference with the publication or *gathering* of news can constitute a de facto censorship equally effective, equally damaging to the press, equally violative, in spirit, of the First Amendment to the Constitution. There was no censorship as Mr. Mellett construes it during World War I, despite the efforts of President Wilson to obtain such a law from Congress, yet every newspaperman knew that the *threat* of legislative or executive action always hung over him and his employer as a penalty for violation of the "voluntary" pledge which had been given. And every newspaperman knows today that, while President Roosevelt may not repeat the mistakes of Wilson, there are perfectly legal means of making it impossible to secure news, and if it cannot be secured it most certainly cannot be published.

Already such means are being employed here and there, as related in the preceding chapter, and it would be a relatively simple matter to shut down almost 100 percent on any recalcitrant correspondent or even on the paper he represents. And that is censorship, call it what you will.

To date, censorship-at-source of government news has been confined principally to the Army and the Navy, although there are examples of it in other departments. But even here there is the widest possible divergence on what is a military secret. The Navy continually withholds news of a sort freely given out by the Army and other departments concerned with defense matters, and patriotic correspondents and editors, willing to co-operate even though they may think much of it is nonsense, are left holding the bag. For example:

In Secretary Knox's famous circular letter on New Year's Eve, as later amended, he requested "voluntary censorship" in these categories:

1. Actual or intended movements of vessels or aircraft of the United States Navy, of units of naval enlisted personnel or divisions of mobilized reserves, or troop movements of the U. S. Marine Corps.

2. Mention of "secret" technical U.S. naval weapons or development thereof.

3. New U.S. Navy ships or aircraft.

4. U.S. Navy construction projects ashore.

5. The arrival in U.S. ports of damaged British ships for repairs under the Lease-Lend Act.

Implementing these requests, the Navy naturally withheld from then on the news items involved, except in cases where it desired publicity for, say, a ship launching; and its information officers consistently refused to discuss such matters when newspapers with independent sources asked for confirmation. Yet here is the way the Army treats comparable news:

1. Freely publicizes the movement of troops within the United States, and of the sailing of transports *after the fact*, withholding in the latter case only the number of men involved; publishes a complete daily register of individual personnel changes and movements.

2. Refrains from discussing secret technical weapons.

3. Publicizes the manufacture of tanks, airplanes, and the like, with public demonstrations of the new tanks as they roll off the assembly lines, although, naturally, it does not reveal details of construction.

4. Makes daily reports on contracts for new arsenals, shell-loading plants, plane factories, and other facilities comparable to "naval construction projects ashore."

5. The Army has no news comparable to the arrival of disabled British ships.

In May and June of 1941 the President by Executive Order transferred certain units and personnel of the Coast Guard to the Navy. On Wednesday, June 4, the *New York Times* learned in New York that some of these Coast Guardsmen were to be employed as crews of Army transports and naval auxiliaries, but when its Washington Bureau asked the Navy about it, the answer was that such information was "restricted" and could not be discussed.

Next morning the Secretary of the Treasury, to whose department the Coast Guard is attached, disclosed the story without prompting. To add to the confusion, the *Times* withheld the news, despite its announcement by a high Cabinet officer, presumably in view of the prior inhibition imposed by the Navy Department.

About the same time the Navy, which long since had ceased publicizing its individual personnel shifts and the movements of its ships, announced that henceforth it would not release the customary daily list of supply contract awards, on the ground that such lists would tend to give aid and comfort to the enemy. It added that responsible persons would be permitted to inspect individual contract specifications at the Department if they so requested. But Hal O'Flaherty, former managing editor of Mr. Knox's *Chicago Daily News* and now assistant to Rear Admiral Hepburn in managing the naval censorship, explained that this meant that if an individual asked to see a particular contract he would be permitted to do so, but that he would have to know that the contract had been let in order to make such a request. Presumably the only way he could find out would be from the contractor, who no doubt is similarly pledged to secrecy! Yet the Army, so far as can be determined, publishes all its contract awards from the largest to the smallest, and considers that the news of a continuing flow of supplies to the armed forces is beneficial to the national morale.

How the publication of the fact that the Navy had ordered 50,000 pairs of dungarees could jeopardize the national security even under war conditions is a puzzle far beyond the ken of this writer; indeed, the withholding of such news could well be a cloak for the grossest sort of incompetence or financial juggling. There is no purpose here to charge such things — the writer believes implicitly in the efficiency of the American Navy, and believes further that the Roosevelt Administration is as financially honest as any in our history; yet the refusal to permit the voters to know how their money is being spent is an extremely dangerous thing and directly detrimental to the very fundamentals of the democratic process.

Regardless of their ultimate implications, these few examples of crossed signals *within the government* make it abundantly clear what extraordinary confusion results when individual officials or departments set themselves up as the final authority on what shall and shall not be printed in the daily press.

From the point of view of the newspapermen, the statement of Lowell Mellett that no censorship is contemplated even in war time must be accepted at its face value, subject to Mr. Mellett's technical definition of the word. The real question is, what means short of blue-pencil censorship will be employed to prevent strategically valuable information from being transmitted to the enemy?

In the first World War, as related, the Congress after bitter debate refused to accede to President Wilson's request that it violate the Constitution by enacting a press censorship law, but in the mean time the President had constituted his Committee on Public Information. This committee, consisting of three or four Cabinet officers, had as its active director George Creel, a newspaperman who believed then that a "voluntary" censorship was possible and made sense. This is the way it worked:

First, the publishers (radio was not then a problem) pledged themselves not to print anything the government did not specifically authorize, with eighteen general subjects listed as taboo. (With due allowance for the inclusion of other departments and for the fact of a shooting war, the list was a very close approximation of that sent out this year by the Secretary of the Navy.)

Second, the Committee on Public Information set up a clearing house through which all authorized news was cleared in the form of handouts. These handouts were supposed to constitute the sum total of what could be published, but in the event a correspondent ran across a piece of news which seemed to fall in no particular category, he was permitted to ask for authorization to use it.

Third, the Committee released a number of straight-out propaganda stories, some of which were later proved to have not the slightest basis in fact. The supposed purpose of these patriotic lies was to make us love America and hate the enemy. A spectacular example was the announcement that the first convoy of American troops to land in France had been attacked by submarines, and that the escorting vessels had gallantly fought off the enemy without the loss of a single life. It just didn't happen, and Walter Duranty, in "I Write as I Please," amusingly and ironically related his experiences in trying to substantiate it for the *New York Times.*

There can be no doubt that Creel worked hard and intelligently to make a success of a job which he soon realized was foredoomed to failure, and there is no proof that he was personally responsible for the out-and-out falsehoods that were disseminated through his office. Yet the experiment was a failure, and Creel in *Collier's Magazine* in May, 1940, explained why, and voiced an urgent appeal against any repetition of such nonsense next time. Perforce, in a country as big as ours, the system had to be decentralized, with the obvious result that what was news in New York was a secret in Chicago; that something everybody in a whole State knew was withheld from the press; that breaches of faith on the part of individual papers, whether innocent or intentional, gave rise to immediate demands from their competitors that they be punished; and finally and most important of all, that the void created by the shortage of news was filled by the most vicious word-of-mouth rumors, more dangerous than the actual publication of any amount of true but restricted news or even of rumor, which once published can be run to earth.

In the final analysis, it is absurd to suppose that real or potential enemies of our country are getting their information from the newspapers. It is absurd to assume that if a newspaper reporter learns by chance that a transport is sailing on a certain date for Newfoundland, he is the only one who has heard of it. It is even more absurd to conclude that enemy spies sit around in luxurious apartments waiting for delivery of the latest editions in order to send abroad their daily budget of military secrets.

If spies are abroad in the land they know the news, beyond cavil, long before it is printed, so that the net result of a press censorship, technical or actual, voluntary or compulsory, is to deprive our own patriotic citizens of much legitimate news at the behest of some narrow-minded brass hat, without putting any real barrier in the path of the informer and the saboteur. What, then, is the answer?

Obviously there are certain limited classes of information which ought not to be published, and no responsible newspaper would publish them, censor or no censor. Such information includes the details of "secret" weapons, which might be translated into blue-prints by an ingenious enemy. It includes war plans of the Army's General Staff and the Navy's General Board. It includes any secret and exclusive processes for the manufacture of weapons, ships or planes. It includes economic plans intimately related to the conduct of a war, and diplomatic projects whose disclosure would defeat them in advance. It does not, generally speaking, require the experience of a military or diplomatic career to recognize this sort of information, and newspapers and newspapermen are continually refraining from publishing such matter without being asked. But outside these categories it is difficult to conceive of many others whose publication would be of particular assistance to enemy spies.

The answer, then, is not censorship of the American press, voluntary or otherwise, but a very close censorship of cables, radio, and foreign mails. No one who has the best interests of his country at heart could possibly object, in time of war, to such restrictions as these. If a foreign spy is deprived of the means of transmitting his information out of the country, then the publication of such news within the country can certainly do little harm. It may be remarked that this does not solve the problem of the saboteur, who relies on no international communications for his effectiveness. True, but the construction of an airplane factory or arsenal, or the institution of field maneuvers by half a million men are not phenomena which can be kept secret by withholding them from the daily press. Anyone can see a factory being built; anyone can see the troops marching out of camp — the only difference is in favor of the saboteur, because he doesn't have to wait for the paper to be printed and pay three cents for it. Thus when HMS *George V* steamed up the Chesapeake Bay to Annapolis carrying Lord Halifax, the new British ambassador, no secret was made of the fact and anyone who could get close enough could take a look. Yet when newspapers subsequently published pictures of the big battle wagon they were criticized. And when the *Malaya*, in broad daylight, her shell holes clearly visible, entered New York harbor, there was a great to-do about the fact that some papers chronicled her arrival.

But if all means of communication with foreign countries were subjected to the closest censorship, then we would have done all possible to prevent the leakage of news valuable to an enemy. This would have to apply to domestic broadcasts as well as to the wireless telegraph, because our huge super-power stations may be heard far beyond our borders, and a carelessly worded news broadcast could readily be picked up by a hostile receiving station. In addition, these powerful broadcasts serve as directional signals which could be as useful to enemy aircraft as a commercial radio beam.

There is every reason to assume that such a censorship — of radio, cable and foreign mails — has already been

planned in detail and would be invoked immediately upon
the outbreak of hostilities. It is too much to hope, however,
that there would at the same time be no censorship of the
domestic press. Some restrictions, more or less irksome, are
virtually certain to be imposed. There are many influential
members of the Roosevelt administration who are unal-
terably opposed to any such device as George Creel's committee. They believe, with Creel himself, that it would be
inefficient from the government's point of view and disastrous from the viewpoint of legitimate public information.
Whether their opposition will prevail when the final decision is pending cannot be accurately predicted, but here is
what they propose as an alternative:

1. All foreign communications and radio broadcasts to
be subjected to the most searching censorship, with the
corollary expression of hope that the censors will be reasonably literate.

2. All government agencies to maintain their present
press relations systems, giving out such news as they consider to be compatible with the public security.

3. The constitution of a central authority to whom any
one of these press officers may appeal for a decision in the
event of a special problem. This authority, at this writing,
probably would be Lowell Mellett.

4. Executive press conferences, including those of the
President himself, to continue as usual. It is obvious that
fewer questions would be answered, that less news would
be vouchsafed in these conferences, than in time of peace,
but the sponsors of the plan consider that nothing could be
better calculated to bolster the national morale than for the

President and his Cabinet members to see the correspondents at regular intervals and report through them to the nation on the progress of the war.

How such a system might work out in the case of the Navy at least was foreshadowed on June 11, 1941, when Secretary Knox pepperily informed correspondents at a press conference that naval news, in effect, should henceforth be what he himself authorized and nothing more. He denounced, without denying, certain statements in a recent Alsop-Kintner column (Alsop at that time held his commission in the Navy) and instructed the reporters that they should print no unconfirmed stories about the Navy. Further, he said the only place to confirm such stories was at the Navy itself. Yet a day earlier Mr. Knox, in a crowded elevator at the Office of Production Management, in full hearing of some fifteen others including at least one newspaperman, discussed details of defense strike policy with the Undersecretary of War, Robert P. Patterson. The reporter, belying the common New Deal implication that newspapers have no morals, refrained from writing what he overheard.

During World War I little news was made directly available by the departments concerned, but was handed out in mimeographed or printed form by Creel's staff. The handout was the story, and no questions were asked, no amplification or explanation permitted. There were no press conferences. At that time the departmental conference had yet to be instituted, and President Wilson's attempt to conduct regular seminars for the correspondents had not succeeded too well, so that he welcomed the excuse to abolish them altogether. In consequence of all this lack of contact, all this suppression of other than sterilized, canned information, the newspapers became in effect transmission belts for officially sanctioned news and officially concocted propaganda.

Such a condition is detrimental to the very institutions we are presumed to be defending, as the experience of France bears witness. No man, no group of men, is capable of passing intelligent and detached judgment on what is and is not legitimate news for the press of a country as large and diversified as ours, and the tendency of the censor, legal or self-constituted, is always to overextend himself. Had normal news publication and the consequent public criticism been permitted in France, the disaster that befell her might just possibly have been mitigated: in any event it would not have come as so rude a shock to an unprepared people. Military censorship was broadened to include political censorship; debilitating rumor took the place of facts, and the German and Italian press both printed far more genuine information than the French.

Presumably in the event of our involvement in war the Army and Navy would be compelled to get together with some impartial and informed arbiter to work out a catalogue of unpublishable information, a catalogue which would be observed by both. Certainly the present lack of system is silly. The real trouble is that all press censorship is silly — silly in its operation regardless of the motive — and the very negation of popular government in its fundamental concept. Censors tend to be narrow-minded if not actually stupid, and yet, if war comes, we are going to have them in one form or another. The one-man court of appeals, whether it be Lowell Mellett with his OGR or some other individual with a passion for unpopularity, is just another word for censor. The press and the public can only hope that whatever system of press control is set up will be managed with a minimum of bureaucratic blundering.

Many honest patriots have feared that another world war at this juncture with the United States an active participant would mean a disastrous setback to all the institutions upon which our government is founded, if not their literal destruction. This writer cannot subscribe to that view, at least not in its entirety. Certainly war is in its very essence the ultimate in criminal stupidity, and the successful waging of it, even by the innocent victim of aggression, always involves a suspension of many of the guarantees being defended. But they need not be suspended indefinitely, and will not be if the people keep alert and informed. The only way the people can keep informed is by means of the press and the radio; with those avenues of democratic communication cut off or fatally constricted, the citizen may well despair.

THE END

For the Uninitiated

Background — Material given a correspondent to "enrich" his comprehension of a story, but which may not be attributed to the source.

Beat — Also known as a scoop: a story obtained exclusively by a single reporter or newspaper; it helps to increase circulation and obtain salary increases for the reporter.

Blacksheet — A Washington phenomenon: a carbon copy of a story provided by one reporter for another who wasn't there.

City Editor — An unpopular former reporter who directly supervises the local news staff.

Copy — Anything a newspaper is thinking of printing.

Copy Reader — The most important, and unpopular, man on a newspaper: he edits copy and writes the headlines.

Cub — A green reporter; for some a perpetual condition.

Desk Man — An all-inclusive term for administrative employees, rewrite men and copy readers; their distinguishing marks are overweight and a worried expression.

Editor — The publisher's mouthpiece: he has the task of interpreting to the public the paper's policy.

Feature — A story valuable as instruction or entertainment more than as news.

Handout — A press release, particularly one written in the form of a news story.

Journalist — A well-dressed newspaper man.

Leg Man — A reporter whose principal job is to gather news for someone else to write.

Leg Work — The physical act of getting news directly rather than from handouts.

Lobbyist — Anyone with an axe for the Government to grind; or his paid representative.

Lobster Trick — The worst job on a morning newspaper, covering the hours of darkness from the final edition to the time when the afternoon papers start publishing.

Managing Editor — The principal news executive: he has no control over editorial policy or the manner in which it is expressed.

Off-the-Record — Credited to Alfred E. Smith, this term describes the least useful information a reporter can have: he is forbidden to use it in any form.

Press Association — An agency devoted to the gathering of news and its sale to papers on a contractual basis.

Publisher — The principal owner, or his salaried representative, responsible for the management of an entire newspaper.

Rewrite Man — A reporter who has advanced (or deteriorated) to the job of rewriting handouts and other men's stories.

Run — Sometimes called a beat: the particular group of agencies or activities for which a single reporter is responsible.

Senator-at-Large — A Washington correspondent who forgets he is a reporter.

Story — Any newspaper article.

The Milkman in Omaha — A press association term for the lowest common denominator in reader intelligence, for whom the press association reporters are supposed to write.

Index

Abell, George, 196, 197
Adams, John Quincy, 42, 206, 208
Agricultural Adjustment Act, 107, 135, 161, 196
Agriculture Department, 139
Allen, Robert S., 189, 196, 197, 198, 201, 203
Alsop, Joseph, 33, 193, 198, 199, 310
American Aviation Daily, 204
American Newspaper Guild, 24, 89
Ananias Club, 56
Anglo-American Relations, 146
Ashburton, Lord (British Minister), 41
Associated Press, 44, 93, 98, 135, 155, 167, 171, 216, 248

Baker, Newton D., 197
Baltimore Evening Sun, 169, 192
Baltimore Sun, 40, 48, 182, 192, 196, 197, 275
Bank of United States, 208
Bargeron, Carlisle, 113, 114, 182
Barton, Bruce, 128
Batista, Col. Fulgencio, 21, 224
Beats (Exclusive Stories), 25
Belair, Felix, 88, 107, 252
Bennett, James Gordon, 40, 187
Benson, George, 80
Bill of Rights, 272
Black, Ruby, 213, 217
Blacksheeting, 47, 48, 49
Blanton, Rep. Thomas, 113, 114
Bledsoe, Samuel, 135
Bloom, Sol, 178, 179
B'nai B'rith, 140
Bolivia, 152

Bonaparte, Charles Joseph, 29
Bonus, Battle of, 114
Borah, William E., 168, 170
Boston Globe, 94
Boston Herald, 56, 57
Boston Journal, 42
Boycott, 29, 30, 181, 182, 225, 293
Bribery, 21, 36, 112, 208
Briggs, Emily Edson, 209
Britten, Fred, 185
Broun, Heywood, 89, 203, 204
Bull Run, Battle of, 46
Bureau of Labor Statistics, 138, 163
Bureaucracy, 94, 128, 137, 166, 312
Bureaucrats, 12, 18, 32, 104, 128, 174, 242, 250, 274, 275, 278, 283, 296
Burr, Aaron, 40
Butler, Gen. Ben, 14

Calles, Gen. Plutarco Elias, 49, 50
Capital Parade, 193, 198
Capper, Arthur, 238
Carmichael, Jesse, 56
Canton (O.) News, 265
Capra, Frank, 111
Carter, John Franklin, alias Jay Franklin, 195, 196, 284
Catledge, Turner, 198, 199
Censorship, 19, 45, 46, 66, 67, 71, 72, 118, 119, 122, 129, 165, 170, 210, 255, 256, 259, 260, 262, 263, 264, 267, 272, 273, 281, 284, 288, 291, 294, 296, 297, 298, 299, 300, 301, 303, 304, 305, 306, 307, 308, 309, 311, 312

315

Chamber of Commerce of the U.S., 140

Charleston Courier, 40

Cheetham, James, 39

Chicago Daily News, 280, 303

Chicago Press and Tribune, 42

Chicago Tribune, 82, 94, 134

Christian Science Monitor, 196, 197, 209

Churchill, Winston, 155

Cincinnati Commercial, 43

Cincinnati Times-Star, 58

Civil Aeronautics Board, 276

Civil Rights Bill of 1866, 37

Civil War, 14, 36, 42, 45

Civilian Conservation Corps, 134

Clapper, Raymond, 187, 189, 201, 202, 203

Cleveland, Grover, 53, 265

Colfax, Schuyler, 36

Collier's Magazine, 265, 285, 297, 306

Columbia University School of Journalism, 97

Columnists, 13, 14, 31, 35, 40, 93, 94, 96, 150, 187, 188, 189, 190, 191, 192, 193, 194, 195, 196, 198, 200, 202, 203, 204, 207, 289

Columns, 15, 188, 189, 190, 191, 192, 193, 194, 195, 196, 197, 199, 200, 201, 202, 242, 252, 253, 284

Commerce Department, 66

Committee of Public Utility Executives, 229

Committee on Public Information, 118, 304, 305

Congress of Industrial Organizations, 127, 140

Connor, Frank, 69

Constitution, 19, 27, 30, 160, 269, 272, 273, 300, 304

Coolidge, Calvin, 58, 62, 63, 64, 65, 67, 70, 81, 147, 167, 181, 289

Copeland, Royal S., 178

Corby, William S., 237

Corcoran, Thomas G., 88, 193

Couzens, James, 165, 166, 177

Creel, George, 118, 284, 285, 299, 304, 305, 306, 309, 310

Crosby, J. L., 42

Currie, Lauchlin, 100

Dana, Charles A., 187

Davis, Senator Garrett, 38

Davis, Matthew L., 40, 41

Davis, Richard Harding, 111

Dean, Gordon, 134

Defense Commission, 130, 260, 261, 275

Defense Mediation Board, 287

de Kauffmann, Henrik, 126

Democratic Conventions, 48, 191

Democratic Republican Party, 39

Denials, Official, 24, 25, 26, 157, 285, 289, 290, 291

Des Moines Register and Tribune, 195

Detroit News, 48

Dies, Martin, 179

DNB, 224

Duane, James, 39

Dunce Cap Club, 90

Duranty, Walter, 305

Early, Gen. Jubal, 78

Early, Stephen T., 76, 77, 78, 81, 91, 120, 122, 125, 126, 127, 128, 130, 249, 259, 264, 269, 300

Eccles, Marriner S., 160

Editors, 22, 25, 26, 36, 38, 39, 45, 48, 49, 66, 76, 149, 154, 155, 192, 198, 201, 203, 206, 211, 234, 244, 259, 260, 262, 265, 268, 271, 273, 280, 292, 293, 298, 299, 300, 301, 303

Eliot, T. S., 73

Essary, J. Fred, 275

Ethics, Journalistic, 23, 24, 27, 32, 45, 111, 153

Farley, James A., 104

Federal Loan Agency, 146
Federal Works Agency, 133
Federalists, 39
Fellows, Dexter, 109
Felt, Truman, 134
Fess, Sen. Simeon D., 22, 23
Fillmore, Millard, 209
Fortune Magazine, 244, 245, 246, 270
Frank, Jerome N., 161, 162
Frantz, Harry W., 228
Free Press (Elwood, Ind.), 265
Furman, Bess, 216

Gales, Joseph, Jr., 52
Gallup Poll, 11
Garner, John N., 169, 170
Gaston, Herbert, 135
Gennerich, Gus, 88
George Washington Bicentennial Commission, 178
Glass, Carter, 175
Glassford, Gen. Pelham D., 115
Gobright, L. A., 44
Graft, 36, 37, 112
Gran Chaco, 152, 153
Grant, Ulysses S., 36
Greeley, Horace, 187
Gridiron Club, 24, 127, 218, 219, 236, 237, 238, 240
Grogan, Lt. Col. Stanley C., 280

Hadden, Briton, 244
Halifax, Lord, 154, 155, 308
Halpine, O. G., 42
Hamilton, Gail, 209
Handouts. See Press Releases.
Hard, William, 68
Harding, Warren Gamaliel, 55, 58, 61, 62, 143
Harding, Mrs. Warren G., 211
Harrison, Sen. Pat, 84
Hassett, William D., 91
Hearst Papers, 51, 94, 187, 201
Heath, Louis Jay, 152, 228
Heflin, J. Thomas, 182
Henderson, Leon, 242

Henning, Arthur Sears, 82
Herring, E. P., 141
Hepburn, Rear Adm. Arthur J., 280, 303
Hinton News, 93
Hitler, Adolph, 155, 224, 225
Holmes, George R., 83
Hoover, Herbert C., 17, 29, 30, 48, 55, 58, 66, 67, 68, 69, 70, 71, 72, 73, 76, 79, 81, 82, 91, 114, 115, 116, 119, 125, 152, 156, 161, 166, 167, 192, 193, 196, 242, 251, 259
Hopkins, Harry L., 107, 134
Horton, Robert W., 261
House of Representatives, 36
Howard, Roy W., 204
Hughes, Charles Evans, 61, 65
Hull, Cordell, 197
Huntress, The, 208
Hurd, Charles, 74
Hurley, Patrick J., 197
Hyde, Henry M., 169, 170

Ickes, Harold I., 75, 76, 101, 102, 107, 131, 132, 133, 134, 138, 159, 163, 164, 201, 203, 268
Impartial Observer and Washington Advertiser, 51
Interior Department, 133, 135, 151, 159, 258
International News Service, 83, 155, 157, 217, 248
Interstate Commerce Commission, 105, 139
Interview, Birth of, 42
Investment Bankers Association, 103

Jackson, Andrew, 41, 87
Jackson, Robert H., 101, 164, 290
Jacobs, Harold, 260, 271
Jefferson, Thomas, 39, 40, 43, 52, 207, 269
Johnson, Andrew, 15, 37, 38, 43, 44

Johnson, Hugh S., 190, 191, 193, 202, 203
Johnson, Magnus, 181, 182
Jones, Jesse H., 113, 138, 146, 161, 164
Joslin, Theodore, 71, 72, 73

Kansas City Star, 94
Karger, Gus J., 58
Kent, Frank R., 182, 192
Kingman, Elias, 39
Kintner, Robert, 33, 193, 198, 199, 310
Kiplinger's Weekly News Letter, 204
Kluckhohm, Frank L., 283, 284
Knox, Frank, 138, 139, 275, 276, 277, 278, 280, 299, 301, 303, 310
Knudsen, William S., 135, 136, 275
Krock, Arthur, 83, 192

Lane, Senator J. H., 37
Lawrence, David, 51, 200
Lawson, William, 136
Lease-Lend Act, 249, 301
Le Hand, Marguerite, 219
Lenroot, Irvine L., 167
Leslie's Weekly, 245
Lewis, Catherine, 214
Lewis, John L., 214
Life Magazine, 244, 245, 246
Lincoln, Abraham, 43, 45, 209
Lindley, Ernest K., 195, 196, 253
Lindsay, Sir Ronald, 219
Lindsay, Lady, 219
Lippmann, Walter, 187, 202
Literary Digest, 244
Little Green House on K Street, 62
Litvinoff, Maxim, 292
Lobster Trick, 26, 27
London Economic Conference (1933), 83
London Times, 41
Long, Huey P., 180
Longworth, Nicholas, 237
Look Magazine, 245

Lopez-Contreras, Eleazar, 229, 230
Luce, Henry, 244, 246, 252
Lusitania, 60
Luther, Hans, 224, 225
Lyons, Eugene, 292

MacArthur, Gen. Douglas, 115, 198
McClure Syndicate, 201
McLean, Ned (Edward B.), 182
MacLeish, Archibald, 88
McClellan, Gen. George B., 36
McCullagh, John B., 43, 44
McDermott, Michael J., 131, 152, 153
McKinney, Guy, 134
McNutt, Paul V., 84
Ma, Chan-Shan (Gen.), 26, 27
Madison, James, 52, 211
Malaya incident, 276, 308
Mallon, Paul R., 74, 75, 76, 77, 78, 167, 183, 189, 201
Mallon, Winifred, 159-160
Manning, Mary, 217
March of Time, 246
Marine Corps, 301
Maritime Commission, 261, 277
Marsh, Benjamin, 293
Marshall, Gen. George C., 150, 279
Medill, Joseph, 42
Mellett, Don, 265
Mellett, Jesse, 265
Mellett, Lowell, 201, 255, 257, 258, 259, 260, 261, 262, 263, 264, 265, 266, 267, 268, 269, 271, 298, 299, 300, 304, 309, 312
Merry-Go-Round (Column), 197, 198
Meyer, Eugene, 201, 202
Michael, Charles R., 64, 65
Milford, Morton, 134, 284
Miller, George E., 48
Miller, Hope Ridings, 213
Miller, Pierce, 157
Minneapolis Journal, 80
Minton, Sherman, 197
Monroe, James, 14, 52, 211

Morgan, J. P., 109
Morgenthau, Henry, Jr., 88, 98, 145, 146, 160, 163, 171, 172, 288
Mussolini, Benito, 250
My Day, 202, 214, 218

National Catholic Welfare Conference, 140
National Emergency Council, 256, 262, 265
National Intelligencer, 51, 52
National Labor Relations Board, 200
National Press Club, 23, 24, 30, 62, 112, 130, 139, 205, 209, 235, 237, 238, 239, 240, 241, 242, 259
Naval Disarmament Conference (1921), 61
Navy Department, 122, 139, 163, 274, 275, 276, 277, 278, 279, 280, 281, 298, 300, 301, 302, 303, 307, 310, 311
New Deal, 80, 82, 85, 107, 108, 120, 121, 123, 124, 135, 137, 159, 161, 163, 170, 172, 176, 194, 195, 197, 213, 242, 250, 252, 256, 259, 260, 261, 264, 265, 266, 268, 269, 284, 286, 310
New Orleans Picayune, 40
New York Citizen, 39
New York Enquirer, 40
New York Herald-Tribune, 40, 179, 187, 195, 198
New York Journal of Commerce and Commercial Advertiser, 40
New York News, 276
New York Sun, 187
New York Times, 23, 38, 42, 48, 49, 64, 65, 74, 83, 88, 90, 107, 172, 179, 192, 197, 198, 230, 248, 274, 280, 282, 283, 284, 285, 302, 303, 305
New York Tribune, 42, 208
New York World, 69, 135

News Behind the News, The, 201
Newspaper Women's Club of Washington, 218, 219
News-Week, 195, 244, 246, 253
Newton, Walter, 71
Noah, M. M., 41
Norden bombsight, 279
Norris, George W.., 229
North American Newspaper Alliance, 199, 201
Northcliffe, Lord, 235
NRA, 84, 135, 136, 137

Ochs, Adolph S., 49, 65
Office of Government Reports, 125, 255, 256, 257, 258, 259, 260, 261, 262, 263, 264, 266, 271, 297, 300, 312
Office of Production Management, 261, 291, 310
O'Flaherty, Hal, 280, 303
On the Record, 193
One Man's Opinion, 203
Oulahan, Richard V., 23, 68, 197
Oumansky, Constantine, 21, 220, 221
Oumansky, Mme., 221
Overseas Writers Club, 24, 240, 241

Pan-American Union, 240
Paraguay, 152
Patterson, Mrs. Eleanor, 51
Patterson, Robert P., 310
Paul Pry, 206, 207, 208
Pearson, Drew, 189, 196, 197, 198, 201, 203
Pegler, Westbrook, 202
People's Lobby, 293
Perkins, Secretary Frances, 127, 138, 163, 219
Perkins, Fred, 91
Philadelphia Aurora, 39
Philadelphia Press, 209
Pic Magazine, 245
Pictorial Review, 245
PM, 171, 172

Police Gazette, 245
Poore, Ben: Perley, 42
Post Office Department, 277
Post, Robert P., 90, 91
Press Agencies (Press Associations),
18, 32, 33, 39, 44, 93, 94, 95,
151, 152, 167, 173, 183, 186,
209, 227, 248
Press Agents. See Press Officers.
Press Associations. See Press Agencies.
Press Conferences, 17, 20, 29, 30,
46, 55, 59, 60, 61, 62, 63, 66,
68, 73, 74, 75, 77, 80, 81, 84,
87, 90, 92, 97, 99, 101, 102,
125, 126, 137, 138, 142, 143,
144, 145, 147, 149, 150, 151,
152, 154, 156, 157, 158, 159,
160, 161, 162, 163, 164, 176,
197, 205, 206, 212, 215, 216,
217, 218, 274, 279, 280, 285,
286, 309, 310
Press Corps, 16, 19, 23, 30, 32, 33,
35, 50, 67, 68, 79, 85, 111, 153,
154, 157, 197, 227, 283
Press, Freedom of the, 18, 20, 27,
32, 75, 76, 77, 78, 85, 101, 142,
160, 166, 183, 272, 298, 299
Press Gallery, 14, 42, 46, 92, 94,
181, 183, 184, 205, 208, 209,
247
Press Officers (Press Agents), 16,
17, 29, 32, 46, 80, 81, 92, 94,
97, 98, 99, 100, 102, 103, 106,
117, 118, 119, 121, 122, 123,
124, 125, 127, 128, 129, 130,
131, 140, 155, 158, 160, 165,
170, 219, 238, 259, 260, 261,
263, 266, 271, 272, 285, 286,
287, 288, 302, 309
Press Releases (Handouts), 16, 17,
18, 73, 92, 94, 97, 100, 102, 117,
118, 119, 121, 122, 123, 129,
132, 134, 135, 137, 138, 139,
140, 141, 162, 164, 281, 282,
285, 286, 287, 289, 293, 305,
310

Press Rooms, 17, 18
Press Services, 17
Price, William W., 53, 54
Propaganda, 18, 20, 21, 92, 119,
120, 122, 137, 225, 226, 228,
232, 246, 256, 259, 263, 266,
292, 293, 305
Public Works Administration, 133,
134, 135, 284
Publishers, 22, 36, 38, 39, 119,
149, 234, 243, 245, 268, 273,
275, 276, 283, 284, 292, 299,
300, 305
Pulitzer Prize, 43

Radio Correspondents Gallery, 205,
247
Radio news commentators, 158,
213, 261
Ramsay, Marion L., 134
Reck, Al, 65
Reconstruction Finance Corporation, 163, 168
Reid, Whitelaw, 42
Reorganization Act of 1939, 256,
260, 265
Republican National Committee,
22, 116
Republican National Convention
(1872), 35
Richardson, Francis A., 14, 15
Richardson, Gen. Robert C., Jr.,
280
Richey, Lawrence, 71
Rigby, Cora, 209
Robertson, Nathan, 171, 172
Robinson, Sen. Joe T., 84
Royster, Vermont C., 277
Roosevelt, Elliott, 213
Roosevelt, Franklin D., 17, 23, 55,
58, 61, 74, 75, 76, 77, 78, 79,
80, 81, 82, 83, 84, 85, 86, 87,
88, 89, 90, 91, 100, 107, 119,
120, 125, 128, 143, 145, 147,
149, 150, 151, 154, 156, 159,
161, 164, 170, 191, 195, 196,
198, 219, 226, 227, 237, 247,

248, 249, 251, 256, 259, 262, 265, 267, 268, 269, 289, 290, 297, 300, 304, 309
Roosevelt, Mrs. Franklin D., 86, 87, 202, 203, 206, 210, 211, 212, 213, 214, 215, 216, 217, 218, 219, 226, 227
Roosevelt, Theodore, 16, 29, 46, 47, 54, 55, 56, 57, 58, 59, 63, 74, 78, 85, 109, 147, 289
Royall, Anne, 206, 207
Royall, William, 206

St. Lawrence River, 156
Saulsbury, Sen. Willard, 38
Scheider, Malvina Thompson, 214
Schwartz, Charles, 135
Scripps-Howard Newspapers, 51, 91, 196, 201, 203, 204, 259, 260, 265, 266, 271
Seaton, William W., 52
Securities and Exchange Commission, 95, 104, 139, 193, 229
Sell, Kurt, 224
Senate Banking and Currency Committee, 109
Sesquicentennial of the Constitution, 178
Sharkey, Gov. William L., 37
Sirovich, William I., 178
Skinner, Carlton, 135
Sloan, Alfred P., Jr., 110
Smith, Alfred E., 192
Smoot-Hawley Tariff Act, 166
Soil Conservation Act, 107
Speers, L. C., 48, 49, 50, 274
Sperry Gyroscope Company, 278, 279
Spofford, A. R., 42
St. Paul Pioneer-Press, 107
Standing Committee of Correspondents, 32, 183
State Department, 151, 152, 162, 163, 164, 196, 221, 226, 247, 291
State Department Correspondents Association, 32

Steagall, Henry B., 175
Stephens, Alexander H., 43
Stettinius, Edward R., Jr., 291
Stimson, Henry L., 156, 157, 163
Stokes, Thomas L., 170
Straus, Michael W., 131, 132, 133, 134, 135, 284
Subsidies, 51, 200, 228
Sullivan, John L., 172
Sullivan, Mark, 68, 200
Supreme Court, 84, 85, 105, 107, 108, 135, 176, 199
Swisshelm, Mrs. Jane Grey, 208

Taft, William Howard, 47, 58, 59, 142
Tammany Hall, 40
Thompson, Dorothy, 187, 190, 191, 193, 202, 203
Time Magazine, 244, 246, 250, 252, 253, 261, 268
Times and Potowmack Packet, 50
Trade Journals, 94, 96, 174
Treasury Correspondents Association, 32, 33, 288
Treasury Department, 162, 164, 288
Trial balloon, 55
Tugwell, Rexford G., 107, 196, 283

United Feature Service, 203
United Press, 152, 155, 167, 170, 201, 217, 228, 248, 279, 292
United States Daily. See U.S. News.
United States News, 51, 200
United States Steel Company, 127

Vandenberg, Arthur, 180
Vanity Fair, 195, 196
Villard, Henry, 42

Wade, Sen. Benjamin F., 37
Wagner Act, 200
Wall Street Journal, 135, 277
Wallace, Henry A., 161, 162
Walpole, Robert, 40

Waltman, Franklyn, Jr., 116
War Department, 106, 122, 163, 173, 260, 271, 274, 275, 278, 279, 280, 281, 283, 298, 301, 302, 303, 307, 311
War of 1812, 52
Washington Chronicle, 209
Washington Merry-Go-Round, 196
Washington News, The, 51, 65, 196, 203, 260, 265
Washington Post, 51, 52, 113, 182, 195, 201, 213
Washington Star, 48, 51, 52, 53
Washington Times (now Times-Herald), 46, 48, 51, 197
Welles, Sumner, 154, 155
Welliver, Judson C., 46, 48
West, Roy O., 167
White, Francis, 152, 153
White House Correspondents, 53, 55, 78, 240
White House Correspondents Association, 32, 232, 237

White House News Photographers Association, 246
White House spokesman, 59, 62, 63, 66, 67, 80
Wickard, 164
Wiggin, J., Russell, 107
Willkie, Wendell, 75, 191
Wilson, Sen. Henry, 36
Wilson, Thomas, 51
Wilson, Woodrow, 58, 59, 60, 61, 118, 300, 304, 310
Winchell, Walter, 191
Windle, Mary J., 209
Windsor, Duke of, 215
Women's Press Club (National), 24, 218, 219
Works Progress Administration, 120, 134, 163, 284
Woodrum, Clifton, 172
World War I, 72, 118, 243, 246, 284, 299, 300, 304, 310

Young, J. Russell (New York Tribune), 42